Rebellion in Laos

Rebellion in Laos

Peasant and Politics in a Colonial Backwater

Geoffrey C. Gunn

Westview Press
BOULDER • SAN FRANCISCO • OXFORD

This Westview softcover edition is printed on acid-free paper and bound in library-quality, coated covers that carry the highest rating of the National Association of State Textbook Administrators, in consultation with the Association of American Publishers and the Book Manufacturers' Institute.

Published in 1990 in the United States of America by Westview Press, Inc., 5500 Central Avenue, Boulder, Colorado 80301, and in the United Kingdom by Westview Press, 36 Lonsdale Road, Summertown, Oxford OX2 7EW

Library of Congress Cataloging-in-Publication Data
Gunn, Geoffrey C.
Rebellion in Laos: peasant and politics in a colonial backwater / Geoffrey C. Gunn
p. cm.
ISBN 0-8133-8027-8
1. Laos—Politics and government. 2. Peasantry—Laos—Political activity. 3. Minorities—Laos—Political activity. 4. Revolutions—Laos. I. Title.
DS555.7.G86 1990
959.4—dc20 90-12385
CIP

Printed and bound in the United States of America

The paper used in this publication meets the requirements of the American National Standard for Permanence of Paper for Printed Library Materials Z39.48-1984.

10 9 8 7 6 5 4 3 2 1

Contents

Tables and Maps ix
Glossary of Foreign Words xi
Preface xiii
Acknowledgments xv

Introduction 1

PART ONE: THE DEVELOPMENT OF COLONIAL CAPITALISM IN LAOS (1893-1954) 9

1 The Political and Economic Incorporation of Laos 11

The Political Development of French Laos (1893-1954), 11
The Political Economy of French Laos, 18
Conclusion, 29
Notes, 30

2 The Colonial State Project in Laos 32

Colonial State Control of the Labor Process, 32
The Colonial State Development Project, 39
The Colonial State Budget and Monopoly System, 42
The Taxation and Corvee System, 47
Conclusion, 54
Notes, 56

PART TWO: THE NON-REBELLION OF THE LAO 59

3 Pre-Capitalist Modes of Production in Laos 61

Pre-Capitalist Modes of Production, 62
The Peasant Condition, 75

Social Class Differentiation in Colonial Laos? 78
Conclusion, 81
Notes, 82

4 Modes of State Intervention in Colonial Laos 83

Modes of State Intervention, 83
Lao Peasant Responses to Corvee, 89
The Colonial State and Religious Hegemony in Laos, 93
Conclusion, 97
Notes, 97

PART THREE: THE POLITICAL ECONOMY OF PEASANT REBELLION IN LAOS 99

5 The Political Economy of the Kha Peasant Rebellions of Southern Laos 101

Peasant Rebellion in Laos, 101
Kha Political Economy, 107
The "Holy Man's Uprising" or the Revolt of Bac My (1901-1902), 109
Ong Man's Revolt (1901-1902), 112
Kommadan's Revolt (1901-1937), 114
Sambran (the White Python): the Kha Revolt of 1936-1939, 126
Sequels to Pacification: The Scandal of Saravane (1937), 130
A Colonial Montagnard Policy, 134
Conclusion, 138
Notes, 139

6 The Political Economy of Rebellion in Northern Laos 142

Revolt of the Lu (1914-1916), 142
The Chinese Revolt of 1914, 144
The Political Economy of Hmong Peasant Rebellion, 149
Batchai's Rebellion (1918-1921), 151
Hmong Clan Rivalry and Opium Tax Policies (1931-1937), 160
Conclusion, 165
Notes, 167

7 Revolution and Counter-Revolution in Laos 168

Revolution and Counter-Revolution: The Montagnards of Laos in the Second Indochina War, 169
The Reagan Doctrine, Rambo and the Right-wing Resistance in Laos, 174
Conclusion, 181
Notes, 181

Conclusion: From Rebellion to Revolution 183

Appendix 196
Bibliography 198
Index 216

Tables and Maps

Tables

Table 1.1 Mining permits issued in Laos (1923-27), 26
Table 2.1 Population of Laos according to ethnic group (1936), 34
Table 2.2 Percentage of Vietnamese employed in the Federal administrative services in Laos, 35
Table 2.3 Participation in education in Laos by ethnicity (1935), 38
Table 3.1 Fiscal revenue in Laos according to tax category (1943), 79
Table 3.2 Absolute amount of tax derived per tax category, 79
Table 3.3 Percentages of the number of taxpayers by revenue class, 80
Table 4.1 Ratio of direct tax to subvention from Federal budget (1931-35), 86
Table 4.2 Amount of subvention allocation to local budget in Laos, 86
Table 4.3 Total budget allocation in Laos (1932-39), 89

Maps

Map 1 The *debloquement* or opening up of Laos, 212
Map 2 Indochina by ethnicity (Indochine "Carte des Races"), 213
Map 3 Montagnard rebel zones in southern Laos, 1910s, 214
Map 4 Military deployments during the Batchai rebellion, 1920, 215

Glossary of Foreign Words

ban (L)	village
bao (L)	entourage
boun (L)	fete
chaufa (H)	messiah
chau (V)	political division
chaomuong (L)	lord
chaosivit (L)	lord of lives
Hosenam (Senam) Luong (L)	King's Council
Isan (L)	northeast (of Thailand)
khene (L)	flute
khoueng (L)	province
kong (L)	district
kounan (L)	intendant for the preparation of festivals
kha (L)	slave
khabot (L&K)	traitor/rebels
lam (Kouang, haou, van (L)	tribal intermediary
Lao Loum (L)	lowland Lao
moi (V)	slave
muong (L)	circumscription (province)
malalecs (L)	partisans
naa(L)	ricefields
nong hoi (V)	peasantry
phi (L)	spirit
phoa thay (M)	king
phou	mountain
phu mi boun (L)	men with merit
pia	measure (of opium)
phnong (K)	slave
pongsawadan (L)	Lao Royal chronicles
phuwiset (L)	man claiming supernatural powers
ray (L)	swidden
sou khoun (baci) (L)	calling of spirits

suan (L)	kitchen gardens
sala (L)	rest house
sadet (L)	king
sin (L)	Lao skirt
sakdina (T)	feudal
tasseng (L)	canton
that (L)	reliquary
tahois (L)	partisans
wat (L)	temple

(L) = Lao (T) = Thai (H) = Hmong
(V) = Vietnamese (K) = Khmer

Preface

A study in historical anthropology, this work focusses on the world historical incorporation of Laos into a colonial capitalist system of surplus accumulation. In so doing, new light is brought to bear upon the non-rebellious and, especially, rebellious responses of the majority (Lao) and minority (montagnard) population of that country, at least as determined by a scrutiny of largely archival-based sources. The approach taken is to combine a general world systems analysis with a concern for the non-economic, moral and ideological forms of colonial and "feudal" domination.

In Part One we address the question of the political and economic incorporation of Laos into a global world system. We then turn to an explanation of the system of colonial monopolies, the labor process and the colonial tax structure. In Part Two we turn to the phenomenon of the non-revolt of the Lao, but to challenge the conventional view that the Lao willingly acquiesced in the colonial system of rule and domination. To this end we outline the complex relationship between tributary and local power in Laos, as well as seeking to establish objective indicators of the Lao peasant condition. Proceeding from this foundation we can identify interventionist strategies brought to play by the colonial state in order to stave off the economic and "political" crisis of the early 1930s. In Part Three we turn to the minority revolts which sundered the **paix francais** for the duration of the colonial epoch in Laos. While both the revolts of the Hmong of northern Laos and the Kha of southern Laos carry strong overtones of millenarianism, the major leitmotif that connected the different groups through the decades, it is argued, was the anti-colonial, anti-tax and anti-corvee dimensions of their protest.

The importance of our findings, then, reveal the degree to which the minority population of Laos was "prepared" during the colonial epoch by its experience of capitalism, however incipient, for the revolutionary sequels of the late 1940s down to "liberation" in 1975.

Geoffrey C. Gunn

Acknowledgments

My thanks go out to those at Monash University who read or commented upon this work as a whole, (David Chandler) or fragments thereof (Ben Kiernan). Likewise I am indebted to Herbert Feith, not only for suffering my participation in his course "Centre-Periphery", but pushing me to greater theoretical self-criticism. Undoubtedly, as well, my understanding of political anthropology was enriched by the participation in this circle of Wan Zawawi Ibrahim. In France, I received encouragement from Christian Taillard. Special thanks to Kelvin Rowley and Kevin Hewison for their respective searing and insightful theoretical criticisms of the whole manuscript.

In Bangkok, I also wish to thank Khun Suk Soongsawang of Duang Kamol Book House for encouragement and support. At Westview Press, I acknowledge the keen editorial assistance of Ellen E. Williams.

Finally, thanks to my wife, Chieko, and son, Kenji, fellow travellers to Laos.

Parts of this manuscript have been published in the *Journal of Siam Society*; Vol.73, 1985, Vol.74, 1986 and Vol.77, 1989, the *Bulletin of Concerned Asian Scholars* Vol. 19, No.3, July-September, 1987 and *Sojourn*; Vol.3, No.2, August 1985. I am, accordingly, indebted to the editors of these Journals for permission to reproduce material to which they hold copyright.

Introduction

> No longer is it possible to take seriously the view that the peasant is an "object of history" a form of social life over which historical changes pass but which contributes nothing to the impetus of these changes.
>
> (Barrington Moore Jr. 1966:453)

> The history of these [African] peasant societies is that of an uninterrupted series of revolts against the domination of capital: resistance to conquest, to administrative machinery, to its forced requirements (corvees) and its taxes, massive uprisings whenever the peasants feel the ability of urban capital to operate in the countryside is weakening....
>
> (Samir Amin 1977:152)

This book is a study of two interconnected themes. First, the incorporation of Laos into a colonial-capitalist system of surplus accumulation; and, second, the rebellious and non-rebellious responses of the majority and, particularly, the minority peasantry of that country to fundamental changes in their moral, social, political and economic order. Both areas of exploration, we will show, are explainable with reference to the general phenomenon of world-historical expansion.

Thematically, the subject of this work is that of a tax engendered revolt by the minority montagnard population of French Laos who were thrust with dramatic speed into the colonial capitalist orbit. The various responses of these people to the confrontation with outsiders, was not necessarily a concomitant of total backwardness nor messianism — although this was also involved — but arose in opposition to exploitative capitalist social relations, displacement and disarticulation. We will further argue that while class relations did not develop in Laos or especially in the montagnard environment in a way analogous to that of the commercial and industrial enclaves of Indochina, namely Tonkin and Cochinchina, the overall dissolution effect engendered by the colonial tax, corvee and *prestations* (labor due) system was much more dislocative of traditional social relations in this backwater than has hitherto been appreciated. The otherwise unexplained phenomenon of the majority participation of these hill people in a modern movement for social and especially national liberation under the banner of the Pathet Lao movement and under the nominal (?) urban working class leadership is brought into perspective.

One of the central issues in the study of the colonial and post-colonial peripheries has been to establish the way peasants react to sweeping changes in their familiar political, economic, moral and social settings. By the early 1950s, modernization theorists had begun to question the value of the hitherto static notions of anthropologists who focussed their attention, albeit descriptively, on such part-societies as tribe, clan, and lineage. For modernization theorists who were concerned with the so-called transition from tradition to modernity or development on a national scale, the process of development in the colonial and post-colonial periphery was seen as following a similar trajectory of growth as that taken by the developed world. However, the theoretical foundations of the belief that the processes of social change are endogenous in the periphery came to be challenged in the early 1970s by varieties of dependency theory approaches. The new approach which emphasized uneven development on a world stage challenged the modernization approach as ahistorical and theoretically underdeveloped. Frank and Amin were representative of such theorists. Similarly Immanuel Wallerstein revealed in the mid-1970s, little work had been done on the processes that made it possible for the capitalist world system to incorporate the non-capitalist social system. The concern that local level economic processes or part systems should be viewed as aspects of the world system has been echoed by the Fernand Braudel Center in the 1980s via its publication, *Review*.

More recently, however, a separate body of literature has emerged which harks back to classical Marxist statements on capitalist accumulation on a world scale and thus posits a corrective to the dependencia theory. Thus while the dependencia theory posits a relationship of domination and dependency between a core and a periphery, between a metropole and a satellite (ie. a world system versus a nation-state as the unit of analysis), the new ascendant "industrialization" theory concentrates directly on the relations of production under imperialism and focusses on class structure and social classes engaged in class struggle. In contrast to the dependencia theory argument which states that imperialism blocks capitalist development in the periphery, the "industrialization" theory suggests rather that during the period of the industrialization of the peripheral areas of the world, imperialist expansion actually helps towards the industrialization of the peripheral regions of the world capitalist system (cf. Berberuglu 1984).

Clearly, while the political implications of these variant readings of Marx and Lenin on the historical underdevelopment of peripheral societies are fundamental to the debate, one of our concerns in this monograph is to critically enter the literature on the incorporationist process. In so doing we limit our area of focus to a case study of the initial imperialist intervention in an erstwhile colonial backwater, that of French Laos. The period is from 1893 to 1954 or from the outset of direct colonial rule to the eclipse of French power at Dien Bien Phu. But aside from the central concern in development studies of whether or not development took place in the colonial or neo-colonial era is the salient question of what were the modes and mechanisms of imperialist domination in the economic spheres? What was the linkage between the subordination of the population to metropolitan capital and the development of a peasant and working class consciousness of its oppression at either a communitarian level or at a class level?

Developing as an aspect of the dependency debate, a new theoretical framework for an understanding of Third World peasants has emerged. Central to the "new" anthropology, and in contrast to the old "descriptive" anthropology it replaces, according to the Malaysian anthropologist, Zawawi, is a concern to delineate the structural relationship of Third World peasants to capitalism during different phases of imperialist contact (Zawawi 1983:198). He further points out that this New Economic Anthropology, with its emphasis on underlying structural changes and transformations, gives little consideration to the formulation of an integrated framework to explain changes, continuity and variations at the level of consciousness or ideology, ie. how peasant actors become ideologically reconstituted as subjects and placed in structure by capitalism (Zawawi 1983:206). Notable exceptions to the neglect of the question of superstructure include Godelier (1977), Kahn (1978) and Scott (1976). Arguably the latter, more than any other scholar, has laid the groundwork for a treatment of the question of peasant ideology and consciousness. But, Zawawi underscores, the task of synthesizing Scott's emphasis with the "new" theoretical framework has yet to be undertaken (Zawawi 1983:201). The matter has also been expressed succinctly by Werner in the preface to her study on the Cao Dai in Vietnam. The Vietnam area, she notes, has become a rich testing ground for both imperialism theories and peasant studies, inquiries only marginal to the old modernization paradigms (Werner 1981:2).[1]

Theoretically, what is at issue here, as the anthropologist Joel Kahn found in his study of Minangkabau social formations, is to determine "those features of the local economy which are externally and those which are internally generated..." This arises out of the recent debate within a debate between world system theorists (Wallerstein) and those who advocate a concept of articulation of modes of production (Rey, Kahn). The set of theses or theoretical prerequisites set out by J. G. Taylor for an analysis of Third World Formations is apposite here. As opposed to functionalist notions of development or underdevelopment, he argues, the problem must be analyzed from within historical materialism. A Third World Formation, he contends, can be seen as "being structured (or determined in the last instance) by an articulation which is produced largely as an effect of imperialist penetration". This articulation involves at least two modes of production; a capitalist and a non-capitalist mode, in which "the former is, or is becoming, increasingly dominant over the other" (Taylor 1983:102-3). Further, he theorizes, the division of labor and the restricted and uneven development produced by imperialist penetration establishes the material basis for a class structure specific to these formations. Moreover, "Imperialist penetration attempts to guarantee the reproduction of its restricted and uneven development through the promotion of political alliances representing its economic class supports. Yet, this in itself, is insufficient, since it also requires an ideological guarantee" (Taylor 1983:102-3). Thus in this work we are concerned not only with the Marxist ideas of modes of production, social formation, relations of production and value as they relate to a concrete historio-specific situation, but with the general problem of under-development, domination and peasant responses to imperialist intervention. Not only does this bring us to the identification, in the first instance, of a mode of production but to an analysis of its reproduction and its future transformation.

Methodologically, our innovation is to combine a world systems approach with a concern to register the non-economic, moral and ideological modes of domination in one colonial periphery. The thesis of this work holds that even in the most remote village of a colonial backwater, peasant behavior was influenced from the outset of the imperialist encounter, as much by the laws of capitalism (unequal exchange and surplus accumulation) as by the transformations engendered by the imposition of the colonial bureaucratic state. Stated another way, the decisions taken by the boards of directors of metropolitan enterprises — the *Sociétés* in the French context — had as much if not more impact on colonial subjects at the periphery as the agents of colonial state power, the Governor Generals, *Résidents* and their local collaborating agents.

Consequently (and characteristically?), hypotheses supporting the case of the peasant as a free market actor, places — in the face of climactic social and economic changes engendered by colonial capitalist impact — an erroneously romantic gloss upon explanations of peasant behavior. The corollary of this argument, then, is that ideological constraints are seldom sufficient to mask social injustices and to stave off simmering discontent and even open rebellion ad infinitum.

In writing on the process of world historical incorporation, Alvin Y. So has pointed out in that a theory of incorporation should include, an investigation of the historical condition under which incorporation initially took place, the particular historical event that initiated the incorporation process and the distinction between State level processes and local level processes, the concept of uneven incorporation, and the distinction between economic and political incorporation (So 1984: 113-4). From these general guiding principles to which we will loosely adhere, at least in the way of combining a world systems approach with a modes of production analysis, several analytical foci or questions emerge. First, given French economic interest in this colony over a period of 50 years, why was it not able to overcome its technological backwardness (the problem that the new socialist order has just begun to confront after decades of warfare). Second, why is class differentiation not an inevitable consequence of the process of colonial capitalism (cf. Kahn)? Third, what is the relationship between the intrusion of the cash nexus, subsistence threats and collective peasant responses? (cf. Scott and Popkin). Fourth, under the impact of the cash economy and the colonial tax system (the raising of primitive capital), can the various responses of the minority peasantry (upon which the burden fell heaviest) be considered as evidence of proto-nationalist stirrings? Finally, given the general condition of passive acquiescence of the majority Lao population in the face of the colonial experience, what ideological superstructural guarantees was the colonial State able to press to its advantage and in a manner reproducing indigenous social hierarchies and relations of production?

Intellectually, far from seeking to set up a false tension between area study and theory, history and social structure — although specialists in all areas might be disappointed — we are wedded to a holistic view of historical reconstruction and social praxis, in the hope that the elucidation of each facet will contribute to a better understanding of the totality. Having said that, it must be emphasized that this study is primarily a work of historical anthropology that seeks to fill a gap in a hitherto neglected area of local Lao history. However, we are equally concerned to set this study upon correct theoretical foundations. Friedman has supplied a sophisticated statement of the problematic; he contends that for a number of anthropologists, history appears opposed to social structure, according to the Marxist approach, history is necessarily incorporated in the field of analysis as the "stream of events" ceases to exist as an autonomous phenomenon. He continues, "The Marxist approach must transcend the false dichotomy between synchrony and diachrony by making the object of analysis the system of social reproduction, a system whose properties can be defined only with respect to time (Friedman 1975:162). Friedman is thus concerned with developing a "complete theory of structural transformation in which determination is correctly located at the juncture of intra- and inter-systemic variation in the process of social reproduction" (Friedman 1975:198-9).[2]

This study, therefore, seeks to contribute to a general understanding of historical movement, the standard social scientist's obsession with causal explanation. Equally it seeks to contribute to a general understanding of the interplay between internal and external economic and political forces. Specifically we are concerned to test the hypothesis whether conservation effects or barriers to capitalist penetration prevailed over dissolution effects as matched by taxation policy and the generation of primitive capital. In common with the peasant studies tradition we are also concerned to enter the literature on how peasants act in adversary situations.

In the absence of a local history writing tradition in the modern sense — and towards the end of demystification of heroic history [Lao communist historiography upholds its minority rebel leaders and personalities as exemplars of revolutionary virtue without much elaboration on the context or detail of the rebellions (cf. Phoumi Vongvichit 1968 passim)], — I have turned, as others before me in the study of Indochinese history, to the colonial archives. In the main, two sets of archives have been mined, first, the holdings of the *Résidence Supérieur* of Laos in Aix-en-Province, designated Aix and, second, the Archives National de France in Paris designated AOM. While the former, as implied, are concerned solely with matters of Laos, for the study of Federal Indochinese matters also involving Laos (eg. the workings of the opium *Régie*), I have recoursed to the latter. The reader should also be cautioned that a certain inbuilt bias attaches itself to colonial archives, apart from the researchers' own bias of selection, namely that the government's not the subordinate's viewpoint is dominant. Moreover, in the case of the colonial history of Laos, the thin spread of documentation, uneven in quality, suffering lacunae and in a state of deterioration, further strictly delimits the scope for a more contextual reading. Additionally, it might be said, any exercise which seeks to document the spread of capitalist relations of production in a relatively backward corner of the colonial periphery is bound to be misdirected as the attention of colonial rapporteurs was obviously upon the zones of greatest economic potential. Laos, we will show, was not only an economic backwater but, as measured off in meters of surviving archival deposits, of negligible concern to capital alongside Vietnam. The choice of Laos, then, sets this study apart from those of the peasant studies tradition which have concentrated upon the more economically developed parts of Indochina (eg. Wolf, Scott, Werner, Race, Popkin).

As a foil to the overwhelmingly archival bias of this study, and in the attempt to counterbalance elite sources with a "history from below" perspective, I have also sought to contextualize via the device of traveller's accounts, published ethnographies, press accounts of the day and fieldwork.[3] The problems of fieldwork in the Lao People's Democratic Republic I confronted full on during the course of doctoral research in 1980-81. Although useful, official interviews in Vientiane were clearly no substitute for participant observation in the village. This lacunae was, however, partially offset by a 1981 visit to a Tai Dam refugee village in the foothills of the Vientiane Plain, as well as a visit to Ban Vinai Hmong refugee camp in northeast Thailand in the same year. No less, wide ranging travels in Sip Song Panna (Xi Shuang Banna) in China in the same year were illuminating. In the pre-1975 period, visits to Hmong refugee settlements inside Laos (1972) and to Hmong and Yao villages in Luang Prabang and Xieng Khouang (1974) were useful. Hopefully the National Institute of Social Sciences, and which emerged in Laos in 1988, will expedite the research needs of foreign scholars in this area. On a separate tack, a number of western-based Hmong scholars have been active in oral history reconstruction, and this endeavour can only be encouraged.

In a separate study [*Political Struggles in Laos (1930-54)*, Duang Kamol, Bangkok, 1988], I address, inter alia, the roots of nationalism and communism in Laos. While I do not ignore the linkage and relevance of the early rebellions to the anti-colonial nationalist and communist struggle of the late 1940s in my 1988 study, neither do I force the connection. Rather, I place the emphasis upon organizational dynamics and transnational alliances. The obverse is the case in the current study. Here I brush over the complexities and minutae of organization but dwell upon the spontaneous and proto-nationalist activities of counter-elites and their peasant followers. While the matter is hard to document, I would submit that at the level of consciousness, a definite convergence occurred in colonial Laos between the ethnic rebel proto-nationalists and their modern counterparts in the Pathet Lao movement.[4]

The Organization Of This Book

In Part One we are concerned broadly with the development of capitalism in colonial Laos. Stated boldly, we are concerned to establish the conditions of existence of the prevailing mode or modes of production. Here we make the major distinction between political and economic incorporation into the world system.

In Part Two we set out to establish the conditions of reproduction of the predominant mode of production, the communitarian-tributary mode of production. This leads us to the endeavor of explaining the non-rebellion of the Lao during the colonial epoch prior to the Japanese intervention in 1945, a phenomenon we will seek to explain with reference to modes of State intervention in the economic sphere, on the one hand, and to the multiple systems of hegemonic superstructural dominance, on the other.

In Part Three we turn to explanations of the phenomenon of revolt by the montagnard population in the face of the transformation of their moral and economic order by the colonial State. While Chapter Five is concerned with the political economy of the Kha montagnard revolts of southern Laos, Chapter Six will focus upon the Chinese, Lu and Hmong revolts of the northern part of the country. A final Chapter will sketch the role of the montagnards in revolution and counter-revolution and up to the present.

A Conclusion will enter the discussion on the links between rebellion and revolution, and how the matter has been perceived in the western and the official Lao communist literature.

NOTES

1. Following in the tradition of Sartono and other scholars of protest movements in Southeast Asia I am concerned to go beyond mere descriptive narrative and to locate the study in an appropriate conceptual framework. Equally I agree that in order to catch the rich textures of meaning and complexities of the various protests the full range of social science disciplines should be at call (cf. Sartono Kartodirdjo 1973:xii).

2. I have expanded upon this problematic elsewhere. See the author's "Approaches to Tai-Lao Studies: From Orientalism to Marxism", *Review*, XII, 4, Fall 1989, pp. 503-533.

3. The problem of striking an independent vantage point over colonial documentation and presenting the point of view of the dominated class is well discussed by Cheah Boon Kheng in *The Peasant Robbers of Kedah 1900-1926: Historical and Folk Perceptions*, Oxford University Press, Singapore, 1988, pp. 6-8. Ultimately he sees the exercise as one of "historical creativity". I would agree although I do not lose sight of the larger forces at work, namely the intrusion of the cash nexus.

4. Noting of otherwise disconnected revolts in the Philippines between 1840 and the early twentieth century, Reynaldo Ileto stresses common features or at least in the way these events were perceived. "There lie, perhaps, not in a certain chain of events, but in the common features through time of a consciousness that constantly seeks to define the world in its own terms" (Ileto 1979:39). This observation, I would submit, is not irrelevant to the Laos context.

PART ONE

The Development of Colonial Capitalism in Laos (1893-1954)

During their whole rule over Pathet Lao, the French colonialists did nothing to develop the industrial potential of the country except for the exploitation of tin ores in the southern part of Patene with a yearly output of 1,500 tonnes. The policy of the French colonialists was to maintain the Pathet Lao in a permanent state of backwardness so that they could exploit it as a source of raw materials and as a market for their goods and use it as a strategic position in Indochina and Southeast Asia.

(*The Liberation Struggle of the Pathet Lao*,
The Pathet Lao Propaganda Committee
for World Peace, October 1952).

1

The Political and Economic Incorporation of Laos

THE POLITICAL DEVELOPMENT OF FRENCH LAOS (1893-1954)

Along with Cochinchina, Annam, Tonkin, Cambodia and Kouang Tcheou-Wan (the treaty port in China), Laos was one of six French possessions in Indochina, each holding a distinct, independent civil personality within the Indochinese Union.[1] The general administration of Indochina was headed by a Governor General seated in Saigon.

While the self-perception of the colonizer of the metropolitan mission in the colonial periphery hardly accords with national versions of history, the following survey and rationale of events leading to the political and economic incorporation of the Lao principalities on the eastern side of the Mekong river into the French colonial empire by one of its servants, Lapomarade, is nevertheless instructive. "History" he wrote,

> ....explains to degrees the loss of vitality of the Lao in the Mekong valley; internecine wars, successive invasions would have consumed a race which, while weakened as it appears today, was nevertheless once vigorous and combative.

To be sure, the rescue theme occurs like a leitmotif through colonial historiographical accounts of "fallen" Laos:

> In the Fourteenth century, at the time the Siamese founded their Kingdom of Ayuthya on the Menam, the Lao, already installed on the upper Mekong, descended the river, driving before them the Khmer, and founding in their turn a Kingdom which they progressively extended towards the South and which, it is said, experienced prosperous years.

In the Nineteenth century, however, a division of families occurred separating Luang Prabang and Vientiane and leading to disunion, bloody conflict and irremediable decadence. Profiting from involvement in the affairs of the country, foreigners then and there created the presumptions of sovereignty, the Siamese in the valley and the Vietnamese on the plateau. Freed from the Burmese menace, the Siamese grew in strength and appetite for treasure and manpower, thus appearing in Laos as conquerors. Relations between the Chakkri and the princes of Vientiane were truly without love, at least judging by the two sackings of Vientiane in 1800 and 1826 and the multiple raids upon its population. On the contrary, it appears that the court of Bangkok had more noble intentions with regard to Luang Prabang, at least helping that Kingdom in annexing Hua Phan (Sam Neua) from the Vietnamese during the 1830s.

The growth of the Chakkri, in any case, coincided with the weakening of the dynasty of Annam, consecutive with the death of Emperor Gia Long. A veritable period of anarchy thus proceeded, to the favor of Chinese bands arriving from the north (ie. those led by Deo Van Tri from a base in Lai Chau and who entered into conflict with the Siamese in 1887 and who sacked Luang Prabang) and the invasion of high country of Laos between the Mekong and the Black River by Siamese regulars arriving from the south. Disorder and insecurity were soon at their limit, and Siam could only profit from this state of affairs. Around 1880 and 1890, the authority of Bangkok was more or less recognized in Luang Prabang and Vientiane while Siamese Commissioners were in place in Cammon, Attopeu and in the province of Bassac encroaching on the territories of Annam and Cambodia.

But, the text continues, an "unforeseen and insurmountable" obstacle arose to stem this "premature expansion", namely France.

France, had recently established its power in Tonkin, then in Annam, substituting the power of a great nation state for the power of a declining authority, namely the government in Hue.

The explorations of the Mekong (Mouhot, Doudart de Lagree, etc.) then the voyages of the missions of Auguste Pavie along the river and in the high region of the north had made known to the French public the existence of the Lao principalities, the historical foundations of their sovereignty, the rights of the empire of Annam in certain territories of the Mekong basin and, by way of consequence, the recent and debatable pretensions of the Siamese.

A western colonial power and a young Asian state in a growth crisis (*en crise de croissance*) thus met and collided on the great Indochinese river, although the forces were a little too unequal for the outcome to be in doubt.

> Siam, however, was tardy in relinquishing its hold. Our hesitations only encouraged them. Didn't the Convention of 7 May 1886 implicitly recognize our rights in Luang Prabang? Although this convention was never ratified, we nevertheless signed it. Another encouragement for Siam came from England. Anglo-French rivalry was at its fullest; the installation of France on the peninsula offered the Indies a dangerous cousin, and the advantage of having the Siamese state as a strong buffer, wasn't lost upon the British cabinet. London supported Bangkok.
>
> This takes us to the opening days of 1893. The situation was tenuous in the extreme: the Siamese government expelled one of our commercial agents from the Mekong. Three columns of colonial troops and militia thus departed from Annam to reoccupy it in the name of the government of Hue, including the five provinces of middle Laos, from Cammon to the northern frontier of Cambodia. Armed conflict ensued, the islands of Khone were the theatre of combat and an Inspector of the militia was shot dead by the Siamese Commissioner as they were entering into discussions.

The events which followed are well known: the forcing of the Menam by gun-boats, an ultimatum addressed to the Royal government, and the acquiescence by the latter in all the claims made upon it.

> The treaty of 3 October 1893 recognised the exclusive rights of Annam and Cambodia on the territory of the left bank of the Mekong and fixed the frontier as the east bank of the river. The Anglo-French declaration of 1896, then the treaty of 24 February 1904, restored to Luang Prabang certain districts on the right bank of the Mekong, thus completing the work commenced in 1893.[2]
>
> French Laos thus came into being.....
>
> (Ministre des Armes, Archives Historique, Tonkin 10H71, Lapomarade, Attaché Militaire de France, Notice Concernant le Laos Francaise et ses Rapports avec le Siam, Bangkok, 1 April 1928).

A contrary view of the background to political incorporation is provided by a Vietnamese source. This account observes that French explorers first appeared in Laos as early as the nineteenth century under the guise of scientific research. Exploration also served the broad goal of establishing commercial routes to southern China. Among them were Henri Mouhot (1861), who explored the area from Paklay to Luang Prabang; Doudart de Lagrée, who explored not only the Mekong basin but the Sekong, Sebanghien, and other regions such as the Bolovens; Attopeu and Saravane, and who arrived in Luang Prabang in mid-April 1867. In addition, missions led by officers such as Harmand (1875-77) and Paul Marie Net (1882) explored the Mekong, its tributaries, and even the mountain regions inhabited by ethnic minorities. In June 1886 a preliminary accord was signed between France and Siam authorizing the opening of a French vice-consulate in Luang Prabang. The following February the French Vice Consul, Auguste Pavie, arrived in Luang Prabang purportedly as an explorer but in fact to prepare the invasion of the country. By early 1892 the French vice-consulate in Luang Prabang was transformed into a trade representative. Semi-commercial and semi-political agencies were set up in several other localities. Later that year the expulsion of two Frenchmen by the Siamese government and the death of an employee of the French vice-consulate in Luang Prabang served as a pretext for French armed intervention (anon, *Laos: An Outline* 1982:34).

Writing of French colonialism in tropical Africa, Suret-Canale notes that to open up the various territories for "development" or colonial exploitation not only had an administrative/military system to be imposed but chiefdoms acting as intermediaries had to be anointed. This was to aid in the raising of taxes, the supply of forced labor, and so on. For people accustomed to living in freedom, he writes, this could not be imposed other than by force. Colonial history dubbed this process "pacification", but it "took the form of a long and cruel series of military operations, aimed at disarming the population and removing any possibilities of resistance among them" (Suret-Canale 1971:95). Africa or Asia, as we shall see, the process was the same.

Three years after the nominal occupation by France of the territories east of the Mekong in 1893, Bouloche, the *Résident Supérieur* on mission in Laos was given the responsibility of giving organizational definition to the newly acquired possession. Accordingly, Laos was divided into two parts each with a certain autonomy. The first, with its capital in Luang Prabang, was upper Laos, and the second, with its capital at Khong, was lower Laos. At the head of the two divisions was placed a *commandant supérieur*, each having the same attribution as a *Résident Supérieur* and both responsible to the Governor General of Indochina. These two divisions were in turn sub-divided into a number of commissariats — six in the north and seven in the south — each approximating the ancient sub-divisions of Laos, the *muong*, or those circumscriptions more recently created by the Siamese. Each commissioner was responsible for the general administration of the *muong* (later renamed *khoueng*) and also police functions, customs duties and tax collection, opium sales, public works, justice, etc. They were helped in these duties by the *Garde Indigène* constituted largely of Vietnamese effectives but also included Lao (Reinach 1911:230).[3]

Sip Song Chau Tai, by some degrees tributary to Luang Prabang, was placed under the administration of Tonkin, and in 1898 part of the territory of Hua Phan (Sam Neua) was attached to Annam (Reinach 1911:230). A dispute over ownership of Muong Sinh with the British was settled in France's favor in early 1896 and following a convention of 7 October 1902 signed between France and Siam, Bassac (on the west bank of the Mekong) was retroceded to France (Boulanger 1931:333 and 342). The last major territorial adjustment occurred in December 1904 when the Governor General of Indochina detached Strung Treng from the administration of Laos and placed it within the boundaries of Cambodia (Sarin Chhak 1964:32).

Following an *arrête* of the Governor General on 6 February 1899, the position of *Commandant Supérieur* was abolished and the two divisions of Laos were united and placed under the authority of a *Résident Supérieur*. Because of unification, French officials hitherto answerable to a separate administrative service, were incorporated into the general Indochinese civil service. The administrative capital, first placed at Savannakhet, was then fixed at Vientiane, the seat of the *Résident Supérieur*. The eleven provinces of Laos, then determined, were Vientiane, Upper Mekong, Tran Ninh (Xieng Khouang), Cammon, Saravane, Bassac, Khong, Savannakhet, Attopeu, Muong Hoa and Hua Phan (Reinach 1911:251). This was in line with an *arrête* issued in the same year determining the establishment of provincial level administrative units on an all-Indochina level. Apart from the provincial administration by civil officials, certain regions of Tonkin and Laos bordering on China were, for security reasons, organized as military territories (Galembert 1924:49).

The system of military forces in Laos was rationalized by a decree of 31 December 1906. The *Garde Indigène*, thus established, was placed under the command of the Governor General, on the one hand, and the local administrative chiefs in the component countries of the Indochinese Union, on the other. Its appointed mission was "to assure internal policing, to undertake escorts of convoys, the surveillance of administrative buildings, the guarding of prisoners and the security of communication routes." The strength of the force in Laos was as follows: two inspectors, fourteen *garde principals*, 29 sub-officers and 625 corporals or *gardes*. It was constituted into eleven brigades based in the main towns in the provinces. Meray, a colonial inspector, observed that in practice each of the brigades revealed a certain autonomy and only came under the very remote control of the *Résident Supérieur*. The *garde principals*, he commented, appear to exercise constraint with difficulty given the ruling which makes them the auxiliary and subordinate of the province chiefs. Indeed, in the majority of the provinces visited by the inspector, the relations between the commissioners of the government and the officers of the *Garde Indigène* were observed to be "very tenuous," especially in Pakse and Xieng Khouang. As a consequence, the administration sometimes recoursed to the employment of the Gendarmerie to exercise duties otherwise reserved for the *Garde Indigène* (AOM Paris NF 95 947 "Etude sur la Garde Indigene au Laos." Maurice Meray, Phnom Penh, 3 March 1914).

The creation of the Fifth Military Region of Laos, with its administrative center located at Muong Khoua (Phong Saly), by an *arrête* of 21 March 1916 upon the termination of military pacification in the region, led to direct military rule in this part of the country up until the time of the Japanese intervention in 1945. The administration of the territory was confided to the chief of the Fourth Battalion with precedence over two delegate administrators in Outai and Bountai. For the *muong* of Phong Saly, the chief of the Fifth Battalion acted as the Commissioner of the territory and was assisted by one *chaomuong* and five Lao officials (AOM Aix Q2, Fifth Military Region). The Fifth Military Region, along with Attopeu, Bassac, Cammon, Upper Kekong, Hua Phan, Luang Prabang, Saravane, Savannakhet, Tran Ninh and Vientiane thus formed the composite provincial administrative framework of colonial Laos.[4]

Writing in 1911, Reinach observed that under French administration, the political institutions of Laos remained largely as they had been constituted before 1893. Following the example of Siam, he asserted, the French allowed their subjects the "greatest liberty" and, insofar as they were "compatible with French institutions," respected their traditions, customs and mores. That was a big caveat, however. If the philosophy of administering a protectorate accorded with a policy of minimal intervention, the French mission, by definition, demanded a profound transformation of the political-religious and social armature, if it was to be efficacious. With under-statement he acknowledged that the French were constrained to revoke certain indigenous authorities who were compromised with the Siamese or whom were otherwise "worthless" (Reinach 1911:231). One of the first radical reforms to be introduced, however, was the suppression of the slave traffic in which Lao notables no less than individual Siamese were involved.

While in many ways special, the indigenous administration of Luang Prabang reflected, par excellence, the common pattern of centralized and hierarchical *muong* administration, typical of Lao (Tai) political systems. In Luang Prabang the head of the *muong* was the *Somdet Phra Tiao*, the first king, known as the "lord of life" and the *Tiao Maha Oupahat*, along with the second king known as the "grand master responsible for the preservation of the well-being." After them, in order of precedence, came the prime ministers, the *Latsavang* (first prince of the right), the *Latsabout* (second prince and minister of the left), *Komakhoune* (third prince and minister of the milieu) and *Kommamoune* (fourth prince and minister of the civil service). All were of Royal blood and all bore the hereditary title

"Tiao". Certain other members of the Royal family in government service, notably those in the *Senam* or *Hosanam Luong* (King's Council), bore the title of *"phaya."* Subordinate to the *phaya* were *"Krommakan"* (judges). Various other mandarins were responsible for tax collection, assembling corvee labor, public service, military affairs, palace affairs, etc. (see Vongsay 1967:92 and Reinach 1911:233-4).

In contrast to the rest of Laos, which was under the direct rule of the French administration, the Kingdom of Luang Prabang, was considered as a country of the "special protectorate" and regulated by a convention with the King signed on 24 April 1917. Thereafter, the King's Council was streamlined to accord with the realities of colonial administration and, following a Royal ordinance of 15 October 1927, was reconstituted with three members; the Director of Internal Affairs, the Director of Justice and Religion and the Director of Finances, Public Works, Commerce and Agriculture. Decisions made could only be rendered executory by the *Résident Supérieur,* however (*Indochine* 1931:20). Additionally, an Inspectorate of Indigenous Affairs was created at Vientiane, a position held by the senior Lao administrator and future Lao nationalist hero, Prince Phetsarath.

In that part of Laos subject to direct French rule, and where local princely prerogatives had been overridden, all administrative matters were the subject of *arrêtes* of the *Résident Supérieur*. In line with traditional practice, the main administrative unit in Laos was the *muong* and the *kong* (outlying districts peopled by non-Lao races). At the head of the *muong* hierarchy were *chaomuong* answerable to the French commissioner or his delegate. In intermediate echelons were *oupahat* and *phousouei,* responsible for the establishment of tax rolls, the recovery of tax and various *muong* services. *Samien* occupied the lowest administrative echelons. The administration of *kong* was conferred upon *naikong*. The *ban* (villages) were headed by *naiban,* helped by *phoban* and advised by an assembly of elders. Villagers grouped into *tasseng* (cantons) were administered by officials of the same name (*Indochine* 1931:21).

By an *arrête* of 13 October 1920, an Indigenous Consultative Council was created in Laos. Presided over by the *chef de province,* it was not composed of elected members but made up of the *chaomuong,* the *oupahat* and other Lao notables chosen by the *chef de province* with the consent of the *Résident Supérieur*. The provincial Council in the province of Vientiane also included three Vietnamese notables. Convened annually, the councils could only tender advice to the *Résident*; their consultation was not obligatory. The next hesitant step towards local political participation was the creation of an Indigenous Consultative Assembly by an *arrête* of 27 April 1923. It was largely comprised of members elected from the Indigenous Consultative Councils along with representatives designated by the *Résident Supérieur* and delegates of the King of Luang Prabang (Galembert 1924:199-200 and 225).

In the course of 1931 — and indeed on numerous other occasions — the monarch, Sisavang Vong, expressed anxiety over the future of his dynasty, on this occasion to the French Minister of Colonies, Paul Reynaud, then on tour in Indochina. His request to place the Kingdom of Luang Prabang on the same legal plane as Annam and Cambodia was rewarded by a letter signed by the Minister of Colonies on 19 December 1931. According to Inche, while the Kingdom of Luang Prabang was now placed on a firmer legal base, the document was to some degree illegal because it was not ratified by the French parliament. What had in fact happened, he argued, was that the French State had appropriated western "secular" sovereignty over Laos, while the Kingdom of Luang Prabang retained the religious and ritual attributes of sovereignty owing to "oriental" civilization (Inche 1935:199).

> France has occupied and administered (Laos) for forty years, but there does not exist a document specifying its legal status. There exists no law of annexation of Laos by France although according to our constitution, a law is juridically indispensable to make a region a French colony. There neither exists an international treaty placing the ensemble of Laos under the French protectorate.
>
> (Inche 1935:11).

While doubtless lost upon the Lao elite, much less the population, debates over the precise juridical status of Laos — whether as a colony or as a protectorate or as both — continued through the entire epoch.

The system was described by Virginia Thompson in 1937 as "an immense success." As in Cambodia, French rule "floated gently on top of the old native administration giving an appearance of modernization to what had always existed and with which it did not interfere...." Compared with Vietnam where the French erred on the side of over-direct administration Laos, "had administrators but no administration" (Thompson 1937:368-9). While this notion contains an element of truth, we will argue that the degree of French administrative intervention in both the infrastructural (economic) spheres and the superstructural (political) spheres was nevertheless not inconsequential.

THE POLITICAL ECONOMY OF FRENCH LAOS

French sentiment by the 1880s was that as colonies were expensive, then they should pay for themselves. The other side of the coin, according to this logic, was that the colonies should be reserved exclusively as French markets. This was codified by the law of 11 January 1892 and which provided that the products of the mother country could enter the colony duty free while those of other countries were subject to the same tariffs as France. In return, Indochinese produce could be imported duty free into France. Robequain remarks that up until the First World War, economic regulation was rather disorganized. Home industries, while having great predominance, were not predominant. Many Chinese and Japanese commodities used by natives were subject to only moderate duties. Conflicting demands of various concerned metropolitan economic interests saw to it that no coherent economic doctrine emerged at that point. But in 1928, a thorough remodelling of the 1892 custom system was brought down. In practice, the claims of local Indochinese groups were "smothered" and led to the enforcement of even greater protectionism. Chinese and Japanese articles were now subjected to ordinary tariff rates. Indochina became isolated behind even steeper tariff walls than metropolitan France. But no sooner had this new customs law come into effect than the depression began (Robequain 1944:128-136). Despite the apparent lack of official interest in stimulating local industrialization, local manufacturing facilities gradually evolved during the inter-war years, especially in Cochinchina. Murray remarks that they developed "within the interstices of metropolitan activities" as ancillary operations, eg. raw materials processing and small to medium scale production for local consumption (Murray 1980:317).

During the war years the Indochina economy obviously became "more directly subservient to Japanese needs than ever was the case vis-à-vis the French". At issue was forced payment for the Japanese occupation army and indirect financing of Japanese purchases of land and businesses (Robequain 1944:370). As wryly observed by two American commentators during the war years, however deplorable the purpose and method of the Japanese occupation it did lead to a broadening of the industrial picture and a breakdown of some of its monopolistic characteristics (Adrus and Green in Robequain 1944:388).

With empirical reference to French colonialism in Africa, and not without relevance to the case of Laos, the French historian Suret-Canale observed "....the first economic aspect with considerable social consequences was the introduction and penetration of the market economy". European penetration, he showed, came mainly through trade, the prime aim of colonization being to achieve "advantageous deals." Administrative coercion via taxation not only burdened the masses with the expenses of administration but sought to produce and (reproduce) the "conditions necessary for business to run smoothly." Thus forced to participate in the circulation of money, the people had to raise tax money (Suret-Canale 1971:59). Further, the development of the market economy accelerated the dissolution of the traditional hierarchies tending to leave isolated individuals. But, according to Suret-Canale in a reformulation of the unequal exchange argument, ".... colonial exploitation in the periphery by monopoly capital differed from the role of usury in medieval Europe in that instead of permitting primitive accumulation on the spot as the basis for the subsequent development of industrial capitalism it robbed the country of this accumulation, which took place instead at home thanks to profits and surplus profits exported" (Suret-Canale 1971:68-69). Moreover, in the trading economy, "agriculture remained almost the exclusive source of production" and even the social group remained essentially unchanged (Suret-Canale 1971:218).

The following observation by Samir Amin is not without interest or relevance. In theoretical terms, he notes, while at the center the capitalist mode of production tends to become exclusive the same is not true of the periphery. The form assumed by peripheral formations are different depending upon the forms and epochs upon which they were integrated into the world system. Indeed peripheral national capital becomes subject to strict limitations, stunted or hypertrophied and subject to extraversion (Amin 1976:202). It is thus the capitalist mode of production which is dominant and "subjects the others and transforms them, depriving them of their distinctive functioning in order to subordinate them to its own, without, however, radically destroying them" (Amin 1976:22). In the following pages we will explore these hypotheses with reference to French colonial capital accumulation in Laos through a pre-monopoly to a monopoly phase.

The Pre-Monopoly Phase of Capital Accumulation (1889-1926)

From the outset of the French conquest of Laos, colonial policy was directed towards helping private metropolitan commercial advantage. Colonial development policy (*mise en valeur*) thus sought, first, to establish the potential preconditions for capitalist expansion and, second, to expand the general conditions of production by fostering basic economic infrastructure.

The general sense of the statist endeavour was revealed even before French political hegemony was secured. Indeed, trade preceded the flag in Laos. Accompanying a second Pavie Mission in 1889 was a commercial and industrial mission including Parisian traders and industrialists. Their mission was called the "Syndicat francais du Haut Laos" and was funded with operating capital of 100,000 francs. Their stated goal was to evaluate commercial prospects in the upper Mekong basin. In 1892 the mission was renamed the "Syndicat Francais du Laos" with its agents bearing the official title of commercial agents of the government and beneficiaries of emoluments from the colonial budget. They were responsible to the Minister of France in Bangkok and to the Governor General of Indochina (Grossin 1933:42). In the war of nerves against the Siamese, they also doubled as political officers.

The colonial State policy of *mise en valeur* in the non-monopoly phase of capitalist expansion centered on the leadership of and the mediation of the metropolitan state apparatus in encouraging and facilitating private investments through public works, loans, concessions etc. (Murray 1980:104). Stated another way, French expansion in Indochina was made possible only by the entrance and circulation of capital. This was raised either within Indochina in the form of duties and taxes or in the form of loans subscribed in France. Private business generally derived its capital from France but sometimes within the colony (Robequain 1944:137). Equally, one should not ignore the role of the colonial lobby throughout the French Third Republic in contributing to the colonial myth. As identified by Percell, the lobby constituted a group of interest groups and long-standing institutions concerned with the growing aspirations of empire despite "its quite limited economic potential" (Percell 1983:1-5).

The pre-monopoly phase in French Indochina, then, was dominated by the growth of merchant capital under the umbrella of metropolitan protectionist policies. In theory, as mentioned, metropolitan goods entered Indochina without duty under the 1892 law and, reciprocally, Indochinese produce imported by the metropole was exempt from duty. This meant free trade was established between France and Indochina, within which the separate countries were dissolved (cf. Robequain 1944:129-30 and see Samphan 1979:30). Although Laos lost its free trade status in 1931, the geography of the country preempted the erection of effective customs barriers around its external boundaries. The underlying rationale of colonial State actors in tandem with its merchant capitalist agents was thus control of markets. The principle was that metropolitan merchandise was sold at high prices and colonial products were purchased at low prices. Non-monopoly capital was dominated by expatriate settlers and fortune hunters whom nevertheless were the risk-takers and pioneers in agro-mineral production, thus setting the scene for the next stage of capitalist accumulation, that is, monopoly finance capital (Murray 1980:98-99).

In Laos, the grandiose dreams of the first merchant capitalists — of exploitation of a huge natural commercial emporium — literally foundered on the Mekong rapids before the new century dawned. Not only an unlikely trade-route to China, the Mekong proved an unreliable conduit to the south. Meray, a colonial official set the task of investigating the reasons for the economic decline into which Laos had slipped in the first decade of the century, noted that out of a total of 273,193,924 francs of merchandise introduced into Indochina in 1912, the corresponding figure for Laos was of "minimal importance," a mere 2,500,000 francs. Between 1908 and 1912 only 2,119,060 francs worth of merchandise entered Laos from other Indochinese countries, while the lion's share, 9,166,366 francs, entered Laos from Siam. Despite the privileged position of expatriate traders in Laos, strengthened by the Indochinese customs union, French merchant capitalists faced competition in colonial Laos. Apart from three French *maisons* (commercial enterprises) engaged in the sale of preserved food and spirits and in the consignment of rubber and benjoin, the Chinese were "masters of the marketplace." Found in the smallest of Lao towns, their shops were in fact the agencies of Bangkok-based commercial establishments. Not only did the Chinese benefit from frequent contacts with compatriots in Bangkok, but they enjoyed certain economies of scale such as the collective rental of transport services. The other side of the coin was that the Siamese market offered a greater outlet for Lao products than did Cambodia and Cochinchina (AOM Paris Indochine H 12 947, "Verification du Service des Douanes et Régies au Laos: Etude sur l'installation de la zone franche," Inspection Meray, Phnom Penh, 10 April, 1914).

It is worth noting here the comment of the French military attaché in Bangkok on the stagnation of French Laos compared to the relative economic dynamism of Siam:

> No roads, little commerce, few schools, no sporting groups — fewer in any case than Siam — no boy scouts, no military instruction to stimulate local patriotism — few indigenous functionaries sufficiently educated to participate in the upper echelons of the administration of the country and a consequent penetration of the administrative and commercial armature of the country by Vietnamese.
>
> (SHTM, 7N3340, Lt.Col.de Lapomarede, Attaché Militaire, 1 April 1928).

In any case direct competition with the entrenched position of the Chinese (and Vietnamese) merchants in the commodity trade was not entertained. Indeed, the activities of non-indigenous middle-men would have been appreciated in a colony where for a variety of reasons local entrepreneurs had not entered into merchant capital ventures. Rather, the comprador role of the Chinese and Vietnamese was viewed as complementary to the metropolitan project. While French capital would pioneer transport and extractive-export oriented industries, together with Chinese and to a lesser extent Vietnamese capital, it would also advance the process of primitive accumulation in the pre-monopoly phase.

The first merchant capital ventures in the transport sector in Laos were the "Compagnie Subventionée de Navigation Saigonnaise," which, from

1894, offered a steamer service on the middle Mekong and, the "Compagnie des Messageries fluviales de la Cochinchine et du Cambodge," the concessionaire of the Khong Island railroad linking the interrupted sections of the Mekong. While of course prospecting preceded investment in extractive export-oriented industries, two companies, the "Société d'Etudes et d'Exploitations Minières de l'Indochine" and, the "Companie fermière minières d'Etains d'Extrême Orient", reorganized tin-mining in the Nam Patene basin on a large scale basis in the 1920s. The exploitation of the agricultural and forestry resources of Laos was pioneered by the "Commerciale du Laos," created in 1922 with a capital subscription of one million francs, while the "Compagnie de l'Est Asiatique francaise" carved out for itself a commercial empire in upper Laos.

The Monopoly Phase of Surplus Accumulation (1926-1954)

As Murray has shown, the renewal of the charter of the Banque de l'Indochine as the bank of issue by the French National Assembly represented the political triumph of finance capital in Indochina and the demise of non-monopoly capital (Murray 1980:140). While in its pre-monopoly phase, the Banque operated as primus inter pares, for instance as opium purveyor to the administration along with the Comptoir National d'Escompte (Anon., 1916-17:11), by the 1930s it had moved into the phase of expanded reproduction, in fact increasing profits through the depression years while consolidating political power with financial power. As Murray points out, in its monopoly phase the Banque became the most powerful economic force in Indochina enjoying all the advantages of a government bank but not subject to government control (Murray 1980:132-154). Interlocking directorates permitted the Banque to operate throughout the Far East, Africa and Oceania while also dominating the principal branches of production within Indochina. According to an official American document, the Banque and three other major enterprises controlled, by 1952, some 119 companies in Indochina. In addition the Banque, along with other private metropolitan-controlled monopolistic trade associations, dominated the rice export and petroleum import businesses (*Foreign Relations*, 1952-54, "Documents relating to the organization of Indochina's rice export trade," The Minister at Saigon (Heath) to the Department of State, Saigon, 9 April 1952).[5]

The monetary system, as Samir Amin has written, "passively" fulfills an important technical function, that of adjusting the supply of money to the need of it expressed in a "state of equilibrium." "Simple reproduction" is the assumption of this function. Although ignored by conventional theory, Amin argues, the monetary system also fulfills another more decisive function, that of making "expanded reproduction" possible. This he calls the active function of money or the increase in the quantity of money necessary if the transformation of savings into investment is to be possible and if capitalist accumulation is to proceed (Amin 1976:84-8). In Indochina, however, the general trend with the piaster — the money having legal tender — was devaluation. Between 1884 and 1930, the value of silver, to which the piaster was then pegged, dropped by two-thirds. This meant that the price of rice produced by the Indochinese peasant farmers, as calculated in bullion, dropped substantially with the devaluation of the currency paid to them (Samphan 1979:83). In 1930, the rules of convertability of the Indochinese piaster were fixed. One Indochinese piaster was made equal to ten French francs (Despeuch 1953:43). However, the linking of the piaster to the gold standard at a time of economic depression, Hémery argues, further exacerbated the crisis, particularly for the rice exporters of Cochinchina trading with Asian marketplaces still operating with silver-backed currencies (Hémery 1975:28-9). For "expanded reproduction" to be successful in the colonial periphery, clearly the programme of primitive accumulation through monetization had to be expanded on a universal basis. In social formations like Laos, however, strong survivals of pre-capitalist structures threw up barriers to the active function of money in circulation, thus creating differential effects of capitalist penetration.

This problem might be illustrated with reference to the montagnard of southern Laos. In her ethnography of the Nya Hon, a southern montagnard group in Laos, Wall explains how at the time of her fieldwork in the early 1970s, the montagnard saw no use for round coins (much less paper bills).

> Les montagnards n'avaient pas l'habitude d'échanger un objet inutile contre un autre representant pour eux une valeur certaine, et mettant en évidence la richesse de la famille ainsi que le prestige social.

Rather, the piaster — still hoarded for their silver value today — were transformed into little ingots, preserving the character of money, but of more aesthetic interest and even acquiring magic potency. In the montagnard scheme of exchange, one large ingot or *lien* equalled one *piaster de commerce de la Banque d'Indochine*, 1906. She found that this form of money was accepted by most of the neighboring tribes, although coexisting with barter (Wall 1975:35-6). Problems of circulation, commoditization and the raising of primitive capital are still being confronted today in socialist Laos.

In any case the foci of monopoly capital and the locus of capitalist penetration in Laos was in the tin mining sphere. The Banque's interest in this area was secured by way of a controlling ownership of the "Etains du Cammon." The highly capitalized tin mining operation in the Nam Patene basin, then, most fully expressed the nature of unequal exchange between the center and the colonial periphery and, as will be argued below, the dissolution and "hybrid" effects of the capitalist mode of production in the localized agro-mineral sphere.

The Boom Years (1926-1929) By 1926, metropolitan capitalists were seized with a new optimism over commercial prospects and quick profits in Laos, almost entirely related to a changed evaluation of the mining domain. As Murray remarks, with the gradual recovery in 1922 of the previously deflated price structure of minerals, a boom was precipitated in the industry, attracting, by 1925, widespread attention among metropolitan investors. An unparalleled upsurge in capital investments in mining took place and "prospecting fever" spread from the principal mining zones in Tonkin to Laos, Cambodia and Annam (Murray 1980:320). This we will characterize as the boom years of colonial Laos, all the more remarkable for the crash which succeeded it.

While a start had been made in capital investment in Indochina in the pre-World War One period, taken as a whole, economic development had hardly commenced in Indochina. In the period between 1918 and 1930 a far more comprehensive program of development had been initiated. Particularly after 1924 large amounts of French investment entered Indochina, in part a consequence of the franc's depreciation and the relative security offered by the Indochinese piaster to metropolitan investors. Equally, Europeans in Indochina borrowed large sums for local investments. The sudden increase in loans issued for the establishment of new companies in the 1926-1929 period, Robequain pointed out, was indicative of the hopes for the development of Indochina's resources (Robequain 1944:164). As an anonymous colonial rapporteur wrote of Laos in the early 1920s:

> ....the interests, the initiatives, the capital turns towards the study and exploitation of the treasures of this Laos, yesterday still ignored, this veritable Far West, this *magasin de reserve* of French Indochina.
>
> (AOM Aix D6, "Rapport sur la Situation du Laos," 1923).

While the mining fever in Laos was as much a manifestation of the psychological climate of the Bourse as of actual development of the new "Oriental Klondike," the country attracted its share of adventurers. Table 1.1 reveals the dimensions of the mining boom on the ground in Laos.

In the single year 1928, 4,000 mining declarations or claims were made and test bores were sunk in various parts of Laos. Mining exploration

TABLE 1.1
MINING PERMITS ISSUED IN LAOS (1923-27)

Year	Prospecting Permits (Laos)	Operating Permits (Laos)
1923	4	36
1923	10	32
1925	68	77
1926	817	895
1927	630	1515

Source: (Deloncle 1930:153)

activity in this "New Bolivia," as it came to be known, far outstripped that undertaken in other parts of Indochina (Deloncle 1930:153).[6]

European exploitation of stanniferous ores in Indochina was first confined to Tonkin, and only since 1920 were operations extended into Laos in a big way. The Nam Patene concession, the center of operations, first attracted the interest of metropolitan capital in 1896 during the pre-monopoly phase of capital accumulation. A "Syndicat minière du Laos" was then formed with a capital issue of 130,000 francs. This amount was later raised to 210,000 by the Société d'études de Hin Boun. By the early 1920s the "Société d'études et d'exploitations minières en Indochine" was formed with a capital issue of 100,000 francs, later raised to 12,600,000 francs. Despite formidable logistics problems, machinery was installed and by 1921 the plant was operational giving employment to fifteen European managers and 700-800 mine coolies.[7] By 1927 profits exceeded two million francs. The *Société* then went public on the Bourse and raised 323 million francs share capital. Encouraged by this success, the *Société* ventured into diverse subsidiary enterprises including the "Société commercial du Laos," the "Société immobilière du Laos" and the "Société Textile du Laos" (Deloncle 1930:153).

A particular characteristic of the monopoly phase of capital accumulation in Laos was the making of fabulous personal fortunes by individual speculators even at the pre-exploration stage. The "Société des étains de l'Indochine" founded in October 1926 with primitive capital of 18 million francs, attracted such attention on the Bourse that by March 1929 it had accumulated 406 million francs capital. This was largely attributed to the acquisition by the *Société* of twenty-six claims in the Nam Patane basin from a certain Dubost. The same enterprising individual also sold for 225,000 francs, and twenty-five percent of the profits realized, a private claim to the "Société des étains du Cammon," founded in February 1927. In October, Dubost created two separate *sociétés*, each subscribed to with share capital to the value of 1,500,000 francs in 15,000 share lots. Dubost was alloted 14,000 shares from these two *sociétés* which attained a value of 102 million francs. He then financed five more *sociétés* listed as mining ventures in Laos. His share holdings then rose to 1,106 million francs. As one observer of this spectacle remarked, a hectare of land at Nam Patane was beginning to acquire the value of gold. The irony was, however, that none of these *sociétés* listed on the metropolitan stock exchange had the least relationship with tin nor with Nam Patene. The "development" fiasco in Laos was undoubtedly symbolized by the creation, on paper at least, of the "Compagnie Minière du Laos" by the banker Meurire. His advertised mining operations in Tchepone were exposed as entirely fictitious and the company exposed as entirely fraudulent (Deloncle 1930:153). As Robequain commented on the 1925-1928 "boom" in Laos, it sometimes reached "tragicomic" proportions. Launching a new enterprise often depended more upon an advertising campaign than a careful study of local conditions. The banks and boards in Paris and the stockholders in the French provinces had only the remotest notion of the actual enterprise. He remarked:

> The stock-market quotations sky-rocketed before a single tonne had been taken out of the fabulous mine. Some time later came sudden collapse.
>
> (Robequain 1944:265).

While the interests of metropolitan capitalists and the colonial state coincided in the sphere of the extraction and export of minerals little investment was ploughed back into the country in a way that would have eased the establishment of pre-conditions for autonomous national development. The same gravitation of capital towards import-export activities reported by Samphan in Cambodia (1979:42) occurred in colonial Laos in the mining and also the non-mining domain.

A State Agricultural Service was established in Laos in 1926 with a view to simplifying the exploitation of the agricultural wealth of the country. The "encouraging" results obtained by several European planters in lower Laos led to the creation in 1928 of the Mixed Chamber of Commerce and Agriculture. Likewise a State Forestry Service was established to help the "rational exploitation" of Lao timber, particularly teak (Meyer 1930:55). The concession was awarded to the "Compagnie de l'est asiatique francaise" and some 12,000 to 15,000 logs of wood were floated down the Mekong annually to Saigon (Lévy 1974:79). Although Laos produced around 350,000 tonnes of rice a year or equal to one kilogram of rice a day per head of population (900,000 at 1930 figures) under normal conditions, it was a net rice importing country during colonial times. While certain provinces such as Bassac usually produced a rice surplus, rationalization of agriculture under the colonial administration never extended to the kind of State-sponsored hydraulic projects necessary to improve yields.

Certain other agricultural products yielded moderate profits for the commercial interests involved, whether colonial entrepreneurs, the embryonic national bourgeoisie or the *lam* or tribal-intermediary most closely involved with the minority peasant population at the point of production. For instance cardamom cultivated on the Bolovens plateau and exported to Bangkok and Cholon realized substantial profits for the French involved in the trade (about 160,000 piasters annually). Of marginally greater significance in the montagnard economy was the sticklac trade. Accruing from natural production and "harvested" by the Kha to the amount of 40 to 50 tonnes per annum, its trade was worth 400,000 piasters annually. The export monopoly of both benjoin and sticklac was held, however, by the Parisian *maison* "Dore Saint Germain". The livestock and skin trade with Siam was valued at 260,000 piasters annually, while the ivory and elephant trade, important during the early colonial period, had diminished in importance during the closing decades of colonial rule. During the Second World War, coffee plantations already established in the highlands of Cochinchina were extended to the Bolovens plateau (Lévy 1974:79). Although more grandiose schemes to develop and "colonize" the Bolovens and Xieng Khouang plateaux were drawn up following the bloody pacification of these temperate regions, little was actually accomplished. As Ennis notes, the fundamental problem, aside from transport, remained the dearth of manpower (Ennis 1936:130).[8]

A Vietnamese source notes the existence in Laos in 1945 of barely twenty industrial enterprises. These included ten rice-husking mills employing between nine to twenty workers, water and power stations in the cities and provincial capitals and saw and paper mills. Besides the tin mines, other export oriented activities included rubber plantations covering some 20,000 hectares and coffee production reaching a yearly output of 3000 tons in 1940-45. The source explains how these spheres of activity were expanded along the lines of "feeding war by war". Thus to service the needs of war and of French forces other activities developed like repair workshops, public transport, import-export companies mainly run by French and Chinese interests as well as gambling dens, bars, hotels and brothels. Hand in hand with the entry of the French expeditionary corps came the "consumer society" and which even invaded the rural society. Overall, however, 95% of the population remained "in a state of small autarkic underdeveloped exploitation" (anon, *Laos: An Outline* 1982: 44 and 70-71).

In Yacano's phrase, it was the metropolitan crisis which implanted its character on the colonies. To be sure, as he indicates, this was not expressed uniformly. Those regions of the colonial periphery subsisting in the natural economy escaped more or less completely from the crisis, at least as expressed by the fall in prices of agricultural produce, the collapse of industrial production, the diminution of currency in circulation and the falling away of trade (Yacano 1971:34). While the combination of geographical isolation and the resilience of pre-capitalist modes of production in Laos shielded the Lao peasant from the direct and most debilitating effects of the crisis suffered with great intensity by their Vietnamese counterparts, even Laos could not be quarantined from the secondary economic effects of the crisis which swept the Indochinese peninsula.

Although the price of tin remained buoyant during the depression years, the global slump meant the dismissal of marginal workers in the mining industry and a general impoverishment of the population of Laos, especially if measured in cash terms. Generally speaking, the crisis revealed the vulnerability of Indochina, as an exporter of raw materials, to the cyclical effects of global economic conditions. The crisis also revealed the dual and contradictory nature of capitalism in the periphery. On the one hand, it revealed the extent of the integration of Indochina into global networks of surplus accumulation and, on the other hand, it revealed the extroverted, and hence restricted nature of the operation of the laws of capitalism in the periphery.

CONCLUSION

While Laos was politically incorporated into the French colonial sphere of influence in 1893, it was not until six years later that administrative measures were taken to integrate the country into a Federal Indochina-wide set-up. Aside from the Kingdom of Luang Prabang, where the fiction of indirect rule was maintained and where, in the main, traditional ideological structures of dominance were allowed to be perpetuated, the rest of Laos was ruled as a colonial protectorate. Historically, the conditions under which incorporation took place, answered to the political need of the French to rebuff Anglo-Siamese hegemony over the east bank of the Mekong. The prospect of a river road to China and the opportunities of exploitation of a natural emporium were of no less consequence in the timing of the act of political incorporation. Even so, as we have seen, trade preceded the flag into Laos.

In the pre-monopoly phase of capitalist penetration in Laos, costs decidedly outweighed gains, and merchant capital enterprise as a result was negligible; although a comprador class, almost exclusively Chinese, had emerged by the first decades of the century. On the other hand, monopoly capital interests developed almost exclusively in the tin mining sphere. While profits steadily realized by monopoly capitalists from tin-mining ventures in Laos could have realized primitive capital for local investment, it did not transpire. Rather, a particular characteristic of this phase was the making of fabulous personal fortunes on speculation in the metropole; whatever local capital was generated gravitated towards import-export activities. Tin-mining ventures in Laos thus fully expressed the phenomenon, not only of unequal exchange but of unequal development. While the Lao and minority population of Laos were, to degrees, shielded from the economic crisis at the center during the early 1930s by the ability to fall back upon the natural economy, migrant labor in the monetized economy, as indeed in the more commercialized zones of French Indochina, proved more vulnerable. The effects of the crisis at the center as translated in the colonial periphery thus reflected the simultaneity of dissolution and conservation effects of capital. As Murray states the problem, while certain structures upheld the surface quality of tradition, in fact these structures were to a large extent penetrated by the laws of motion of the capitalist mode of production. Accordingly certain modes of production prevailed and certain modes dissolved (Murray 1980:7-8).

NOTES

1. For the sake of conformity with colonial era usage I have retained the French names for the units of the Indochinese Union, however, I consistently designate the dominant peoples of Tonkin, Annam and Cochinchina as Vietnamese. In dealing with the post-1945 situation, I employ the more acceptable national designation, Vietnam. Likewise, I employ the name Siam when that is the official designation of that country and Thailand when that is officially acceptable.

2. The French protectorate over Laos was definitively established on 3 October 1893, the date of the signing of the Franco-Siamese Treaty by which Siam renounced all rights over territories on the east bank of the Mekong. On 13 February 1904, by another French-Siamese Treaty, Siam renounced all anterior rights of suzerainty over the region of Bassac and that part of the Kingdom of Luang Prabang on the west bank of the Mekong (Galembert 1924:38).

3. See McCoy (1970:68-75) for an account of the French conquest of Laos.

4. According to *Annuaire Statistique de l'Indochine, 1936-1937*, Laos hosted a population of 1,012,000 in 1936, dispersed through 63 *muong* and *kong* and 8,457 villages.

5. That the Banque de l'Indochine only opened its first office in Laos on 9 April 1952, reinforces the point that, within the Indochinese Union, Laos was

treated as a peripheral economy. (R. Martin "Le Banque de l'Indochine Laos" in *La Revue Francaise de l'elite Europeene,"* No. 203, October 1967). Neither was there an impelling need in Laos for credit organizations to finance loans for land purchases. As a consequence Laos was the only country of the Union not hosting such an institution, (at least by 1943) (*Geographical Handbook Series*, 1943:364).

6. According to Robequain, the mining law of 26 January 1912 was based upon the principle of the claim stake. Any individual provided with a personal authorization could secure exclusive prospecting rights over a certain area. This could, upon fulfilling certain conditions, be converted to a permanent grant. The applicant was not required to prove that the enterprise was technically or financially practicable. As Robequain commented "Under this very liberal law, mining has not progressed at a steady pace" (1944:250).

7. Operations at Nam Patene were rationalized in 1926-1929 and placed under the control of the "Compagnie Fermière des Étains d'Extrême Orient". As one witness described the production process: "Work is done by gangs and goes on continuously since the machines can only be stopped at great expense, at night this isolated basin, surrounded by rugged mountains and dotted with electric lights which furnish illumination for the coolies as they work to the accompaniment of the mill's unrelenting rhythm, is a striking picture" (Robequain 1944:260).

8. Writing in 1936, Ennis notes that the colonization schemes sponsored by the Indochinese governments in other parts of the peninsula had not touched Laos. One exception was the coffee growing operation on the Bolovens carried out by the Société de l'Houle Pakhout. Ennis foresaw no improvement until the Tanap-Thakek railroad was completed (Ennis 1936:130). At least one attempt was made in 1936-7 to colonize the Tran Ninh plateau with ex-French military personnel (SHTM Indochine SPC1438, "Le plateau du Tran Ninh." 1936-7).

2

The Colonial State Project in Laos

As developed in this chapter, the colonial State project in Laos involved three distinct but interrelated processes. These are control of the labor process, the development of infrastructure and fiscal and money control. Thus the opening up of the country by river, road and rail was to further simplify the integration of Laos into an Indochina-wide economy. Considered inept and incapable of great industry by the French, the Lao were to be merged into an expanded pool of free labor fed by infusions of more "dynamic" proletarianized immigrants from overcrowded and more developed regions of Indochina. In the interim, the Lao and minority peasant producers were to be forced into the money economy by a combined fiscal and labor policy that demanded labor dues and head taxes. A special feature of the political economy of Laos was the economic niche to be carved out for Hmong peasants as producers of poppy, the primary source of revenue for the system of colonial monopolies.

Aside from the opium monopoly, it might be objected that despite the continual efforts of administrators to develop new sources of revenue in Laos, the colony was a permanent drain on French resources. Even if the matter was otherwise in the more developed and hence more exploitable regions of Indochina, there was no demonstrable exploitation of Lao in Laos. How does one square this fact of life with the general thrust of world systems analysis which would see the central feature of colonial domination as the unequal exchange between center and periphery? While seeking answers to this question in this chapter we will return to the problem in a conclusion.[1]

COLONIAL STATE CONTROL OF THE LABOR PROCESS

In Laos, where the preconditions for capitalism were non-existent, the colonial State created them in the mining sphere almost exclusively. This was not achieved without considerable violence, particularly in the control of the labor process. As a country of low population, low population density and with a minuscule indigenous proletariat, the colonial State sought to alleviate the chronic manpower problem of Laos by recruiting free Vietnamese labor from the labor reserves, particularly of Annam. State coercion of the migrant labor of the Nam Patene mines or "death valley" as it was called, through rigid control of the entire labor process, had its political correlate in the 1930s. This is a reference to the emergence of the first generation of communist revolutionaries in Laos and the face-to-face confrontation of labor and capital at the point of production (cf. Gunn 1988).

As Murray has written, the central dynamic underlying colonial mining operations was the metropolitan capitalist's domination of the labor process. Murray offers two general conditions of capitalist production. After Marx these are, first, the formal separation of sufficient numbers of producers from the principal means of wage laborers, second, the fusion of the sphere of circulation and production, meaning that metropolitan capital actually functioned to create surplus value through actual control of the labor process itself (Murray 1980:335 and 315).

But the Lao were universally decried by colonial agents as unreliable and unwitting proletarians. Typical of such sentiments is the following statement from a *Résident Supérieur* of Laos:

> The reputation of the Lao for laziness has not only been ascribed by 'men of action concerned to turn quick commercial profits and to register their short sojourn', but also by those who have lived long in this country where numerous Europeans have passed their entire careers. Without doubt this reputation necessarily requires modification. Properly speaking the Lao is not lazy but independent, or, if one prefers, whimsical, caring only to work at the task he likes and when it suits him. He is hostile enough to regular, sustained work; this repugnance translates itself into an indifference....
>
> (Moretti Report: education).

As one "neutral" observer, Thompson, pointed out, "the Lao have no sense of time, and a thousand obstacles and superstitions interfere with the accomplishment of work at a fixed date." She concedes, however, that the European residents, themselves, who might otherwise have been a motive force behind any change, invariably succumbed to "the prevailing atmosphere of *su su*, the Oriental equivalent of *dolce far niente*" (pleasant idleness) (Thompson 1937:381).

What, then, was the demographic condition underlying the colonial State's control of the labor process? According to a study by Cam Van Thu, the relatively high rate of growth of the population of Laos from 1911 to

1921 (2.5%) can only be attributed to immigration. In the first decade of the French protectorate, the new administration faced, on the one hand, a shortage of administrative and technical personnel for the operation of the public administration and, on the other hand, a lack of manpower, both skilled and unskilled, for the construction of public works, as well as for private agricultural and commercial enterprises. Also, Chinese and Vietnamese merchants were attracted to Laos by commercial opportunities, thus swelling the ranks of the foreign colony in the interior and in the newly emerging urban centers (Cam Van Thu 1973:175-6).

Between 1921 and 1936, however, the rate of demographic growth weakened to 1.43%, due to the world economic crisis of 1929-30 and the particular financial crisis that surrounded the bursting of the private investment speculation bubble, notably in wildcat explorations in the tin-mining domain in Laos. In these circumstances, as production tapered off, so did man-power demands and, so accordingly did immigration into Laos from Vietnam. In the second phase of capital accumulation in Laos, or that of expanded reproduction, man-power requirements further declined to the degree that the operations became capitalized and mechanized. The figures offered by Cam Van Thu on this question are quite eloquent of this trend. A total workforce of 6,000 at the Nam Patene mines in 1929, had fallen away to 1,157 by 1932. By ethnicity, this latter figure comprised 921 Vietnamese, 156 Lao, 70 Thai, seven Afghanis, two Cambodians and one Chinese. In the same period Vietnamese manpower was rechanneled either forcibly or voluntarily from the overcrowded delta regions towards the rubber plantations in the highlands of Vietnam and the French Pacific possessions (Cam Van Thu 1973:175-6 and see Table 2.1).

TABLE 2.1
POPULATION OF LAOS ACCORDING TO ETHNIC GROUP (1936)

ethnic group	population
Vietnamese	27,000
Lao	565,000
Other Tai	100,000
Indonesians (proto-Indochinese)	247,000
Cambodians	2,000
Chinese	3,000
Indians	200
Europeans	1,000
Others	20,000
total	**1,012,000**

Source: Annuaire Statistique de l'Indochine, 1936-1937.

The increase in the rate of growth of the population of Laos in the 1936-1943 period (1.84%), Cam Van Thu attributes to the moderate successes attained in the realm of public health, especially in controlling malaria and epidemics — which hitherto took a huge toll especially upon the montagnard population and also on corvee laborers — and to the steady development of urban centers, fed by an influx of Chinese, Vietnamese and Indian artisans. To be sure, ethical questions aside, there was a cost benefit analysis involved in ensuring the public health, particularly that of the corvee laborers and mine-coolies. The exceedingly low rate of growth (1.12%) of the population in the 1943-1946 sub-period, was directly related to the massive population shifts occasioned during the nationalist revolution and which saw the exit from Laos of most of the Vietnamese population to Thailand (Cam Van Thu 1973: 175-6).

The Vietnamese minority in Laos were mainly urban dwelling and few were engaged in agriculture. The majority were workers, traders or government employees. An *arrête* of May 1935 formalized the creation of Vietnamese villages and outlined the rules whereby notables were to be appointed as head-men and as intermediaries in dealing with the colonial authorities. While representing little more than 2% of the population of Laos, their representation in administrative positions far outstripped their demographic strength. This situation was not without its political consequences, especially following the 1945 August Revolution in Vietnam. Out of 396 positions in the Federal administration in Laos in 1937, only 54% were held by Lao. Table 2.2 gives the percentages of Vietnamese employed in the various bureaux of the general Indochinese administrative services in Laos.

TABLE 2.2
PERCENTAGE OF VIETNAMESE EMPLOYED IN THE FEDERAL ADMINISTRATIVE SERVICES IN LAOS

Service	Percentage
Clerks and secretaries	70%
Military orderlies	90%
Sûreté agents	70%
Navy personnel	70%
Veterinary service employees	30%
Government printshop workers	40%
Professional school tutors	75%
Primary teachers	35%
Medical assistants	50%

Source: (AOM Paris Indochine 271 2398(2), *Résident Supérieur* of Laos to the Governor General of Indochina, 15 April 1937).

Those colonial officials like Moretti, who were in favor of drawing the line on expanded employment by Vietnamese in the Indochinese administrative service in Laos, argued that while the Lao were indeed educationally ill-prepared to fulfil administrative duties, and lacked the capacities and aptitudes of the Vietnamese, that was the fault of the educational system. While appointment by merit was not a principle that could be objected to, he argued, an increased number of subordinate positions not requiring "book culture" could be reserved for the indigenous population. He also intimated the desirability of mollifying the Lao population against perceived job discrimination:

> It is incontestably regrettable to have to take into account the incompatibilities of temperament and also of racial friction which besets the two ethnically antagonistic groups.
>
> (Moretti Report: education).

Such sentiments, however, were characteristically treated with bureaucratic dissimulation.

Moretti evidently hit a raw nerve, however. Defending the administrative practice of employing Vietnamese auxiliaries in the Indochinese service in Laos, the *Résident Supérieur* argued that:

(a) dating from the Pavie campaigns, the French owed the Vietnamese a debt.

(b) insofar as the Vietnamese taxpayers subsidized the Lao budget to the tune of fifty percent, a certain obligation was owing to them.

(c) a second generation of Vietnamese was born in the country, assimilated to local conditions and therefore should not be discriminated against.

(d) the press in Annam, particularly in Hue, had echoed sentiments of reverse discrimination and "humiliation" suffered by their compatriots in Laos (Moretti Report: education).

For instance, as expressed by a Vietnamese journalist in the pro-French newspaper *La Depêche Coloniale*:

> When in 1899, the Governor General Doumer conceived his great work of creating the Indochinese community, he had also by the same act set down the conciliation between rights and obligations of each of the constituent countries. In this sense, Vietnamese, Lao and Cambodian should join in complete solidarity, at the risk of becoming tributary to their neighbors.... the common administrative services that were established are none other than organs bound to create an exact correspondence between respective interests. Make this great colonial conception our own. And, in our turn, let us reinforce this Indochinese

> unity which would permit it to lead the state to perfection — this equilibrium between the different ethnic elements in our Far Eastern possession.
>
> (Hoang Van Co, "La question des Annamites au Laos," *La Depêche Coloniale*, 12 May, 1936).

Such arguments were not lost upon the *Résident Supérieur* of Laos. He believed that whatever measures the Administration took to protect the Lao population from Vietnamese domination of employment opportunities would be interpreted by the latter as a "bromide." Rather than increasing the small percentage of positions reserved for Lao in the federal administration, the *Résident Supérieur* held to the view that the Lao should first distinguish themselves educationally (Moretti Report: education). Generally speaking, such attitudes prevailed in official French circles in Laos during the entire colonial epoch.

Of all the countries of the Indochinese Union, Laos hosted the smallest Han Chinese population. The province of Bassac accounted for more than half of the 2,000 odd Chinese in Laos, the rest being dispersed in towns and villages through the country. For matters of administrative and political expediency the Chinese communities throughout Indochina were organized into *congrégations* headed by nominated community leaders. In Bassac, for instance, there were two Chinese *congrégations*, one for the majority Hakka and one for the Teochiu. While many Chinese were immigrants in Laos during the colonial era some had established themselves on Khong island during the Siamese period and uncertain numbers were *métis* and acculturated into Lao society. As stated, the Chinese community were considered as indispensable by the French, given their role in servicing the local import and export business (Coulet 1929 and Haudebert 1933:411). A similar role was played by Yunnanese traders in north Laos.

Education

The quality of education offered in colonial Laos appears as the other side of the coin of the manpower crisis. The proportion of public expenditure on education in Laos was always weak relative to the other countries of the Indochinese Union. In 1935, for instance, only 8.45% of total public expenditure in Laos was allocated for education, versus 18% in Annam, 15% in Cochinchina, 12.87% in Tonkin and 11.60% in Cambodia. While the overall compression in the Lao budget from 1932 to 1936 was 30%, expenditure in education in Laos over the same period was reduced by 38%, from 407,508 piasters in 1932 to 252,649 in 1936. As one colonial inspector noted, the extension of elementary education in

Laos was less developed than in Siam, despite the fact that the amount of public expenditure in Siam was proportionally even less than in Laos (AOM Paris Indochine H12 NF 287/2495 (2), Rapport 33, "L'Enseignement au Laos," Mission Moretti).

Table 2.3, showing ethnic participation in education in Laos in 1935, is revealing of the gravity of the crisis.

Obviously a disproportionate number of Vietnamese relative to Lao participated in education — particularly higher education — in colonial Laos. Minorities in Laos had even less access to education of any kind.

In 1935 only 378 ethnic minorities were receiving any kind of officially sponsored education, 132 Thai, 105 Lu, 47 Kha, 34 Phu, 26 Hmong, 14 Youn and 20 non-specified ethnic groups. In practice this meant that in 1935, the percentage of indigenous peoples receiving the *Certificate Etudes Primaire Franco-Indigène* was 32% (including three Hmong and two Kha), while 68% of these certificates were awarded to Vietnamese. Of diplomas for senior studies, 48 were earned by Vietnamese and 28 by Lao (AOM Paris Indochine, H12 NF 287/2495 (2), the Director of Public Education in Indochina to Moretti, the Inspector General of Colonies en mission, 20 May 1936).

One should nor ignore the fact that official public education was supplemented by *wat* (temple) education. In the period from 1932 to 1935, the temples managed to enroll twice as many pupils as government schools had been able to accomplish in the preceding 34 years. By 1935 the number of *wat* schools had risen to 387 with 7549 pupils. Moretti noted that as in Cambodia, the influence of religion and the authority of the bonze was undeniable. The head of the *wat* moreover, had a moral obligation to provide education for the *sangha* (community). The *wat*

TABLE 2.3
PARTICIPATION IN EDUCATION IN LAOS BY ETHNICITY (1935)

	Number of Pupils		
	Lao	Vietnamese	Total
Elementary schools	4196	1083	5279
Primary schools	702	554	1256
College Pavie (includes 8 French)	45	53	106
No. of pupils	4943	1960	6641

Source: (AOM Paris Indochine H12 NF 287/2495 (2), "Rapport fait par M. Tenzenas du Montcel sur la penetration scolaire et les ecoles de pagodas au Laos a l'epoque du 6 April 1936," Mission Moretti, Service de l'Enseignment au Laos).

schools, however, rather than supplementing the official education system, were strongly inclined towards Buddhist moral education. In comparison with *wat* schools in Cambodia, those of Laos were regarded as being notorious for poor attendance, low standards, and with low professional quality of the bonzes as educators (Mission Moretti: education).

The stimulus to education in Laos, when it came, was in response to the emergence of Thai irredentist sentiment in the early 1940s. The first schools for the minority population were established in this period, boarding schools and "mobile" schools for the Kha of Saravane and Attopeu opening in 1939-1941 and the first government schools for Hmong opening in Xieng Khouang and later Nong Het in 1940-1942 (AOM Aix D3, "Education", 1941-2). The first *lycée* to open in Laos, the *Lycée Auguste Pavie*, did not open until July 1947 with a curriculum keyed to that of France (AOM Aix R, nd.).

While in theory, students from Laos could continue with higher education in Saigon and Hanoi, few but the sons of the mandarin class made that transition. Even fewer were afforded the opportunity to study in France. Decidedly, the Lao had vastly reduced educational opportunities compared with the Vietnamese, or for that matter, Thai students, a privileged few of whom had already graduated from British schools in the late 1920s. Indeed, the advent of the modern printing press in Laos was probably later than in any other French colony. Although official bulletins were published throughout the colonial era,[2] the first newspaper to be published in Laos was the *Lao Nhay* (Great Laos) which appeared between 1941 and 1945 along with the *Pathet Lao*, a Lao language supplement. In substance, French colonial efforts to establish a modern educational system in Laos did not extend beyond the imperative of cultivating a loyal "feudal" elite in the administrative mores of empire. Not surprisingly, Laos supported the highest illiteracy rate in the region.

THE COLONIAL STATE DEVELOPMENT PROJECT IN LAOS

The author-economist Pierre Deloncle likened Laos to Sudan in French West Africa, colonies of low population density isolated from the sea, the Mekong, as with the Niger, limited in its navigation possibilities by rapids. Writing in 1930 for a metropolitan audience, he advocated a continuation of the project of development in Laos, otherwise interrupted by the First World War. The key-stone of this undertaking, as reiterated in numerous official reports, was the *debloquement* or opening up of Laos and its concomitant integration into a wider Indochinese economic structure (Deloncle 1930:135). As the limitations of the Mekong as a transport conduit became obvious in the early colonial period, the emphasis was to be placed upon the opening up of motorable roads, railways and aviation links. Thus while in Laos corvee labor was also employed on the construction of public buildings and other projects, the "development" of the country was almost coterminous with road construction. No large scale hydraulic works were undertaken in Laos, as happened in other parts of the Indochinese Union, although the creation of towns was an obvious visible symbol of colonialism. Indeed, with the exception of Luang Prabang with its Court related activities, all towns in Laos were products of the colonial intervention.

Echoing official opinion, Deloncle argued that the project of *mise en valeur* in Laos required changing the entire "natural and historical" orientation of the country. To be sure, he observed with candor, this posed a dilemma if good relations were to be upheld with Siam. Writing in 1930, he noted that the Siamese railheads had been advanced to Chiang Mai, Ubon and Khon Khene, the latter just 200 kilometers from Vientiane. Already these communications links were "draining" Lao trade towards the port of Bangkok. Undeterred by the human and capital costs of the Yunnan railroad, the construction of a rail link from Annam to Laos across the Annamite Cordillera was given priority. The work was to be financed by colonial loans ear-marked for Indochina and, as a measure of confidence in the project, the route from Song Gia via the Mu Gia pass to Thakek was surveyed and a service track constructed. Although the first locomotives were timetabled to arrive in Thakek in 1936, the scheme was eventually abandoned, a sacrifice to the Great Depression (Deloncle 1930: 155). A large scale irrigation scheme under study was evidently a victim of the Second World War, (Lévy 1974:79) as were more grandiose plans for State-sponsored colonization of certain temperate upland regions.

According to a British consular report, however, the expected cancellation on 31 August 1937 of the government subsidy to the French company "La Compagnie de Navigation et de Transports", which hitherto ran steamer services on the Mekong, caused considerable local opposition "among those who consider that the result will inevitably be to make French Laos economically dependent upon Siam". But intra-imperialist economic rivalry was also at stake. The report also noted the appearance in the markets of the larger towns in Laos of such Japanese goods as natural and artificial silk, footwear, Thermos flasks, tinned provisions and metalware in the markets of the principal Lao towns. Fifteen tons of this merchandise entered Savannakhet per month during 1936 while 65 tons entered Vientiane during the same period (PRO FO 371/19868, British Consulate General, Saigon, 29 October 1936). Clearly the economic no less than the political incorporation of Laos into the Federal Indochina set-up proved to be problematical.

As the *Résident Supérieur*, Eutrope, commented, the opening up of the various provinces of Laos to the rest of Indochina served both an important political and economic role. From the political point of view, he remarked, the opening up of the country had greatly assisted the military-security operations of the administration on the Bolovens Plateau and in the valleys of the Upper Sekong and Upper Sekamane. Northern Laos, he noted, previously "closed" was now within hours from colonial garrisons, whether located in Tonkin or in Annam. It was unlikely, he speculated, that the "bloody" events of 1915 and 1920 (Chinese incursions and Hmong rebellions) would be repeated. At the same time incursions into Indochina from Siam, Burma and Yunnan could be effectively neutralized (AOM Paris Indochine NF 286/2493, Eutrope's comment on Moretti Report: education).

The first major *route de pénétration* constructed in Laos, then, was that linking Tourane with Savannakhet (Route Coloniale 9), and was followed by roads from Vinh to Thakek (RC 12) and Vinh to Tran Ninh (RC 7). By 1934, the Pakse to Saigon link (RC 13) was opened and by February 1936, the road from Luang Prabang to Annam was completed, a laudable achievement for corvee laborers concerned given the nature of the terrain and the technical problems involved. The scale of this exercise is conveyed in Robequain's account of the construction of the Pakse-Kratie road. It was finished between 1935 and 1937 in less than three dry seasons, thanks to the systematic organization of the work which mustered a total of 6,500 coolies in an "unhealthy and sparsely populated region" (Robequain 1944:102).

The broader rationale of opening up Sam Neua, then, was to ease the entry of Lao products onto the world market, through the port of Haiphong. Roads constructed in Luang Prabang and Attopeu were foreseen as enabling the export of forest products, agricultural products and cattle. Upgrading of RC 13 connecting Pakse to Saigon was seen as imperative if the development of lower Laos was to take place. Development in this sense meant turning the traditional trade flow of Laos away from Yunnan and Siam and redirecting the commercial current towards French Indochina (AOM Paris Indochine NF 286 2493 "Eutrope's comment on Moretti Report: fiscal").

Certainly, as Forest muses in a study of the colonial process in Cambodia, the construction of roads touched on one of the central myths of colonial civilization — a country could not be civilized without roads. In Laos, as in the rest of Indochina, the roads stood as the most visible manifestation of colonial power. The irony was that their utility at the time of their construction was entirely dubious, no matter the long term benefits (Forest 1980:236). For the colonial State, they stood as symbols of progress and the *paix francais*. For the corvee laborer, which in Laos probably never embraced less than 20% of the population, they stood as symbols of folly and unmitigated colonial oppression. For all the political expressions of support for road building in Laos, however, it should be borne in mind that the system was meant to be self-supporting in terms of financing. While fifty percent of budget expenditure was absorbed by public administration, only one percent was allotted to road-building (Thompson 1937:369). (See Map I).

Along with the monopolies and colonial taxation system, the resort to corvee labor by the colonial State in Laos was one more manifestation of the process of "primitive accumulation." As Murray points out, the colonialists were compelled to apply outright coercion in order to initiate economic activity that could not have been accomplished by market forces alone. Thus corvee labor was the most dependable means of obtaining a proletariat or part-proletariat in the shortest time possible. The legal obligation to work and the forced separation of small-scale cultivators from the means of production was part and parcel of the generalized system of colonial coercion and violence over the labor force (see Murray 1980:81-82).

THE COLONIAL STATE BUDGET AND MONOPOLY SYSTEM

In 1892, for the first time, the local budgets of the existing protectorates of Indochina were denied regular metropolitan subsidies, with the exception of funding for military operations. In a further rationalization undertaken during the Doumer administration (1897-1902), the five local budgets of Indochina were separated from the general or federal budget of the Indochinese Union. Thus armed with a centralized budgetary authority, budget deficits that had been characteristic of earlier administrations were effectively eroded. This fiscal reform, Murray shows, had the effect of establishing the colonial State as a capitalist in its own right. Between 1902 and the end of colonial rule, he notes, the *régies* or State monopolies along with customs duties secured a steady guaranteed income for the general budget (Murray 1980:72-74).

A basic distinction in the Indochinese financial system was the restriction of indirect taxation to the general budget and of direct taxation to the local budgets. Indirect taxation which generally contributed over seventy percent of the revenue of the general budget was derived from customs duties and from the *régies* on the sale and consumption of alcohol, opium, salt, mineral oils and tobacco. The main source of revenue for the local budgets was direct taxation in the form of capitation and a land tax. According to an American account, this rigid separation of the two forms of taxation could not have been a satisfactory arrangement as it tended towards a lack of equilibrium in the financial structure of the country. Likewise it gave way to a considerable contraband and evasion (*Geographical Handbook Series, Indochina,* December 1943).

The budget system in Laos was created by an *arrête* of the Governor General in 30 September 1895. The deficit incurred by the first colonial budget in Laos, that of 1896, set the pattern for the entire epoch. From the beginning, local resources were insufficient to cover expenses, the deficit being made up by annual subventions from the general budget. At the time of the creation of the Lao budget, the general budget was supplied according to the following ratios: Cochinchina, 6/13ths, Tonkin, 5/13ths and Cambodia, 2/13ths. Taking the 1896, 1900 and 1910 Lao budgets as bench marks, Reinach calculated that the average per capita expenditure for the budget in Laos was 2.42 francs of which local receipts contributed only 1.10 francs, leaving a deficit of 1.32 francs to be made up by subvention from the general budget (Reinach 1911:224). A recurring theme in colonial administrative memos throughout the whole epoch was the imperative to bring the local budget into equilibrium by minimizing the deficit, although the complete elimination of the deficit was never viewed as a realistic course of action. It is obvious that the burden of this fiscal support operation was placed upon the tax-payer in Laos, more so in periods when a diminution in the subvention earmarked for Laos was impelled by the demands of a greater fiscal stringency on the part of the central budget authority. Thus, for instance, revenue accruing to the federal budget from the sales of opium produced in Laos did not figure as a receipt for the Lao budget. Calculations about whether Laos was an overall drain on the Federal Indochina budget or, indeed, on the colonial budget, is complicated by this local fiscal arrangement and by the general insufficiency of the data base and the questionable reliability of colonial statistics on financial matters.

Between 1902 and the end of colonial rule, the "triple-headed monster of the monopolies"; opium, alcohol and salt, formed the basis of colonial tax exploitation and never contributed less than half the revenues of the general colonial budget (Murray 1980:74).[3] The Indochina customs service *(Douanes et Régies)* was only established in Laos in 1905. Before that time customs dues had not been collected across the Mekong, although a customs post and a sub-directorate had been established in Vientiane in 1904. In 1912, because of staffing problems, the local service was reattached to that of Cambodia.

Writing in 1914, Meray observed that the contribution of customs receipts collected in Laos to the general budget in that year was an "insignificant" \$600. In fact no primary customs excise was collected at all in Laos. In that year, of least importance were the matches, tobacco, mineral oil and alcohol monopolies which had been established as in other parts of Indochina to attract more revenue to the Federal budget. Of slightly more importance in Laos was the salt monopoly, providing $13,500 to the Lao office of the Indochina customs service in 1914 (AOM Aix F4, Delpit, "Chief of the Economic Mission of Laos to the *Résident Supérieur*", Savannakhet, 11 September 1915).

The most significant source of revenue to the service in Laos, however, was from the sale of opium. Of $297,450 received by the *Douanes et Régie* in Laos in 1914, $265,000 was contributed from opium sales. Until disbanded in 1900, opium produced in northern Laos had gone to the *bouillerie* (boiler) in Luang Prabang, while that produced in middle Laos was sent to Saigon. Indeed, the promise shown by opium as a revenue winner prompted Meray to urge the reestablishment of the disbanded Luang Prabang *bouillerie*. Likewise, as a way of under-cutting the activities of smugglers, he recommended that the *Douanes et Régie* move actively to assert its monopoly prerogative in the purchase, not only of Hmong opium, but also of opium emanating from Yunnan and Burma. Indeed the cultivation of opium in Indochina had been "provisionally" authorized by Article 87 of an *arrête* of the Governor General of 7 February 1899. By 1914, the cultivation of poppy in Tran Ninh by Hmong hill peasant farmers was said to be "well enough developed." The 1914 harvest was estimated at between 150-200 kilograms, the sale price of which was $26-50 a kilo (AOM Paris Indochine NF 95 947 "Verification of the Douanes et Régie service in Laos: Study on the installation of a free zone", Meray, Phnom Penh, 10 April 1914).

As Delpit, chief of an economic mission to Laos observed, the bulk of the Hmong opium surplus was sold to Ho traders who came in mule caravans from Yunnan to purchase cheap opium for sale at Yunnan-fu (Kunming). He cautioned against heavy-handed attempts to prevent this contraband, given the potential of the Hmong for mischief. The latter would be well enough disposed to sell their opium surplus to the *Régie*, if the price was right, he asserted (AOM Aix F4, Delpit, Chief of the Economic Mission to Laos to the *Résident Supérieur*, Savannakhet, 11 September 1915).

Although important purchases of Hmong opium were made in Laos by the *Régie* in 1924, it was decided in 1925 to reduce the amount solicited to an annual maximum of 3,500 kilograms at a price of $12-15 a kilogram. However, by 1927 purchases by the *Régie* had tapered off to only 15 kilograms and no official purchases were made in 1929.[4] An enquiry by the *Résident Supérieur* concerning the reason for this shortfall was inconclusive. Clearly, the leakage of opium revenue from Laos was an embarrassment to the local administration. The *Régie* estimated that surplus production in Laos was probably three to five tonnes a year. By 1928-1930, the *Régie* had managed to purchase 800 kilograms a year by following a policy of purchasing directly from the producer and not from the numerous intermediaries. As Inspector Conte pointed out, Indochina in 1930 was a "non-producing" country of opium, meaning that it was a net importer of the drug.[5] Compelling reasons were advanced to change that situation. Expanded opium poppy cultivation in Laos would serve a dual purpose: (1) the revitalization of the metropolitan alkaloid industry (which was itself a subsidiary of British and German industry) and (2) the reduction of opium imports from India. By 1930, then, the *Régie* had definitely decided upon a policy of the expansion of opium cultivation in the High Region of Laos and Tonkin (AOM Paris Indochine 282 2480, "Le Conte, Inspector General of the Colonies", 18 February 1930).

From 1935 onwards, opium producers in Laos had been granted the facility to sell their produce via the *Régie* to the manufactory in Saigon. By 1938 the trade was realizing an average annual influx into Laos of 50-60,000 silver piasters presumably as payment to the producers (*Discours prononcé par M. le Résident Supérieur, Eutrope*, September 1938, p.5). Indeed, by 1938 the opium monopoly supplied the general budget with 12,388 thousand piastres out of a total revenue of 82,455 thousand piasters, a considerable amount by any measure (*Annuaire statistique de la France*, 1938:291).[6]

Cut off from the rest of the world during the Second World War, and divested of alternative sources of local revenue, the colonial administration leaned ever more heavily on the opium *Régie* in order to meet its budgetary demands. The Hmong of northern Laos were to play the leading role in this fiscal operation. Not being able to suppress the activities of smugglers, the *Régie* opted to out-do them. According to Charles Rochet, then the Director of Education in Laos, the "enormous" purchases of opium effected by the *Régie* in northern Laos were matched by a "vertiginous ascending curve" on the price scale. This meant that the country was flooded with an amount of silver more than that which it could absorb without economic dislocation. According to Rochet, "economic disequilibrium" was compounded by "demoralization." Although northern Laos was "rotten" with silver, its people could no longer afford to feed themselves. Even wage-earners could not afford the inflated cost of commodities. When opium was "God" in northern Laos, all who could indulge in the traffic did so, and not excluding the Royal family. Those who were unable to take part in opium hunts financed expeditions. Rochet comments that the absence of a Press in Laos protected these profiteers from exposure (Rochet 1946:104).

The Japanese *coup de force* of March 1945 broke down the Federal Indochinese budget system. Bereft of the subvention, both the Japanese occupation administration in Laos and the Provisional Lao Issara Government fell back upon opium as a source of local revenue. While statistical evidence is not forthcoming for this turbulent period of Lao history, it would be no exaggeration to say that Lao Issara fiscal policy was coterminous with its opium procurement policy. The Lao Issara Chamber of Representatives of the Lao People adopted a ruling on the purchase, fabrication and sale of opium in Laos on 27 December 1945. The monopoly was vested in the *Lao Issara Douanes et Régie* service and opium exploited as a "direct *régie*." This was achieved by instituting a licencing system for dealers and smokers; the product being marketed in the *Lao Issara Douanes et Régie* labelled bottle (AOM Aix U "Prime Minister's ruling on the Opium monopoly," nd.).

In the post-war period, the French Indochinese government engaged in international conversations over the closing down of the *Régie*. A decision taken by the High Commissioner of Indochina, Bollaert, on 18 May 1948 concerning the reduction of sales of opium by the *Régie* at the rate of 20% a year was influenced by the recommendations of a conference held in Bangkok during that year on that subject. Another *arrête* of 3 September 1948 scrupulously laid down the regulations for the functioning of the monopoly, even prescribing the doses for registered addicts (Luce 1974:297).

When Laos became a constitutional monarchy within the French Union on 11 May 1947, the system of the general budget was no longer operative and in theory Laos and the other Associate States, Cambodia and Vietnam gained control of their own budgetary resources. No longer would the Indochinese *Régie* siphon off revenue derived from Lao opium to the benefit of the general budget, although it was not until the Pau Conference in 1950 that commercial interests between France and the Associated States were finally settled.

The rewards to the Lao state from expanded opium revenue were all too obvious in this period. Despite gathering international censure of the trade, as McCoy explains, all across northern Laos, the hill tribe peasant had been transformed into cash crop opium farmers. The annual head tax was raised from three silver piasters to an exorbitant eight piasters. The possibility of paying in kind (three kilograms of opium) stimulated an opium cultivation boom in northern Laos (McCoy 1972:83). In this interregnum period, as the following memo makes clear, the Lao *Douane* took over where the Indochinese *Régie* left off:

> Do not ignore that this product supplies important resources for our budget. It is up to your unreserved co-operation to the Purchasing Commission. You should thus dispatch, as happened in the past, one of your most honest, devoted and experienced officers...
>
> I particularly stress the importance of this collection, if the goal of 1943 and 1944 is obtained (45 tonnes) our budget will have sufficient

> resources to permit us with assurances to broach the suppression of already heavy personal taxes and the unpopular *prestations*.
>
> The interest of collecting opium is thus of national priority. Every functionary and citizen who lends his collaboration can be proud to have performed useful work. Equally it follows that the representatives of the government act reasonably in a way that producers are not too exacting on the price. Equally I profit on this occasion to address myself to our cultivators of opium inviting them to deliver the surplus of their harvests. I assure them that if they themselves deliver their harvests to the purchasing center, they will be paid as intermediaries. It is thus in the interests of the producers to eliminate the intermediaries by offering to deliver their opium directly.
>
> It is in replying spontaneously to my appeal that you will aid us in relieving the fiscal charges of all, the goal that we aim at in pursuing this opium campaign.
>
> (AOM Aix F17, "Thao Leum, Minister of Finances of the Kingdom to the Chaokhouengs of Luang Prabang and Xieng Khouang," Vientiane, 8 November 1948).

In theory, then, the means existed to finally relieve the Lao peasant of the head tax. The relief would have been equally welcome in 1943-1944 when the Indochinese *Régie*, as intimated above, derived substantial revenues from the sale of opium produced in Laos. At 1943-1944 piaster values the profits realized from the sale of opium would have been sufficient to balance the Lao budget without recourse to the subvention. Stated otherwise, Lao opium funneled through the Indochinese *Régie* was a major prop to the general budget in 1943-1944, a remarkable turnaround in fiscal policy in just 13 years. By 1943, however, the Lao *Régie* would have been in competition in the opium purchasing business with Viet Minh agents, whose commercial contacts in the clandestine arms, currency and opium business ran from Bangkok to Hong Kong.[7]

THE TAXATION AND CORVEE SYSTEM IN COLONIAL LAOS

As Murray has demonstrated, the taxation system became an important institutional lever in forcing the population out of subsistence economy and into the money economy. The taxing mechanism demanded from the population not only compulsory payments in money form but forced them to share the burden of strengthening the European-dominated export activities. With a view to making Indochina a self-supporting colony, traditional taxation systems of the Indochinese countries were overhauled. The most sweeping change was that which required payment in cash in lieu of payment in kind. Under the colonial tax system, as

Murray argues, the social category of non-tax payer (or one whose poverty precluded paying taxes) was removed. It was criminal to be poor (Murray 1980:68-70).[8]

In the more developed parts of Indochina, the taxation system and the system of *prestations* (labor dues) was set down in the course of the latter half of the 19th Century. *Prestations* were gradually abolished, first in Cochinchina, Tonkin and Annam, until, during the 1930s they basically only remained operative in Cambodia and Laos:

> ....where an insufficiency of the communications and a feeble population density obliged its recovery, although more and more rarely to the degree that the penetration of the country was accentuated.
>
> (*Indochine* 1931:169).

It should be borne in mind that in its role as appropriator of agricultural surplus and as mobilizer of manpower, for whatever reason, the colonial state in Laos (as in the other countries of Indochina) was heir to the historical tradition and prerogatives of centralized State power.

Although the general taxation system of Laos was fleshed out by various *arrêtes* between 1900 and 1935, the basic system was pioneered by a convention with the King of Luang Prabang dated 3 December 1895. From this time, taxes and corvees raised in the Kingdom by the monarch were subject to the consent of the French Commissioner in situ and to the approbation of the *Résident Supérieur* in Vientiane. Personal tax was required of all Lao males from the age of 19 (later 20) to 60 years of age at the rate of 2 piasters a year. Additionally, all were obliged to serve 20 days of corvee labor annually, five of which were to be served in the taxpayer's place of origin. The Kha, formally released from various kinds of slave bondage, were required to pay one piaster annually and to serve ten days corvee. The *tasseng* and the Kha chiefs concerned were made responsible for collecting the personal tax. Their reward for faithful collection of the taxes was a remission of the tenth part of the total amount received. In recognition of the special status of Luang Prabang, a local budget was drawn up by the King and Commissioner. Additionally, the Royal treasury was beneficiary of one half of the net profits received by the French administered Opium *Régie* (AOM Paris Indochine NF 614 (1) and (2); "Project de convention avec la Majesté le Roi de Luang Prabang", 3 December, 1895). While subject to important modifications in later decades, the original system as applied in Luang Prabang, in essence, remained the model for the duration of the colonial epoch.

A note on the pre-colonial tax system would be apposite. Was the burden just as onerous? Or were the subject peoples in the pre-colonial system cushioned by bonds of reciprocity.

Bourotte, a French author, notes that with the Siamese occupation of Laos following the sacking of Vientiane in 1827 and with the posting of Siamese dignitaries in Attopeu, Bassac, Strung Treng and Oubon, the tax burden on especially the mountain peoples increased. The Siamese levied a tax payable in gold in addition to gifts made to minor mandarins. Some villagers were required to pay in gold dust the weight of 2.5 or 8 grams of rice per inhabitant. The matter was policed by Lao militiamen. This burden combined with the slave trade led to the mass migrations and desertions from the *ray*. "The hill tribes led an existence of unspeakable wretchedness" (Bourotte 1951:57-8). As shown below, if the colonially imposed system of taxes and corvees was marginally more humane, or at least less arbitrary, than those collected by local and foreign tributaries in the historical past, they were, however, of a qualitatively different order.

In Laos and Cambodia, then, when the French were congratulating themselves on the suppression of slavery or at least debt bondage, the institution of State corvee was reinstituted and revived on a more efficient basis. As in traditional times the *prestations* were required to be requited during "dead times" following the harvest season. As in other parts of colonial Indochina, the collection of taxes was a major preoccupation of the *Résident* and a role which was also delegated to local indigenous authorities (see Forest 1980:210). This most despised of colonial institutions known as the *kouang, lam, haou* or *van* has been characterized by the Lao communist historian Phoumi Vongvichit, as a "ferocious regime of exploitation" (Phoumi Vongvichit 1968:36).

Details of the method of tax collection in the early colonial period are set out in a report by Maurice Meray. Village tax rolls were now drawn up by the *tasseng* at the end of each year, more rigorously than in the pre-colonial period. The number of *inscrits* (registered taxpayers), the number of *prestations* (labor dues rendered), as well as the number of houses, arms and elephants in each *tasseng* were documented and transmitted to the *chaomuong* for verification. He, in turn, submitted them to the French Commissioner. As the interface between the French administration and the indigenous bureaucracy, the *chaomuong* were subject to close surveillance, all the more so in view of their proclivity to encourage tax-collectors in the field to perform their duties with excessive zeal (AOM Paris Indochine NF 95 947, "Inspection Meray," 20 February and 12 March 1914, Phnom Penh).

As Meray noted of the *prestation* system enforced by local authorities in Laos in the early phase of the colonial administration, there was not only considerable local variation but there was a very loose interpretation of the regulations. For instance, he noted that while the ratio of the amount of corvee redeemed in kind (ie. actually worked) versus the amount of *prestation* recovered in cash was never prescribed in any of the *arrêtes*, it was fixed according to a certain rule of thumb. Indeed, as he pointed out, the equilibrium of the budget depended upon a certain guaranteed cash redemption. For instance, at a session of the Provincial Council of Vientiane in 1910, it was determined that, for the benefit of the local budget, 100,000 corvee days would be obligatorily redeemable in cash in the *muong* of Vientiane for the following year. In the *muong* of Tourakham, it was determined during the same year that a part of the corvee would be redeemed in cash, while another part would be redeemed in labor. At a session of the Provincial Council of the province of Bassac, the Commissioner made it known that owing to a lack of local credit and towards the end of balancing the budget in Laos, 75% of the corvee in the *muong* would be obligatorily redeemed in cash. One quarter of the amount recovered would be for the benefit of the *muong* budget (AOM Paris Indochine NF 95947, "Inspection Meray," 20 February and 12 March 1914, Phnom Penh).

As Meray intimated, the dominating preoccupation was to swell the local budget with extra receipts gained from the cash redemption of corvees. In the period from 1909 to 1912, the number of *prestation* days redeemed was increased to a rate almost equal to one half of the total contribution of resources to the budget. Corvee laborers were employed in a variety of projects linked with the colonial State project of *mise en valeur*. The first road construction projects introduced in the early decades of the century in Saravane and Xieng Khouang were built with corvee labor. In such provinces where public works were in progress, the corvee laborer was set the task of clearing bush and tracks around the villages. Responsibility rested with the *chaomuong* over the manner of local employment of the corvee laborer. Apart from the twenty days of obligatory corvee, the *inscrits* could still be liable for other duties such as repairing the telegraph line, courier duty, portage services, clearing rocks from the Mekong, etc. For instance, in one week 300 coolies were requisitioned at short notice to transport the baggage of officers of the Service Geographique. In Savannakhet, the *Service* reclaimed 22,500 corvee days in 1912 and 36,000 in 1913, a "real abuse" according to Meray, although the pioneering role of the *Service* in carrying out surveys for future mineral prospectors should not be overlooked. Commenting on the "evil" Meray remarked with some acerbity:

> ....in view of the fact that requisitions also exist for the Public Works service, navigation, Post Office and personal transport, one would not be astonished to see a discontented population nor to see almost entire villages passing onto the right bank...experienced by the Inspection to procure precise information on this point indicates that it is profound and owes above all to habit, become almost usage, which it follows would be very difficult to eradicate.

Merchant capitalists also benefited in diverse ways from the State-sponsored corvee. In 1913, 27,600 corvee days were worked in the single post of Khone in the province of Khong which only mustered 5500 *inscrits*. Their unremunerated labors were so much gratuitous profit for the concessionaires of the Khone Island railroad on the Mekong river rapids bypass, the Messagerie Fluviale (AOM Aix Indochine NF 95 947, "Fonctionnement de l'impot de prestations au Laos", Inspection Meray, Phnom Penh, 12 March 1914; and see Mogenet 1980:73-93).

In summing up the system of fiscal administration in Laos in his 1936 report, Inspector Moretti observed that it rested upon "three super-imposed *capitations* (poll taxes) personal tax, *prestations* and alcohol tax. The latter consisted of an annual per capita tax of 0.50 piasters payable by each registered taxpayer on alcohol or fermented drinks whether or not the person consumed alcohol (see Mogenet 1980:77 and Moretti Report: fiscal).

In contrast with other countries of the Indochinese Union there was no tax on property in Laos. In accord with local custom, the State continued to be the sole owner of the land and the subsoil, no matter the nature of the exploitation. Tenure of land, however, was submitted to certain conditions. The occupier of the land was bound to keep it in a state of cultivation. After a lapse in cultivation of three years duration, the land reverted to the State and the right to usufruct could be claimed by the new occupier. As Reinach remarked, in Laos there was neither private domain, nor public domain nor reserves, there was only State domain (Reinach 1911:242). If the proprietorship of land was a consuming question in "feudal" and colonial Vietnam, land shortages as such were unknown in Laos. The situation was bound to change, however, and the first official recognition of the question was displayed by a tax on land and rice fields introduced on 19 May and 6 June 1935 (see Mogenet 1980:77), although considerable capacity for evasion existed in this area.

In 1937, certain measures were set in train to make the personal tax structure less regressive by giving the appearance, at least, of shifting the burden onto those better capable of paying. To assure that the "well-to-do" taxpayer with acquired wealth did not escape tax obligation, further taxes on the holdings of productive rice-fields were included as well as a tax on ownership of large herds of cattle. Special tax in the form of a *prestation* on the owners of draught animals and carts was also enforced, with an obligation to lend them to the service of the State. As reported by Eutrope to the Lao Consultative Assembly in October 1937, the administration lowered the amount of personal tax from 2$50 to 2$00 while the rate of redemption was lowered from 0$50 to 0$20. Because these "well-meaning" measures, he averred, the local budget recorded a 400,000 piaster or twenty-five percent diminution of receipts in the 1932-38 period.

With consummate irony, Eutrope told the assembled Lao delegates and mandarins:

> I should say that there exist few countries in the world outside of France where taxpayers have benefited from such considerations.

In the same breath, as it were, Eutrope then argued before the delegates that experience had only proven that lowering the number of obligatory days to be served had only proven counterproductive, especially in remote regions where travel time to and throe to the work site consumed an excess of time. Accordingly, he elevated the number of days required for the Lao to fourteen while holding the amount for the Kha constant. As a concession to the Lao, the rate of *prestation* commutation was lowered (*Discours Pronounce par Résident Supérieur Eutrope*, 22 October 1937).[9]

By 1940, the tax net had been spread wider, not only to embrace land and property, but to accommodate a more complex and differentiated system that had evolved in tandem with the albeit limited extension of capitalist relations of production into the countryside. This was implied in the revised five tier personal taxation system that applied to indigenous people.

Category 1 — those paying 20 piasters personal tax, 25 piasters or more land tax and 355 piasters or more for commercial licenses. There were nine categories of exemptions, including the Royal family, *Tasseng*, *Naiban*, bonzes, military personnel etc. The indigent had no excuse and were not exempt from paying personal tax.

Category 2 — those paying at least 10 piasters personal tax, those paying 10 to 25 piasters land tax and over 15 piasters for commercial licence fees.

Category 3 — those paying at least 5 piasters personal tax, those urban land-holders paying land tax from 5 to 15 piasters and those paying commercial licence fees from 4.5 to 15 piasters per annum.

Category 4 — those Lao, Vietnamese and "evolved" montagnards such as the Hmong, Man, Lu, Yao and Kha Loven whom paid 2.5 piasters a year personal tax.

Category 5 — those montagnards such as Kha and Phoutheng who paid 1.5 piasters per annum personal tax (*Devoirs* 1940:19).

By 1940, the annual *prestation* liability was established at fifteen days for the Kha, fourteen for the Lao, Hmong, Man, Lu etc. The former could, if desired, redeem their *prestations* at 0.16 piasters a day and the latter at 0.30 piasters a day. After January 1941 these redemption rates were raised to 0.20 piasters and 0.35 piasters respectively. The administration reserved the right to request that *prestations* be redeemed in cash or by furnishing such commodities as wood, rice, maize and tobacco. Officially a nine hour day was operative, but if work could not be found for corvee laborers then they were still obliged to redeem their obligation in cash. While medical care on the job-site was officially provided, it was the corvee laborers' own obligation to feed themselves for the duration of their duty. The work-day computation did not include travel time to the job site. Twelve categories of exemptions existed. Owners of draft animals and carts were also obliged to render obligatory services to the State (*Devoirs* 1940:19).

The 1940 brief on tax regulations revealed the conviction of the administration that the *tasseng* and the *naiban* had received sufficient education in the school system and in the pagoda school system to be able to read instructions relating to the tax administration in Lao. Accordingly severe sanctions were levied against those *tasseng* and *naiban* who indulged in tax fraud. For instance, a charge of misappropriation of public funds could incur a one to five year prison sentence and a fine double the amount of money misappropriated. On the other hand rewards and promotions awaited those Lao officials who conscientiously acquitted their duties (*Devoirs* 1940:19).

In a departure from past practice, then, *naiban* and *tasseng* were jointly held responsible for the preparation of tax rolls, although they were to be assisted by a delegated *muong* official. *Tasseng* and *naiban* were held responsible for the collection of two categories of tax, those registered on the rolls and those collected on receipts from the delivery of various permits and licenses. Of the former category, certain were as specified in the past while others were inherent in the nature of the expanded tax collection basis that had become characteristic of the late colonial era in Laos. Thus added to the duty of collecting personal tax from indigenous residents and foreign Asians, was added the duty to collect stay-permit tax from foreigners and a tax on the manufacture and consumption of alcohol. To the familiar duty of collecting *prestation* redemption fees on people and on animals and carts, was added the burden of collecting forest *prestations*, licence taxes, various property and rice field taxes, the elephant *capitation* tax, the bicycle tax and the arms permit tax. A whole range of taxes, however, were not collected by the indigenous authorities but directly by the French. These included the collection of personal tax from Europeans, a general tax on income, urban property tax, vehicle tax and departure tax. Seventeen categories of registration fees were likewise collected by the French authorities, ranging from court fees to theatre fees (*Devoirs* 1940:19).

In the post-war period, following the French restoration and the establishment of a constitutional monarchy, the tax system was established on a "modern" footing. In 1949, a national tax system was introduced in replacement of the dual personal tax and *prestation* tax system. With the exception of a newly introduced "turnover" tax, the principle of taxation was to be shifted from a tax on people to a tax on objects. Indirect taxes which had formerly constituted an element of the Federal budget revenue, such as salt and alcohol, now accrued to each of the constituent "Associated States of Indochina," including the Kingdom of Laos. Given the penury of the Lao National Budget, the new policy impelled the authorities towards collecting tax arrears. To the same end, the working population was urged to step up production in the expectation that increase profits would translate into greater direct tax revenue (AOM Aix L12, Sayaboury, 3 June 1949).

A Vietnamese source comments that French economic policy essentially showed no change in the post war period. As seen in the previous chapter, French capital continued to monopolize mining and the import export trade. In fact the corvee system continued but under new circumstances. Each Lao was obliged to offer his labor to the French expeditionary corps and the government for five to six months. Additionally, local authorities requisitioned labor for work duties. Each Lao citizen had to pay a 120 piaster head tax a year as well as contributions to "national salvation" funds arising from the war effort. Nevertheless the budget deficit kept increasing in the early post-war period (53 million piasters in 1952 and 381 in 1954). From self-sufficiency in rice in the pre-war period, after 1950 Laos was importing up to 30,000 tons of food a year (anon, *Laos: An Outline* 1982:71). To be judicious, corvee was also an obligation to those — especially minority peoples — living under the Pathet Lao administration.

Politically, the source continues, the French speeded up the formation of a "national army" in implementation of the Franco-Lao agreement of 6 February 1950. In December 1950 the US signed agreements granting military aid to the Kingdom of Laos. Notionally, Laos received its independence on 22 October 1953 with some administrative and technical services handed over to the "national government" (anon, *Laos:An Outline,* 1982:71).

CONCLUSION

The central dilemma for the French project of *mise en valeur* was that of labor. A modern State and capitalist process could not exist without a minimally educated population, on the one hand, and a pool of capable wage labor, on the other. Neither having fostered education of the Lao or having succeeded (after Marx) in separating producers from their means of production, the French turned towards the reserves of Vietnamese migrant labor to fill this gap (the political consequences of which turned out to be momentous at least in terms of communist activity). The colonial State project, we found, was almost coterminous with road building. This served, not only the generation of erstwhile unwilling consumers of the marketplace, the product of a disciplined labor force, but served a direct political role (assisting troop movement and the pacification of the country) and an economic role (facilitating the extraction of raw materials and trade flows).

The imperative of the colonial bureaucratic State as the major claimant on scarce peasant resources and as the leading arbiter of developmental decisions (in much the way as the pre-colonial State but with much more formidable instruments of passive and active coercion), was to minimize the chronic budget deficit. Of the State monopolies in Laos, the only viable income source was from locally grown opium and the only viable producer was the Hmong. While accruing to the Federal as opposed to the Lao budget up until the Second World War, opium supplied not less than one sixth of the Federal budget revenue. During World War Two, the State leaned more heavily on the *Régie* and particularly the Hmong to meet budgetary demands. With independence, the means in theory of channeling all opium derived revenue to the Lao State finally existed. Paradoxically, one of the least technologically advanced and most geographically isolated communities, the Hmong, were most strongly drawn into the monetized economy, thus expressing the generalized phenomenon in the colonial periphery of the destruction of the natural economy. Parenthetically, a late twentieth century parallel would be the role of Bolivian Indian peasant producers of coca leaf to the external economy.

With respect to the *prestation* system what set Laos off from the rest of Indochina was its longevity. The rule of thumb on the part of local tax agents was to maximize recovery in cash rather than in kind. The bind, however, was that the burden of corvee fell upon those least capable of requiting the *prestation* obligation in cash, that is the minority population of Laos. Clearly the racially differentiated tax system in colonial Laos became the most important lever in forcing the population into the money economy. At first *chaomuong* and then *tasseng* and *naiban* were the key collaborators in this enterprise. In general the tax net grew more comprehensive and complex as the colonial era progressed and as social groups and classes became more differentiated. It was not until 1949 that the tax system was placed on a more modern footing.

To address the question posed at the beginning of this chapter, it is relevant to consider the arguments of one student of the colonial process in Portuguese Africa, W. G. Clarence-Smith. In a careful study of the economic history of southern Angola, he finds evidence which refutes what he calls the "uneconomic imperialism school of historiography". This would hold that notwithstanding chronic budget deficits, natural poverty and drain on resources in putting down rebellions, colonialism in late nineteenth and early twentieth century Portuguese Africa was not economically motivated. Clearly, he argues, lack of economic returns does not negate economic motivations and expectations of profits. The Portuguese expectations of a "second Rand" in southern Angola, we have shown, had its analogy in the hype surrounding French hopes of a Laos eldorado. More importantly, he continues, public deficits must be carefully distinguished from private profits. As with Portuguese Africa, French private concessionaires certainly made their pile in Laos as did various import monopolies in commodities, banking and communications. One feature of the colonial State was to mediate between powerful capitalist groups, classes and fractions. Related to this was the emergence of local colonial capitalist lobbies that demanded the State invest in communications infrastructure and to ensure security in the interior and to otherwise undergird a system which maximized the extraction of profits. In the case of Laos (and Cambodia) local capitalist networks syphoned off economic surplus to sub-metropolitan Saigon, the center of the rice trade, branch headquarters of metropolitan commercial houses, maisons, banks, communications and government. French Laos stood with southern Angola of Clarence-Smith's description, as a classic case of uneconomic imperialism (cf. Clarence-Smith 1979:4).

NOTES

1. I wish to thank Kelvin Rowley for making an observation along these lines.
2. An example was the *Chot Mai Het Lao* (1939).
3. For an overview of the workings of the Opium administration in Indochina, especially in the pre-State Monopoly phase in the late nineteenth century, see Murray 1980:75-77.
4. In 1927, as an official French report revealed, without taking into account Kwang Tcheo Wan, the estimated maximum base of a "rational" per annum supply of raw opium required to fulfil consumption demands in Indochina would be 14,000 kilograms of local opium supplemented by 90,000 kilograms of Indian "Benares" opium (AOM Indochine NF, carton 282, Dossier 2480).
5. While the French delegate to the League of Nations argued that the receipts to the *Douanes et Regie* were actually falling — as if to convince the world body that France was cleaning up its house over the opium question in Indochina — it was patently obvious that within Indochina, people were smoking more and more. The reasons for this apparent contradiction were pointed out in an article in the Cochinchinese newspaper, *L'Argus Indochinois*, 26 January 1929. The system worked like this. Three quarters of the Benares opium supplied to Indochina was re-exported (smuggled) to China. The last quarter was mixed with inferior Yunnanese opium made available to local smokers as Benares at the price of

Benares but without any of the esteemed qualities of Benares and all to the advantage of a certain "well known black treasury". ("Comment on renseigne la Société des Nations sur la question de l'Opium", *L'Argus Indochinois*, 26 January 1929).

6. The official statistics for the amount of prepared opium consumed during one month (February 1940) is equally revealing of the scale of the operations of the *Régie*. While Tonkin and Cochinchina consumed the lion's share, 3.1 and 2.5 million kilograms respectively, Laos consumed 111,960 kilograms for the month.

7. According to an official French memo, the purchase price for opium in the 1948 buying season was to be fixed between 2,600 to 2,700 piasters a kilogram. Payment for this inflated sum was to be in fine silver tissue (AOM Aix F17, March 1949).

8. As one British observer commented of the Indochinese tax system following a visit in 1928: "There can be no doubt that the Indochinese under French protection (cf. British and Dutch) are subjected to a rather high rate of taxation and very few things can be done without being subject to an impost of some sort" (Bell 1928:267).

9. According to Forest (1980:224), if calculated on a per capita basis, the Cambodian peasant was the most imposed upon by the Indochinese taxation system and a victim of an enormous injustice and bias on the part of the general budget. As with Forest in respect to Cambodia, we cannot produce complete statistics on taxes collected in Laos on account of the general budget. The veracity of Forest's assertion depends of course on the period under review. In Laos the contribution to the general budget expanded proportionally to the development of opium poppy cultivation, especially in the late 1930s. Contrary to Forest's assertion, the *prestations* were more onerous in Laos than in either Cambodia or Annam for the entire colonial epoch.

PART TWO

The Non-Rebellion of the Lao

....there has been no evidence of agitation on the part of the indigenous population of Laos. This country has loyally remained aloof from these activities which disturb public order. Underpopulated, not accessible to political intrigues and living in a country with abundant territory with appreciable forest resources, the Lao appears satisfied with his lot. Content with protection which has otherwise put an end to incessant incursions from across the frontier regions, benefitting from numerous incremental advantages offered by the Administration, Laos must be classed as the most faithful and devoted of the Indochinese countries to the French cause. These few acts, however slight, of social undiscipline, otherwise unknown in the territories between the Mekong and the Annamite Chain, originate exclusively from Vietnamese elements.... The existence of the inhabitants of the country remains as it otherwise was, that is to say as simple as possible. They remain without ambition, their needs are extremely limited as are their resources....

(AOM Aix F4 Bulletin Politique, the Résident Supérieur of Laos to the Governor General in Saigon, Vientiane, 24 December 1936).

3

Pre-Capitalist Modes of Production in Laos

It should be borne in mind, as Scott affirms, that rebellion is one of the least likely consequences of exploitation (1976:192), and that only a collective "shock" or a series of "shocks" of substantial scope provides a reason for a large body of peasants to defensively react or rebel. The resort to defensive actions, he argues, might be related to ecological vulnerability, price system vulnerability, or mono-crop vulnerability (1976:194). In other words, the "brittleness" and "explosiveness" of the agrarian structure, according to Scott, is a product of interacting forces, partly demographic-ecological, partly in response to market forces and partly owing to the growth of the State (1976:196). Popkin adds that in seeking to explain why peasants in colonial Annam eventually overthrew their notables and reorganized their villages, one should not assume that their moral bonds had withered but should "concentrate on the ways in which colonial influences increased social stratification by adding to the comparative political advantages of the notables thus aggravating peasant grievances" and which finally gave way to support to revolutionary movements (Popkin 1979:201). Scott's contention that in the context of depression in Annam, the continued collection of fixed taxes posed the immediate threat to subsistence (1976:132), would not contradict Popkin's conclusion.

To make sense of the question of why the Lao did not openly rebel against colonial rule during the depression years — when faced with adversary economic conditions — we should not only consider normative assumptions of the peasant eye view (cf. Scott, Popkin), but equally attempt to identify the circumstances and forms in which surplus accumulation, transfer and redistribution took place. This leads to an identification in this chapter of the pre-capitalist modes of production in Laos. A subsequent chapter is reserved for a consideration of the array of strategies mustered by the colonial State to actively stay off the crisis and to nip rebellion in the bud.

PRE-CAPITALIST MODES OF PRODUCTION

In polyethnic Laos some sixty-five ethnic groups have been identified, at various stages of social, economic and cultural development. The three major expressions of local community, tribal or village-based power with which we are concerned in this essay are those represented by the three major ethno-linguistic groups found in Laos, the dominant and majority Tai-Lao-Lu (*Lao Loum*) and the subordinate Kha (proto-Indochinese or *Lao Theung*) and the H'mong (Meo)-Yao (*Lao Soung*). (See Map II).

The main feature of the human demography of Laos, is the vertical pattern of ethnic distribution. In general, the minority tribal people live at higher altitudes than the majority Lao. The Tai, constituting about one sixth of the population of Laos, characteristically dwell in upland settlements in the mountainous northeast of the country. Technologically less advanced than the Lao, they nevertheless share their cultural origins. Also dispersed throughout northern Laos are the Hmong (Meo) and the Yao (Man) tribes representing as much as one tenth of the population. These two groups occupy approximately a similar ecological niche, only seldom settling during colonial times below an altitude of 1000 meters. Having migrated out of China in the modern historical period, the Hmong possess many Chinese racial and cultural traits. About one quarter of the population is made up of the autochtone *Lao Theung* (Kha) who occupy the high ground and hills between the Lao and the Hmong-Yao. Characteristically the diverse Kha tribes cultivate upland rice and practice slash and burn agriculture. Not converts to Theravada Buddhism, the religion of the Lao, they are considered by this section of the population as political, social and technological inferiors. A major feature of the human demography of landlocked Laos is that members of each ethnic group are actually more numerous in such neighboring countries as China, Thailand and Vietnam (cf. Le Bar and Suddard 1960:25-6, 35).

Two topographical features dominate the landscape of monsoonal Laos, the Mekong river and the Annamite Cordillera. The Mekong in the main marks the boundary with Thailand (Siam) while, with certain exceptions, the Annamite Cordillera marks the eastern frontier. It is this mountain range which figures as the main natural divide in Indochina, separating the watersheds of the eastward flowing rivers leading to the China sea and the southward tending rivers of all Southeast Asia including the Mekong. While the Annamite Cordillera has proven a formidable and historic and cultural barrier to movement, the Mekong and its east bank tributaries serves as the major north-south communication conduit. Ecologically it is the narrow flood plains of the Mekong which both supports the highest population density, and constitutes the heartland of the *Lao Loum*. While the waters of the Mekong provide protein in the form of fish, wet rice cultivation forms the basic human activity of the Lao. All the larger towns and settlements of Laos are located on the banks of the Mekong. The Lao thus form a roughly contiguous settlement between the north and the south of the country, especially on the fertile lowlands but occasionally in isolated fertile pockets of the mountainous interior.

For a variety of historical, cultural and economic reasons the plains and river valley dwelling Lao are at the pinnacle of the power hierarchy in the country to which they lend their name. As Woodside has observed, although pre-revolutionary Vietnamese villages possessed hierarchical structures as complicated and as rigorous as any in Southeast Asia, village life in Laos and Cambodia, by contrast, was "amazingly egalitarian". To support this thesis, he cites a study by Charles Robequain who observed that as travellers from north central Vietnam moved west towards the Mekong river and Laos the "simpler" they discovered village nobility to be. In contrast to hierarchical Vietnamese villages where the local nobility based its power directly upon concentrations of landed wealth, the Lao — as observed by Vietnamese activist intellectuals — did not fight with each other over who should sit in the highest place at village meetings (Woodside 1976:120). While access to prime land may have developed into a social issue in Laos, in pre-colonial and colonial Laos, it should be stressed, land was never in short supply.

In contradistinction to the hierarchical political as well as territorial system of the *muong*, as represented by the *muong* at the central state level and the lesser *muong* which the former englobes as principalities and as districts, stands the Lao peasantry at the level of "democratically organized" villages. According to a typology developed by Condominas, the system of *muong* exemplifies "extended social space" (*espaces sociaux larges*), as indeed do Vietnamese (and Buginese) social systems. This, he explains, should be contrasted with "confined social space" (*espace sociaux restreints*) as typified by proto-Indochinese village systems. Social space, he defines as the "space determined by the ensemble of relations characteristic of the group under consideration" (Condominas 1980:14 and 53-61). Sharing this Durkheimian conceit, the geographer, Christian Taillard, recognizes three levels of space in which the Lao village is situated; "inhabited space" or the area surrounding the village and pagoda but which also has a ritual character, "utilized space" or the area embracing the *naa* (rice-fields) without intensive irrigation systems, the *suan* (kitchen gardens) and the *ray* (swidden) on the way to being converted to *naa* and a periphery which shades into forestland and finally "acknowledged space", quintessentially expressed by the *muong* as a natural unit — a mountain valley or plain — in which individual villages compete for prestige (Taillard 1977:45).

In an essay treating the concept of village power in Laos, Taillard comments that the Lao village presents itself more as a human community than as a territorial unit. This he attributes to the under-population of the country and, by inference, the lack of demographic pressure upon the land. The community, he explains, functions on several levels (economic, religious and territorial) and constitutes the central element of village life. Economic solidarity manifests itself through mutual aid whether in offering financial support to a relative or in the community construction of a house or in great works, eg. harvesting or planting. The economic solidarity of the village rests in turn upon religious solidarity, expressed by reverence to the protective founding deity of the village, the *phi ban*, and through membership of the *sangha*, the community of Theravada Buddhist adepts and the temporal Buddhist hierarchy (Taillard 1977:42).

According to Condominas, worship of the *phi ban* is the most emphatic expression of the *phi* cult and an act which involves the participation of the entire village. Yet, he affirms, in the Lao village Buddhism remains the dominant faith on both the religious and sociological level, the *wat* (temple) being both symbol and the center of the rural collectivity (Condominas 1970:17 and 88-97). Social integration of the Lao community is also cemented by the calendrical cycle of rites and rituals notably in the way of performance of the pre-Buddhist ceremony known as the *sou khoun* or *baci* (the calling of spirits) and the *boun* (festival) the otherwise ceremonial expression of the Buddhist desire to make merit and express social equanimity (see Zago 1972, Archaimbault 1973).

Taillard explains that community conflict in the Lao village is arbitrated by the elders, although village political organization is founded upon the principle of unanimity. The prerogative of raising motions is vested in the village chief who acts with the consent of the abbott of the local *wat* or other leaders. In any case, questions are not debated in the western sense of the term especially if agreement on a problem is sufficiently well advanced. Once arrived at, the village chief coordinates the execution of decisions. Taillard comments that the system of village unanimity and consensus as the basis of village power has enabled the basic system to be replicated down through the centuries (Taillard 1977:42).

As suggested by the calendar of agrarian rites and rituals, Laos is an overwhelmingly agrarian society with 95 percent of its polyethnic population deriving its livelihood from the cultivation of wet-field or dry-field rice, fishing, hunting and other agricultural pursuits. While important changes in the economic life of the Lao and non-Lao peasantry of Laos were set in train at the point when circuits of commodity circulation were inserted into the economy at the outset of the colonial era, a majority of the peasantry continued to subsist in what Lenin, Luxemburg and Phoumi Vongvichit, among others, have described as a "natural economy". This might be defined as self-sufficient family units under autarkic conditions engaged in economic activity that encompassed a complete cycle of acquisition of raw materials to their final preparation for consumption. While an idealized version of reality, the "natural economy" concept is useful in reference to those elements of non-capitalist modes of production which contradict the spread of capitalist modes of production, and, by extension, the colonial State project. As Murray points out, the natural economy stood opposed to commodity exchanges and circulation, in general (Murray 1980:6-7).

As Samir Amin reminds us, the identification of the predominant mode of production in any particular formation is essential as this permits us to know the predominant form of surplus, whether tribute, rent in kind, commodity form, (surplus value) or profit. Then we need to know in what way the given society lives on that surplus and, the extent to which that surplus is transferred from other societies (trade) and the distribution of this surplus among social classes in relation to different modes of production characteristic of this formation (Amin 1976:18). Clearly, identification of the predominant mode of production in a peripheral social formation is a primary task if we are to comprehend the broader process of this formations' world historical incorporation, the emergence or the blockages to the emergence of class-divided society, the phenomenon of conservation versus dissolution effects under colonial capitalist penetration and the persistence of vestiges of non-incorporated traditional economic systems and ideological modes into the colonial and even post-colonial periods.

Samir Amin's fivefold categorization of modes of production is relevant in this context. These are (1) primitive communal (2) tribute paying (3) slave owning (4) simple petty commodity and (5) capitalist (Amin 1976: 13-14). Typically, he explains, these do not exist in a pure form, but rather articulate in complex groups of "classes" or "social-group" divided forms. With reference to the production process, and the generation of surplus within the Lao social formation, the specific class-divided modes of production that will be taken into consideration in the following analysis are those sets of opposition between *Lao Loum* lords and peasants, *Lao Loum* lords and "slaves", majority and ethnic minority peasants and free petty craftsmen, commodity producers and merchants, and, in the colonial capitalist phase of surplus accumulation, a national and comprador bourgeoisie and proletarian class, albeit incipient. The "debate" on the development of socio-economic formations in Laos (and Vietnam) is of course embedded in the communist history of these two countries. Thus official Lao spokespersons see pre-colonial Lao society as "feudal" with lingering survivals of "pre-feudal" social formations (cf. Kaysone 1980:54).[1]

The Tributary Mode of Production

While the connection of the proto-Indochinese with pre-Angkorian and/or Dongsonian civilization points to a dual process of devolution from and evolution to tributary formations, particularly in the way of accommodation of "indigenous" political systems to Indianized or Sinic forms of statecraft and kingship, the relationship is both complex and controversial. While certain proto-Indochinese tribes share collective memories of anterior civilizations as reinforced by myth and ritual (cf. Hickey 1982:121-143), the dominant tributary or "Asiatic mode of production" to which the colonial power deferred was centered on the Lao Kingdom of Lan Xang (Luang Prabang).

Lao history proper begins with the formation of the Kingdom of Lan Xang in 1353 and the statist orientation of that kingdom set the pattern of *Lao Loum* Theravada Buddhist hegemony at the center over the marginalized and the peripheralized minorities — the tribal and largely non-Indianized Lao Tai and the indigenous proto-Indochinese *Lao Theung* or Kha. The Lao court chronicle version of history indicates that Fa Ngum, as the bearer from Angkor to his capital at Luang Prabang of a powerful symbol of legitimacy — the *Prabang* image of miraculous origin and community beneficence — created an indigenized version of Asoka's Buddhist state by adapting to strong native traditions the Angkorian version of Theravada Buddhism and Indian notions of statehood (cf. Gunn 1982:79).

The model of the traditional polity was thus that of an ideally divinized king at the center of a cosmologically ordained socio-territorial ordering, which implied the opposition of more or less benevolent spirits/demons against, in descending order of spiritual and social rank, court nobles, then commoners (the Theravadin *Lao Loum* peasantry), and in darkness, as it were, the ritually subordinate and peripheral Kha tribes. At a general level of abstraction, the towns of medieval Laos were the seat of a politico-religious power exercised by an hereditary nobility (ministers who had considerable power) in the name of a *Buddharaja* (god-king) and ensured of support by a local Buddhist clergy, the whole buttressed by the principal economic exchanges that flowed from more remote tributaries. *Chaomuong* (chiefs of the provinces) were also of the nobility and acted as veritable kings with respect to the administration of the principalities (Gunn 1982:79).

Relative to stronger anterior regional tributary formations, most notably that based on the Angkorian mode of production which reached its apogee in the ninth to twelfth centuries (cf. Sedov 1974:327-343), the Lao tributary formations based on the Kingdom of Lan Xang and Vientiane from the fourteenth to the nineteenth centuries, were weaker in terms of mobilizational capacity, surplus accumulation and in the construction of great works (cf. Manivanna 1974:309-325). The eclipse of the pre-Angkorian and Angkorian formations, which had previously held sway over southern and central Laos, by the invading and conquering Tai peoples, however, had the consequence of a corollary deracination and marginalization of the indigenous proto-Indochinese peoples. This was expressed at both the ideological-ritual and economic levels. Economically, the appearance of a tribute collecting Lao social formation in the fourteenth century was matched by the emergence of incipient social class divided society, between lord and peasant and peasant and slave.

This authentic provincial autonomy of the *chaomuong*, in the estimation of Lévy, conferred on Laos a "quasi-feudal" status, the evident source of the economic and political feebleness of the center, whose power, in any case, turned out to be more religious than real. Thus the traditional political entity of Laos is characterized by Lévy as being riven with "internal contradictions and class antagonisms" between nobles and commoners, free men and slaves, and *Lao Loum* versus other ethnic groups. As a result, states were unable to support their fragile existence for long (Lévy 1974: 21-2 & 58-9). Martin Barber, by contrast, in a study of "traditional" political relations between village and town, observes that the political ideology of the outlying villages remains basically independent of the ritual and the ideological involvement with the concepts of Kingship. Although, he continues, "control over the villages had to be maintained at the level of political bargaining, through the perceived mutual advantage of military protection, economic support and the settlement of disputes". Barber affirms, however, that only through religion was there any ideological link between the villages and the king in the capital (Barber 1979:243 and Gunn 1982:79).

Elsewhere (Gunn 1982), I have argued that the essential bifurcation between the State and the village community was upheld in a manner expressive of the Asiatic mode of production. Indeed in the context of the debate over the validity and the applicability of the Asiatic mode of production carried out in the French journal *La Pensée*, it has been argued by Keo Manivanna that in fact Lan Xang did conform to the model, though it lacked great works, specifically, that it was without the mobilizational capacities of Angkor) and that tax and the control of commerce (long distance trade) did play an important role in the accumulation of wealth in the hands of the aristocracy and State.

Moreover, at the superstructural level, the transformation of the State and the appearance of the kingdom accompanied fundamental religious changes, namely the adoption of the Angkorian version of Theravada Buddhism. The emergence of a differentiated aristocracy, a class of priest specialists, artisans, and soldiers at Luang Prabang set apart the centralized Lao State from the ancient Tai political structure, the *muong*, such as that existing in Sip Song Panna (southwest Yunnan) and the Sip Song Chau Thai of northeast Laos and the Dien Bien Phu region of Vietnam (Manivanna 1968:56-69 and cf. Gunn 1982:79).

It is accepted here, after John G. Taylor, that a particular characteristic of the Asiatic mode of production is its "changing yet unchanging" history, a phenomenon that results from successive rulers occupying State power, yet retaining intact the functions of the previous ruler and economic relations with the villages. So while one dynasty or family replaces another in the State apparatus of domination (in Laos, this involved the shifting of the locus of the kingdom to Vientiane, its subsequent florescence during the reign of Souligna Vongsa (1637-94) and the eventual reduction of the kingdoms and principalities of Laos to tributary status at the hands of the Burmese, the Vietnamese and the Siamese, the overall structure of the formation may remain highly stable (Taylor 1979:181). To be sure, as Lévy has pointed out, the idea of a Lao nation is not only the consequence of the French protectorate but appeared long before in the ancient tribal solidarity of the *chaomuong* (Lévy 1974:59 and cf. Gunn 1982:80).

Amin likewise characterizes the tributary mode of production as existing in a class divided social formation. Typically, he points out, the ruling class, "...monopolizes the functions of the given society's political organization and exacts a tribute (not in commodity form) from the rural communities" (Amin 1976:15). Economic structure was based on the village community with its "indestructible" autarky. As a production-consumption unit unto itself, the village community had not yet separated agriculture from handicrafts. With reference to the ideological level of control, typically the king represented the "superior unity" in the personification of the state, itself mediated through the bureaucratic apparatus (see Mazzeo and Antonini 1978:75 for a discussion of the Asiatic mode of production concept with reference to Angkor). Known as the "*chao sivit*" or the "lord of lives", the monarch at Luang Prabang exercised a more powerful hegemony over his subjects on the religio-ideological plane than on the economic plane, especially in comparison to the "archetypal" hydraulic-agricultural "oriental" societies.

It is well at this stage to delineate the contours of the Asiatic mode of production and to distinguish it from the feudal mode of production. Suffice is to say that the forces of production and the relations of production taken as a whole constitute a mode of production. The relations of production or the socially structured relations between men, into which they must enter as a result of their participation in the process of social production form the substructure of society, on which rises a superstructure of laws, politics, religion, etc. Structure and superstructure taken as a whole constitute a social formation. Corresponding to each mode of production are specific forms of the appropriation of the labor of others. Thus under the Asiatic mode, the land belongs in the last resort to the State and the labor of the village community is subject to the collective corvée (Melotti 1977:68). In the Marxist schema, Sawer explains, the Asiatic State is not only part of the superstucture of society but also part of the productive base, the State being required to provide public works to satisfy agricultural needs. It is, then, the only mode of production that is geographically-ecologically circumscribed (Sawer 1977:53 and 104-9). Under feudalism, by contrast, the king is only primus inter pares and the feudal lord is the direct exploiter, claiming hereditary superiority and control over the land and the people on it (Melotti 1977:68). But the theoretical implications of the concept of the AMP, as suggested by Althusser, are that in relation to the pre-capitalist modes of production, which largely characterize the Lao social formation, centrality must be given to the non-economic structures, notably at the political and ideological levels (Sawer 1977:229 and Gunn 1982:80).

While according to Samir Amin (1976:15), the tributary mode of production inevitably becomes feudal when the ruling class ousts the community from *dominum eminens* of the soil, a major feature of the Tai-Lao mode of production was its replication and continuity down until modern times. This condition, we would ascribe to the lack of demographic pressures on the land in Laos and to the nature of the ideological reproduction of social relations specific to Tai political systems. The debate by indigenous and non-indigenous scholars over the characterization of the Tai-Lao *sakdina* system as a feudal or an Asiatic mode of production continues unresolved, however (cf. Keo Manivanna 1974, Chit Phumisak 1974, Condominas 1976, Taillard 1974, Elliot 1978, Turton 1980, Gunn 1982). As a general statement, we hold with Amin's revised opinion (1976:73), which views the tributary mode of production as the general form in pre-capitalist social formations and the feudal form as a particular kind which did not receive dominant expression (as was the case in Laos).

The Slave Mode of Production

Contrary to Condominas' assertion that the existence of slaves in the Thai *sakdina* system proved Marx's phenomenon of "generalized slavery" in relation to the Asiatic mode of production (Condominas 1980:313), we hold with Turton that the Lao-Tai social formation could not have been dominated by a slave mode of production because no actual production occurred (cf. Turton 1980). Manivanna describes four basic kinds of slaves existing in the medieval period of Lao history. There were war slaves, debt slaves, slaves who had not acquitted their taxes and hereditary slaves whose origin was in either of the previous three categories. These slaves were placed under the patronage of the king, the princes and the congregations of Buddhist monks. They could be bought, sold, lent or transferred but liberated only by royal amnesty or other specific conditions (Manivanna 1974:318). As Lingat has demonstrated, the institution of slavery in Siam is not to be directly compared with that which existed in classical antiquity or as practiced in the colonies of the European nations or in the American slave states. By the middle of the nineteenth century, slaves in Siam and Cambodia and Laos were not a separate social category but, for the most part, existed in a form of debt bondage (Lingat 1931:1 and 236). Clearly in Laos, as in other Tai political systems, slave labor at no time formed the principal basis of production and there were no labor processes specific to slaves.

As in the nineteenth century Thailand, slaves in Laos originated from both outside and inside their respective social formations. Typically, those from outside originated from other states or were drawn from the proto-Indochinese population. Indeed, the pejorative appellation "*Kha*" means "slave" in Thai-Lao versus "*Thai*" which means "free". Those from within the social formations arose in slavery for reasons of indebtedness and juridical confiscation (Turton 1980:289). Stronger montagnard tribes, notably Sedang, Ta Hoi and Jarai preyed upon weaker tribes, selling captives for profit to Siamese, Lao and Khmer mandarins in the slave markets of Phnom Penh, Bangkok, Bassak and Strung Treng (Murdoch 1974:51 and Hickey 1982:34).[2]

To be sure, slavery was the most important form of private property in a society where land theoretically belonged to the king. In Laos, the institution of slavery was organically linked with the ideological superstructure of control by the *Lao Loum* lords and buttressed by notions of Hindu and Mon Burman law. Repugnant to the French sense of republicanism, the colonial administration attempted to eliminate the system by phasing it out, although in fact the slave trade on the east bank of the Mekong had been disrupted — although not altogether eliminated — before it came under French control in 1893 (Murdoch 1974:52).

A major problem facing the French administration in Laos in the elimination of the system of debt contract slavery was resistance on the part of slave owners. The progressive elimination of the system in Laos was linked with a number of measures. These included the liquidation of debt bondage upon the death of a slave and the corresponding emancipation of children born into slavery (at the age of fifteen) and the implementation of a meaningful timetable for the full redemption of debt leading to full emancipation (AOM Aix E6, "De l'esclavage pour dettes et des modifications a y apporter" nd.). As will be seen, the emancipation of slaves in Laos under the colonial order did not, however, remove their liability to render taxes and corvees to the colonial State. At the outset of the French administration in Laos, then, the average value of an adult male slave (26 to 40 years old) — in Vientiane at least — was 56 ticals (30 piasters or 75 francs) while for women (21 to 30 years old) the value was 48 ticals (28 piasters or 70 francs) (Raquez 1902:467). Dauplay, a colonial administrator, noted that when he took over control of Saravane province in January 1906, slaves were being exchanged at the rate of one slave per flint-lock rifle, a practice that persisted into the following decade (AOM Aix E16, Dauplay to the Résident Supérieur of Laos, Saravane, 5 May 1919). It was also the case, however, that some Kha felt more secure in a relationship of bondage than as victims of the colonial tax-cash nexus.

The Commodity Mode of Production

After Amin, the simple commodity mode of production is marked in its pure state by equality between free petty producers and the organization of commodity exchanges between them. It never became the predominant mode of production (Amin 1976:15). Rather, the communal and tributary mode of production (with slaves as a commodity) was anterior to, and coexisted with commodity production at the point of its emergence as a mode of production. In Laos, as in other pre-capitalist social formations, the existence of a commodity mode of production was anterior to the integration of the social formation into global capitalist relations of production. Stated another way the commodity mode of production is frequently a sphere governed by simple commodity relations, eg., the sphere of handicraft production where this has been sufficiently dissociated from agricultural production.

In Laos, handicraft production developed and concentrated in certain regions and according to a certain ethnic specialization. As revealed most strikingly by temple architecture, *Lao Loum* craft, notably in wood sculpture, attained a highly developed state. Gold craft, paper manufacture, pottery, the manufacture of piroques and wagons, the preparation of salt, the manufacture of steel instruments, resin torches etc. attest to a relatively high level of the advancement of the forces of production (see Phoumi Vongvichit 1968:17). It might also be noted that in royal towns like Luang Prabang separate quarters or villages for craftsmen specializing in religious paraphernalia or other crafts testified to a significant dissociation of free petty producers from agricultural production. However, the degree of craft specialization in Laos lagged behind that of Cambodia, Thailand and more markedly that of Vietnam, China and India. As Khieu Samphan noted of mid-nineteenth century Cambodia, the essentially "static" subsistence economy had not yet been transformed into a mercantilist economy (Samphan 1979:34). The same would essentially hold for Laos up until and including the early twentieth century.

Phoumi Vongvichit notes that nearly all montagnard villages possessed forges for the fabrication of instruments and knives, especially in the areas where good quality iron ore was found (Phoumi Vongvichit 1968:11). A survey of Kha industry undertaken during colonial times, which may be taken as representative of pre-capitalist Kha activity generally, revealed the following range of manufactures; forge-made knives, hatchets and ploughshares, cross-bows, cane-matting, cords, fishing lines and woven *sin* (skirts) and fabrics. These woven items were produced by Kha women at the rate of one *sin* and three fabrics a year. It was observed that the number of peasant laborers who produced a surplus above the needs of the family was rare. While there was a limited exchange of knives, cross-bows and basket ware against salt or clothing, it was observed of the montagnard communities in Saravane that there was no family industry sufficiently developed to even give place to a minimum commerce with neighboring provinces (AOM Aix E7 Saravane, Grossin, Commissioner Administrator of the Government to the Résident Supérieur of Laos, 29 August 1930).

Although typically existing within the "natural economy", the Kha did not succeed in living in strict autarky; they were compelled to undertake trading relations with the outside world that went beyond the demands of requiting tribute. The Kha Leu, for instance, as non-weavers, were totally dependent upon outsiders for clothing. While possessing the knowhow to work iron, they were ignorant of the process of the extraction of the ore. Although in need of jars to store rice, they had no knowledge of ceramics. Above all they were in need of salt, a scarce commodity in the highlands (Barthelemy Report). As Wall noted of the Nya Hon, buffaloes — the most usual commodity of exchange — were bartered for pigs from other tribes (Wall 1975:35). Indeed, during colonial times there were four great "natural" markets for the Kha, especially catering for the buffalo trade. These were at Tchepone, Muong Nong, Khesanh and Calu. Until the outbreak of fighting between the French in the Viet Minh in that region in 1946, Khesanh was a major destination for Kha caravans where they traded their forest products against jars and cloths from Vietnamese or Chinese merchants (Barthelemy Report).

According to Phoumi Vongvichit, the Hmong have a level of production more elevated than that of the *Lao Theung*, but inferior to that of the *Lao Loum* (Phoumi Vongvichit 1968:22). Characteristically, the Hmong practice a (relatively) ecologically destructive type of swidden agriculture, growing crops such as maize, opium poppy, rice and fruit trees in *ray* on three different altitudinal levels. As a consequence of the search for suitable calcareous soils for poppy cultivation, the Hmong are by economic necessity more nomadic than the *Lao Theung*. They also have some reputation as stock breeders and as weavers and metal forgers. While largely subsisting within a natural economy, the Hmong have a history of commerce with the plains dwellers.

Currency had made its appearance in the pre-colonial era and even before the Indochinese piaster was established as a uniform medium of exchange, a hodgepodge of local and foreign silver-based currencies were already circulating as well established standards for the barter trade (see Robequain 1944:137). Other "currencies" such as salt and opium coexisted with metal-based currencies up until colonial times. The anthropologist Charles Archaimbault noted that from the market places of the high region of Laos to the Bolovens in the south, salt was the object of an "intense" internal commerce and constituted a medium of exchange between Lao and Kha traders (Archaimbault 1973:1).

Commodity exchange within the pre-capitalist Lao social formation was also well developed in the sphere of mining. Iron was mined by Lao producers at Ta En (Sam Neua) and at Lat Boua (Xieng Khouang), rock salt from Ban Keun (Vientiane) and Bo Ten (Phong Saly) and gold was extracted from various rivers (Phoumi Vongvichit 1968:11). Before mining rights were conceded to metropolitan capitalist enterprises in Nam Patane, the tin deposits were worked in a rudimentary way by local peasant labor, the ores being crudely smelted on charcoal fires. Indeed, the *Lao Loum* peasant communities of the Nam Patane valley lived solely from tin mining. They neither engaged in handicraft and weaving activities nor did they work in rice fields and tend buffaloes as did the typical *Lao Loum* peasant. Their annual production was around 1,200 kilograms. This quantity of tin was sufficient to produce a surplus necessary for simple reproduction, a small surplus being bartered against clothing, food and other commodities. During the period of Siamese domination of Laos, a certain number of villages in the Nam Patane valley were obliged to pay an annual tribute of tin (in fact ninety kilograms) to the *Chaomuong* of Lakhone (Gosselin 1900:259).[3]

The role of long-distance trade within and between tributary formations should not be underestimated. Initially involving barter of exotic natural products, slaves and tribute itself, by the late nineteenth century European manufactured commodities had already entered the trading circuits of pre-capitalist social formations at the periphery. Francis Garnier observed during the course of his exploration of the upper Mekong during the 1860s that Nong Khai, with a population of 5-6,000, was the most important commercial center on the Mekong from Phnom Penh to Luang Prabang and had inherited, in part, the commercial importance of Vientiane since its destruction at the hands of the Thai some forty years prior. As witnessed by the French traveller, d'Orleans, during the 1890s, the village of Nong Khai was a great commercial entrepot at the terminus of the Bangkok-Korat route, its trade dominated by Sino-Thai merchants (d'Orleans 1894:416-422).

To this center came from Bangkok such European manufactures and commodities as cloth or silk manufactured in Lyon, Japanese matches, calicut, false jewels, buttons, thread, pencils, conserved milk and a "thousand other items invariably of English or German manufacture". From Luang Prabang, itself a local trading entrepot, came local produce as well as opium, musk, tea, vermicelli, carpets from Dali and Lhasa and lacquer from Burma. To this list might be added a general regional trade in gold powder, lead, salt, iron, ivory, feathers, skins, horns, benjoin, cinnamon, wax and other forest products. During the early years of the colonial administration, the barter trade from lower Laos to Siam and Cambodia was dominated entirely by such forestry or agricultural products. In rank order of importance these were cardamom, buffaloes, elephants, padi. The trade even included tiger bones. Thus at the outset of the colonial administration in Laos, the four major commercial currents followed closely the traditional barter-trade routes; the land routes towards Yunnan via Muong Sai, Muong Yo and Sse Mao, the river and land route to Bangkok, the route to Annam via Muong Phine and the Ai Lao pass and the Mekong river route to Cochinchina via Cambodia (Picanon 1901:267).

It is clear then, that neither the commodity mode of production nor the tributary mode of production existed in pure states but rather in formations that on the one hand combined modes of production and, on the other, organized the relations between local societies and other societies. This was expressed by the extension of long distance trading relations. According to Amin this assumes an important role when the surplus that can be extracted from producers is limited, owing to the less advanced level of the development of productive forces, national conditions or local resistance. In other words, it makes possible the transfer of part of the surplus from one society to another. The very condition of class-divided formations, Amin goes on to argue, is the development of productive forces (Amin 1976:16-18). Typically, in Tai-Lao social formations wealth or the excess of production over consumption was consumed as luxuries by the lord of the *muong*. Notwithstanding the existence of an incipient commodity exchange, specialization of economic function and the insertion of an incipient, albeit foreign (Sino-Thai and Yunnanese) merchant class between the State and other communities, the preconditions for indigenous capitalism were not impressive in pre-colonial Laos.

THE PEASANT CONDITION

We would do well at this point to bear in mind Wolf's consideration, namely as to what kind of peasantry we refer to when we speak of peasant involvement in political upheaval. In anthropology, he reminds us, differences in behavior and outlook between tenants and proprietors, poor and rich, cultivators and craftsmen, between peasants involved in town affairs and the market have important bearings on revolutionary outcomes. Wolf thus defines peasants as "populations that are existentially involved in cultivation and make autonomous decisions involved in cultivation regarding the processes of cultivation". Thus unlike primitives, peasants are subject to the dictates of a superordinate State. Unlike farmers, peasants have not fully entered the market (Wolf 1971:xix). Clearly peasant as a category is imprecise and lends to different readings from the literature. Our argument, has been to stress the "peasantization" of primitives and the commoditization or erstwhile autonomous peasant producers.

The foregoing also raises the epistomological question as to the discovery of the peasantry in French Indochina. Joel S. Kahn has raised this question with reference to the Netherlands East Indies finding that the Indonesian peasantry, as a specific mode of peasant existence and a "product of given historical, social, economic and political conditions", was "discovered" by Dutch scholars and colonial advisors in the 1920s (Van Doorn, Scheltema, Van der Kolff, Koens, Boeke). The Dutch Indonesianists, he reminds us, were significantly influenced by Chayanov's "Theory of Peasant Economy" published in German translation in 1924 as well as German historical economics since the 1870s. Kahn is also mindful of the attraction of the Indonesian communist movement in the 1920s to strongly peasantist ideologies (Kahn 1986 passim).

I would argue that a similar dialectic was at work in French Indochina, engaging not only administrator-scholars (Gourou, Robequain, Yves Henri) but also middle class members of the burgeoning anti-colonial nationalist and communist movements. While I do not wish to be sidetracked by a discussion of the roots of the nationalist movement in Indochina, the following official perception of the political conscientization of the (Vietnamese) *nha que* (peasantry) is apposite here:

> The peasant stooped in his rice-field does not appear until now to have been seriously affected: but it is certain that, from some time to another,

> by means of a letter from a relative, by way of conversation with a boy or with a petty indigenous functionary, through a fragment of a newspaper discussed among friends, there reaches the villager an attenuated echo of the dreams which carress certain of the town dwellers; he hears talk of emancipation of Indochina and now and then he pricks up his ears at the announcement of land reform.
>
> (AOM Paris Slotfom 111, 56, "Le Communisme et les colonies", 1927).

Normative evaluations aside (cf. Chovanes 1986), the study of the peasantry in the colonial periphery would be incomplete without scrutinizing objective indicators of living and working conditions. The major obstacle to such an undertaking in Laos, however, is the absence of valid data, moreover, faced with fluctuating exchange rates in the colonial era, piaster values must be taken as relative only.

In their study of the peasant question in Indochina in 1936-38, Truong Chinh and Vo Nguyen Giap state that a Vietnamese agricultural income was 11.90 piasters per annum. Expenses (including head tax and supplementary tax was four piasters), the total being 34.15 piasters. Therefore, they reasoned, if the peasant did not have additional income from land or from serving as a landlords' tenant, he and his family would be reduced to one basic meal a day or even less. In consideration of the Tai society of Sonla and Lai Chau, analogous to the Tai-Lao society of northeastern Laos, a class of transport coolies or road construction coolies employed by the State, earned .16 piasters a day without food, therefore 58.4 piasters if they were fully employed at that rate on a yearly basis (Truong Chinh and Vo Nguyen Giap 1974:31-32).

Between 1926 and 1930, the average daily wage of adult male mine workers throughout Indochina increased from approximately .40 piasters to .70 piasters. However, soon afterwards, daily money wages declined sharply to .45 piasters in 1933. Low rates for average daily money wages was even further exaggerated by the fact that nearly all wage laborers earned money wages during only part of the year (Murray 1980:337). Marked differentiation in wages between the regions of Indochina was also apparent. For example, in 1931 wages paid in Saigon were twice those current in Hanoi. Average daily wages in northern Indochina in 1931 ranged downward, from a piaster a day for blacksmiths to .95 piasters for *cai* (labor recruiters) to .24 piasters for female manual labor to .20 piasters a day for child labor (see Dumarest 1935:172-174, Thompson 1947:180-184, and Murray 1980:352).

The following journalistic portrait of a cake vendor in Phnom Penh is illustrative of the dilemma of the marginalized town dweller in colonial Indochina seeking to sustain a living or to accumulate a surplus in the face of the unrelenting claims of the colonial tax agents. According to a reporter for *La Presse Indochinoise*, typically the vendor would earn 15 to 20 centimes a day from working capital of 60 centimes a day and after having wandered around town all day. The vendor would hardly have left his or her house, however, when approached by a municipal tax collector claiming from 3 to 5 cents for whatever reason. Naturally, as he had to support a family, he paid without protest. This amount was nothing much in a town which disposed of hundreds of thousands of piasters, the report continued, but it constituted an important sacrifice for honest workers, especially when viewed on a yearly basis. Multiply three or five centimes by 360 days and the figure of 10.80 piasters and 18 piasters is arrived at. That meant that the petty cake vendor actually paid more in Cambodia or elsewhere in Indochina than the tax payer in the top tax bracket. Moreover, even if the vendor did not earn even fifteen centimes every day, he or she was still obliged to pay (*La Presse Indochinoise*, 1 July 1936).

According to a colonial account, the monthly salary of a day laborer in Laos in 1930 was 8 piasters or 96 piasters a year. The day laborer, it was reported, paid on an annual basis 2.50 piasters personal tax, 2.40 piasters to redeem corvees and, in addition, 0.10 piasters to the chiefs responsible for the recovery of tax, thus a total of 5 piasters. The special category of *piroquiers* or river boat coolies in Luang Prabang earned a maximum of 12 piasters a month or 144 piasters a year. Altogether they paid a total of 7.40 piasters per annum in taxes or equal to the eighteenth part of their annual income (AOM Aix Q2, Chef de Battalion, Ayme to the *Résident Supérieur* of Laos, Phong Saly 27 September 1930). While this wage level appears inflated relative to that obtaining during the 1930s in other parts of Indochina the tax burden is also excessive if one takes into consideration that the wage earner characteristically supported a family and even if unemployed or underemployed at any time during the year still had to pay the tax burden as well as meet the *prestation* obligation.

The preceding official account of the wage-tax structure can be weighed up against ICP reports on social conditions in Laos. According to one account, the wages of urban push-cart coolies were between 0.30 piasters and 0.80 piasters a day during 1934, making possible only a "miserable" existence (AOM Paris Slotfom 54, 111, Annex to NP 35 2nd tri 1935, "La Situation Politique de nos ennemis", 6 September 1934). This would translate into 100 piasters a year and 288 piasters a year, respectively, if the coolie were fully employed. While the urban coolie in Laos admittedly had greater earning capacity than his upcountry counterpart, it was also the case, as revealed by the portrait of the Phnom Penh cake vendor, that the ability to escape the tentacles of the tax system was considerably reduced in the urban area.

SOCIAL CLASS DIFFERENTIATION IN COLONIAL LAOS?

But neither can we neglect the question of social differentiation and relative deprivation if we are to come to terms with the question of peasant exploitation. To evaluate the five tier taxation revenue system, as outlined in Chapter Two, the results of a study of this question carried out by Pietrantoni, a colonial administrator, are illuminating. Working from surveys conducted in Laos in 1932 and 1942, he calculated the average amount of personal tax contributed by each category of tax-payer and additionally by certain key ethnic minorities. Extrapolating the results of his study to encompass the whole of Laos, Pietrantoni was led to generalize about the "division of wealth by tax-revenue classes" both within Laos and between Laos and Tonkin. While he acknowledged that revenue was not the only element to be considered in determining social classes, he argued that it was sufficient to arrive at a "first approximation of social equilibrium" in Laos. The sense of the latter, he derives from Pareto: "the state of society attained at any given moment when the ensemble of factors that condition it have produced their effect" (Pietrantoni 1968:192).

The following three conclusions emerged from Pietrantoni's study:

> (i) ...a country with a very strong middle-class whose level and kind of life are very reconciled with that of the leisure class and the simple class and poor class and where authority is not derived principally from wealth but from prestige owing to traditional function (King, mandarins, notables).
> (ii) ...Laos has benefited from fifty years of the *paix francais* in the course of which the stability of its social equilibrium has not been seriously endangered, local incidents never having economic nor even political motives in relationship to the social ensemble.
> (iii) ...the social equilibrium would only be troubled by a profound economic modification of activity or by the action of another society which, at the time of writing, was excluded by the existence of the French prefectorate.

While Pietrantoni was in no position to predict the Viet Minh intervention in Laos, it is worthwhile examining his sociological findings in some detail. As shown in Table 3.1, he quantified fiscal revenue derived in Laos in the sample year of 1943 according to tax category. Additionally, this includes the numbers of taxpayers per category not liable to pay the personal indigenous tax. The first category includes Europeans, foreign Asians and canton notables. The second includes all these plus members of the Royal family, the third includes Phoutheng and Lao notables, while the fourth category includes the latter as well as a number of auxiliary officers.

TABLE 3.1
FISCAL REVENUE IN LAOS ACCORDING TO TAX CATEGORY 1943

Tax Category	No. of Taxpayers (1943)	No. of Taxpayers not liable to personal tax	Total	%
1. 20$	430	1,600	2,030	.90
2. 10$	1,070	3,800	4,870	2.10
3. 5$	2,300	3,500	5,800	2.50
4. 2$	149,910	9,500	159,400	70.40
5. 1$50	54,640	54,650	24.10	
			226,750	

Source: Pietrantoni 1968:185

Having established the number of taxpayers per category, he then determined the average total tax revenue derived from each tax revenue bracket as well as from certain sub-divisions from within tax brackets — notably Hmong and their opium brokers. By extrapolation he was then able to determine in round figures the absolute amount of tax derived per category and sub-category, and hence the relative percentage contributed to the total budget per tax-category relative to their absolute and relative demographic strength (Pietrantoni 1968:185). This is shown in Table 3.2.

TABLE 3.2
ABSOLUTE AMOUNT OF TAX DERIVED PER TAX CATEGORY

Categories	No. of taxpayers	Average revenue derived per category and sub-category	Total revenues
1.	2,230		
	500	3,600$	
	1,730	3,600$	8,030,000$
2.	4,870	1,800$	8,770,000$
3.	17,800 (1)	850$	15,130,000$
	147,200 (2)		
	92,400 (3)[a]	470$	43,430,000$
	54,800 (4)[b]	330$	18,030,000$
5.	5,650	200$	10,940,000$
	226,750		104,330,000$

a. middle class or those taxpayers with revenue derived from property.
b. modest class or those hiring out their services as day laborers, agriculturalists or porters.

Source: Pietrantoni 1968:189

Revenues collected from category four tax-payers were found to average $470 for group A and $320 for group B. Some 12,000 opium poppy cultivators (Hmong and Yao) sold an average per capita 4 kg of opium to middlemen for $90 a kilogram. This in turn was resold by the middlemen to the *Régie* for $160 a kilogram. Already placed in group A of the fourth tax category by virtue of their agricultural and pastoral resources, the Hmong and Yao, as beneficiaries of an average total revenue of $830 ($470 and $360) were elevated to category three. The 200 opium brokers rose from the fourth to the first category. For the first three categories, a certain upward allowance was made for tax evasion. Pietrantoni found that the average revenue in the first category was surpassed by around 500 persons including opium intermediaries, merchants, notables and members of the Royal family and Europeans. Apart from beneficiaries of the Royal civil list, the highest income of any individual in the first category was $24,000 allocated for Prince Phetsarath (Pietrantoni 1968:189).

TABLE 3.3
PERCENTAGE OF NUMBER OF TAXPAYERS BY REVENUE CLASS

Revenue class	Laos	Tonkin (ethnic Vietnamese)
rich and	3	0.5
very rich	7.1	2.5
well-off middle (A)	39.9	7
modest (B)	25	65
poor	25	25

Source: Pietrantoni 1968:190

Pietrantoni adduces from the diagram (Table 3.3) that there was an equivalence in Laos between the number of taxpayers and the percentage of tax revenue. The well to do, he concludes, have not ruptured solidarity with the middle classes — both are part of the same milieu. Of the simpler classes, he argues, there is no oppression of a class of *misérables* by other categories of the population. Their traditional lifestyle, he continues, would have preempted consideration of them in terms of the "Marxist" sense of economic exploitation. With respect to Tonkin, however, insofar as the majority Vietnamese population were taken into consideration, the profile of that country was found to be very different from that of Laos. Firstly, the average income per taxpayer was found to be only 78 percent of that of Laos. Moreover, a proletariat outside of traditional institutions existed in Tonkin. With reference to the evidence provided by the graph distribution of revenue classes in Tonkin, Pietrantoni concluded that the condition of "poverty and misery" in Tonkin did not prefigure the "guarantees of stability" as indicated by his study of Laos (Pietrantoni 1968:190). Indeed Pietrantoni's findings would tend to reinforce Barrington Moore's central thesis that where the links between overlord and peasant community are strong, the tendency towards peasant rebellion (and later revolution) is weak (Moore 1966).

CONCLUSION

We would not contradict Pietrantoni's assertion that class formation in Laos was incipient when compared with Tonkin. Clearly such preconditions of capitalist relations of production as the exclusion from the village community of part of the rural population, the accumulation of money capital and the general commoditization of labor had not occurred. The opium brokers had not inserted themselves as a separate class between peasant community producers and the colonial State, but rather they appeared as appendages of tribute collecting Lao lords.

We would argue, however, that the "guarantees of stability" implied by this affirmation of social hierarchies was fictitious. As our scrutiny of the corvee system has revealed, the taxation system as an ensemble irrevocably dissolved the equilibrium model of social stasis that the colonial State sought to buttress as an imperative of indirect rule. Even though class relations had not developed in the countryside sensu stricto, an emerging contradiction between the countryside and the towns of Laos — mostly of colonial creation — had developed during the colonial era. As with Durkheim, Radcliffe Brown and Parsons, so Pietrantoni, to use Chovane's language, blunts "the excesses of any exploitative relationship" by "promoting the general equilibrium and survival of society" (Chovanes 1986:228). Such a method avoids the central problematic of analysis of the way in which surplus is generated in a social formation, between social formations and among social segments within that formation.

Our argument has been, after Amin, that an analysis of a concrete formation demands we discover how one mode of production predominates over the others and how modes of production are interconnected (Amin 1976:18). Our world system perspective stresses the unifying effect of center capitalism upon even the weakest peripheral outpost, although to be sure whether dissolution effects prevailed over conservation effects is a complex question.

While it is clear that by the late twentieth century certain "strong" post-colonial successor States have been able to dictate the terms of their transfer vis-à-vis the center, one should not depreciate the ability of the colonial State in the periphery to strike advantageous political deals. The nature of such bargains will be taken up in the next chapter.

NOTES

1. According to Samir Amin, social formations constitute a: "dominant mode of production and the articulation around this of a complex group of modes of production that are subordinate to it" (Amin 1976:16).

2. Alan Winnington, in a study of the Wa, a Mon-Khmer group found in southwest China, draws attention to the phenomenon of intra-ethnic slavery. He shows that slavery, which attained about five percent of the population, had its origin in the practice of usury and the inability of debtors to meet interest payments on loans. While slaves could be bought, sold and exchanged, he acknowledges that they did not constitute an important factor in Wa society as the level of Wa production was so low (Winnington 1959:162-177).

3. The weakness of the indigenous forces of production in Laos, however, is starkly revealed by the following statistics for the number of artisans in Indochina in 1939. Relative to a figure of 95,670 for Tonkin and 15,323 for Cambodia, the corresponding figure for Laos was 1,225. Of this number, woodworkers followed by metal workers constituted the largest categories (see Thompson 1947:1979), in any case not a propitious base upon which to build a capitalist society or indeed, in which a capitalist class-divided society would emerge.

4

Modes of State Intervention in Colonial Laos

To be sure, different social class fractions in Laos were affected to different degrees by the global economic depression. There was, however, no direct analogue in Laos to what Scott calls the "depression rebellions" in Nhge Tinh (Central Annam) or Lower Burma where "depression delivered the *coup de grace* to an agrarian order already weakened by structural changes well before 1930". Neither do we find in Laos a chronological link between a drop in the price of rice and expressions of peasant resistance (Scott 1976:144-120). Onerous the tax-corvee burden may have been upon the polyethnic peasantry of Laos, but it was not "murderous", with respect to the majority Lao peasantry at least, as was definitely the case in famine and dearth-ridden Annam.

However, the notion of non-rebellious adaptation by peasantries must guide our analysis of social change in Laos, as this was the more generalized experience. Under a "repressive" rubric versus a "false consciousness" one, Scott outlines four basic adaptive strategies open to the peasantry to buffer or secure themselves from collective shocks. These are: reliance on local forms of self-help, reliance on the non-peasant sector of the economy (capitalist development or scavenging), reliance on State-supported forms of patronage or assistance and reliance on religious or opportunistic strategies of protection and assistance. Scott concludes that out of an array of possible strategies, the nominated forms are not mutually exclusive and that each represents a different "scenario of development" (1976:204).

MODES OF STATE INTERVENTION

The State played an important role in Laos in mitigating the worst structural impact of the depression on the population facilitated also in this endeavour by a number of safety valve escape mechanisms largely intrinsic to the political economy, ecology and geography of the country. One cannot discount time honored mechanisms of the communitarian Lao peasant villager in coping with subsistence crises, no matter the nature or the trigger of such a condition. At the same time, however, the conclusion cannot be avoided that the State was held responsible by certain classes and social groups for the worst effects of the crisis.

For example, the introduction of a new customs regime in Laos in 1931, in part at least designed to increase State revenues from cross-Mekong transactions, was strongly opposed by local traders. The conservative Chinese-dominated Chambre Mixte de Commerce et d'Agriculture issued a statement of protest against the new measure at a meeting held on 8 September 1931. This was seconded by a petition issued by leading business house proprietors in Vientiane (AOM Paris A2 NF 328 2649, September 1931). From September 1931 until May 1933, some 25 traders had closed shop in Vientiane and emigrated to Siam, 59 others had either let their licenses lapse or demanded a reduction in the fee. All in all, 1,688 piasters were foregone to the budget as a result of the new customs law. Encouraged by the Siamese authorities, these recalcitrant merchants established a new commercial center at Si Chiang Mai, on the opposite bank of the Mekong from Vientiane (AOM Aix NF 328 2649, May 1933). The point is that the colonial State in Laos, more often than not, was in competition with or worked against the interest of both the national as well as the comprador bourgeoisie.

In general terms, the Lao peasant responded to the economic crisis by withdrawing from the marketplace. Not only were they devoid of the material means to purchase manufactured goods, they also lacked the cash in hand to acquit their personal taxes and to redeem *prestations*. In the words of a colonial official:

> He relies upon himself in his rural system living off the land and the forest — buffaloes and food production, living a life of ease, philosophically serene, in customary indolence and in a circumscribed economy which has only marginally suffered.
>
> (AOM A2 NF 328 2649, January 1932).

While colonial officials found confirmation of their belief in the "lazy native" syndrome in Laos, it was also the case that the ability of the Lao peasant to return to a pre-capitalist subsistence setting spared them the consequences of immiseration as suffered by the peasant farmers of Annam and Cochinchina, especially those engaged in commercial monoculture.

The non-participation of the Lao in the agro-mineral extractive industries in Laos and the flow back to Nghe-Tinh of superfluous Vietnamese migrant labour in the early years of the depression were likewise factors favorable to the management of the crisis in Laos.

By 1935, colonial observers remarked that while commerce had tapered off considerably in Laos during the depression years, owing to the fertility of the soil and the abundance of land (relative to demographic pressures), the Lao peasant had not suffered unduly. For the first time, however, the dangers of monoculture were commented upon and the desirability of economic diversification into such areas as cattle raising, tobacco and cotton growing were discussed (AOM Paris 329 2657, June-November, 1935). To this end, the State intervened to stimulate economic exchanges with neighboring countries. In 1936 an economic agreement was signed with Cambodia and Cochinchina for the export of Lao cattle from southern Laos to markets in Saigon (AOM Aix E25, Résident Supérieur in Laos to Governor General in Saigon, December 1936, Vientiane).

A more striking instance of State intervention in mitigating a potential subsistence disaster was revealed in a dispatch from the *Résident Supérieur* of Laos to the Governor General in 1936. He noted that relative to a 1935 harvest of rice which stood at 258,123 tonnes, deteriorating conditions augured a harvest shortfall for 1936 with an estimated harvest of 204,200 tonnes. In Thakek province, in particular, the fear of dearth was acute. While Laos had evidently been able to uphold its status as a net rice exporting country up until 1935, that situation was no longer tenable given the rice deficit in even the traditional rice exporting provinces of Laos. In a major departure from a situation of traditional sufficiency in rice, the *Résident Supérieur* requested urgent supplies of rice to be dispatched to Laos from Tonkin and Annam. Particularly pressing was the requirement to meet the consumption needs of the migrant labor force in the sensitive Boneng and Phontiou mines (AOM Aix E25, Résident Supérieur in Laos to the Governor General in Saigon, December 1936, Vientiane).

State intervention also extended into the area of exchange and prices control. According to the *Résident Supérieur*, whereas the devaluation of the franc in 1936 had facilitated economic recovery in other parts of Indochina, it had only exacerbated the crisis in Laos "which not only had nothing to export but did not suffice to meet its own needs...". A major difficulty concerned confusion over the exchange rate with Siam which in any case was manipulated by Siamese traders to the disadvantage of Laos. To counteract price inflation on all but imported goods a Price Control Commission was established in Vientiane and which met twice a month (AOM Aix E25, Résident Supérieur in Laos to the Governor General in Saigon, December 1936, Vientiane).

TABLE 4.1
RATIO OF DIRECT TAX TO SUBVENTION FROM FEDERAL BUDGET (1931-1935)

	1931	1932	1933	1934	1935
Direct tax	34.2%	35.8%	41.5%	41.5%	49.1%
Subvention	53.4%	53.2%	48.1%	44.1%	45.3%

Source: (Moretti Report: fiscal).

Revenue for the local budget in Laos was derived from two principal sources; direct taxes and subventions from the general Indochinese budget. Variations of the two elements conditioned its equilibrium. Stated another way, a greater return from direct taxes was required to the degree that the subvention from the general budget was diminished. The relative importance of the two elements in the budget revenue for 1931-1935 is revealed in Table 4.1.

The figures reveal that between 1931 and 1935 there was an 8.1% diminution in the subvention and a corollary increase in collection of direct taxes of 14.9% during the same period. In absolute figures (and which may not represent constant piaster values in a time of economic depression), the subvention allocation over the same period was as represented in Table 4.2.

This meant that in the 1931-35 period there was a diminution of almost fifty percent in total funding made available to the local budget in Laos.

Because of a general deficiency in receipts arising from the depression crisis in Laos, a reserve holding was created in 1930. However, by

TABLE 4.2
AMOUNT OF SUBVENTION ALLOCATION TO LOCAL BUDGET IN LAOS

Year	Amount
1931	2,359,660$
1932	2,258,660$
1933	1,800,000$
1934	1,500,000$
1935	1,300,000$

Source: (Moretti Report: fiscal).

September 1934 this reserve was depleted to a minimum and no advance withholding was anticipated for 1935, when a ten percent reduction in public expenditure was prescribed leading to a 65,000 piaster cut in the 1935 subvention allocation. In the face of diminishing support from the general budget, local initiative in meeting the shortfall or at least in striking an equilibrium between direct taxes and the subvention was seen as the only panacea (Moretti Report: fiscal). It would be illustrative to examine the measures taken by the State in Laos to steer the colony through the economic-budgetary crisis of the depression years.

Between 1931 and 1933 a considerable reduction in receipts from *prestation* tax was registered (this being the money paid to redeem corvee labor obligation), falling from $833.063 in 1931 to $606.806 in 1933. This was attributed to a general impoverishment in money terms of the population during this period. To rectify the situation and to derive greater cash contributions to the local budget, the administration undertook, in 1934, to carry out new public works employing corvee labor. Increased expenditure had been allotted for the opening up of more roads as well as for improving river communications. In 1935 alone, there was a fifty percent increase of credits for public works operations. Yet the receipts from *prestation* tax were down to $375,000 in 1935, in part attributable to a lowering of the daily rate of redemption for *prestations*. Other direct taxes, including the personal indigenous tax, also suffered an appreciable diminution in 1935. Various other kinds of receipts were likewise reduced during 1935, notably mining and commercial registration fees. This state of affairs was attributed to unfavorable economic conditions for mining and commercial exploitation and because of the non-cooperation of the population (Moretti Report: fiscal).

In contrast to 1934, overall expenditure during 1935 was down by fourteen percent with a corresponding diminution in economic and agricultural services. Credits for public works projects had been expanded by fifty percent, designed — as in the former year — to absorb more corvee labor and to help make up the budget deficit (maximization of *prestation* obligation meant more tax redemption money for the public coffers). More efficient tax collection was also undertaken. In particular, the authorities in Luang Prabang were instructed to tighten the tax collection net, as this province, along with the *Delegation* of Packlay, alone accounted for thirty-one percent of the total non-recovered taxes in Laos (AOM Paris Indochine NF 286 2493 "Comment on Moretti Report").

In the period between the promulgation of the *arrête* of 18 January 1929 and the *arrête* of 21 June 1934 pertaining to tax-rates, the rate of commutation of corvee was increased to 0$30 a day for tax-payers other than Kha and 0$15 a day for the latter. This was an increase in 0$05 and 0$03 per day for non-Kha and Kha, respectively, over the rate fixed in

1914. The days of obligatory corvees remained fixed at 20 for the Kha and 16 for the others. An *arrête* of 5 December 1935 introduced three modifications to the corpus of the regulations on taxation and corvees. The first permitted the number of days spent travelling to and from the work site by the corvee laborers to be deducted, within reasonable limits, from the total of days owing. Alternatively, a salary was to be paid for those days. Secondly, the commutation of corvee could be effected by means other than cash in the way of providing a corresponding amount of commodities for other corvee laborers (most probably rice). Thirdly, the commutation-value of the work day was reduced by 20% for the Kha and 16.33% for the non-Kha. While these provisions had been foreshadowed years before by previous *arrêtes*, the slippage between law and practice — as will be seen — was often considerable (Moretti Report: fiscal).

As explained in Moretti's report, these modifications were in response to belatedly admitted malpractices and anomalies, the political implications of which were all too obvious. Before the reform, the corvee laborer had to provide his own subsistence. The dearth of cash in Laos during the recession years, however, obliged the taxpayers to redeem their labor dues *en nature*. At a time when the number of indigent corvee laborers increased, and when the local budget was only collecting two-thirds of its taxes, credits were not available for the purchase of commodities to support them. Out of experience, the administration conceded that a certain number of days of labor owing on the part of the corvee laborer could be replaced by furnishing commodities useful for his fellow workers. While discharging their obligations, impecunious corvee laborers were freed from State burden and, at the same time, permitted a greater stimulation to the circulation of commodities (Moretti Report: fiscal).

As the *Résident Supérieur* of Laos, E.H.R. Eutrope, pointed out in his speech to the opening session of the Consultative Assembly in Laos in 1937, the crisis had been just as severe in other countries of the Indochinese Union. Insofar as the Governor General had been solicitous to Laos in the past, Eutrope argued, it was imperative on the part of Laos and its people to demonstrate a willingness compatible with its capacities in order to increase as much as possible its own revenues. (*Discours Prononcé par Résident Supérieur Eutrope,* October 1937 and September 1938).

It would appear that Eutrope's strictures were taken seriously. As the figures for the total budget allocation in Laos reveal (Table 4.3), by 1938 Laos had managed to overcome the worst effects of the fiscal crisis.

It should be emphasized that the growth in revenues for the 1939 budget (actually $222,090 over the previous year) was attributable not to an increase in the subvention from the general budget, but from resources

TABLE 4.3
TOTAL BUDGET ALLOCATION IN LAOS (1932-1939)

Year	Amount
1932	4,250,000$
1935	2,867,000$
1938	3,546,000$
1939	3,656,250$

Source: (*Discours, Eutrope* September 1938).

derived from within Laos. The subvention amount was constant at $1,518,600 for 1938 and 1939. Only an allocation of $35,410 for the *Garde Indegène* increased. A supplement of $186,680 was derived from the *Reserve Caisse* and from increased tax revenue (*Discours, Eutrope,* September, 1938).

LAO PEASANT RESPONSES TO CORVEE

If still far short of rebellion, the majority Lao population nevertheless revealed their dissatisfaction with expanded public works developments promoted by the State during the colonial years by defaulting upon their corvee obligations. For instance, a political report dating from late 1930 drew attention to the gathering complaints against corvee labour on RC 4 in Luang Prabang by the Lao population. These had been formulated through official channels, namely by the *Naikhoueng* to the "*Conseil du Royaume*" on the occasion of the Festival of the Grand Oath. Particularly resented was the method of requisitioning labor and the conditions under which corvee labor was employed on the work-sites. The official account revealed a massive desertion of the local population from the districts where corvee labor was requisitioned. This involved the flight to Siam of between 600 to 800 families. Not doubting the desire of the Lao mandarins to cooperate with the administration, the *Résident Supérieur,* following discussions with the King on this problem, was compelled to act in a manner to rectify the situation (AOM Aix E12 "General Report", Luang Prabang, 4th tri. 1930). This and other spontaneous defensive reactions by the Lao against threats to their moral and economic order were typically met, not by violence as was frequently the response of the ethnic minorities, but by time-honored means of escaping the excessive demands of the lords of the *muong;* flight (see McCoy 1970:83).

Neither did the Lao notables prove immune from the malaise. In 1932 numerous officials were compromised in a "wave of embezzlement" of public monies. A *tasseng* and several *phoban* were imprisoned. Substantial public monies were also recovered by way of auction of the property of deceased officials. The *chaomuong* of Kengkok, fearing an investigation of his accounts, fled from justice (AOM Aix E25, "Situation Politique General de la Circumscription, Savannakhet, 1 June 1935).

It remains to be seen, however, if other collective expressions of discontent with the corvee labor system by the Lao and the ethnic minorities, especially in central and southern Laos during the mid 1930s, were entirely spontaneous or, whether, they were provoked or led on by outside elements.

Typical of the "labor strikes" which threatened to sabotage the colonial public works programme in 1935 was that demonstrated by three successive shifts of 120 corvee laborers in the *muong* of Khantabouli who were employed on RC 13. Several hours after they arrived on the job-sites, they deserted en masse, an unprecedented action in colonial Laos. They protested that sixteen days was the limit to their work obligation. They also rejected the demand by the authorities that they requit unfulfilled *prestation* obligation from the previous year. In the event, work resumed after the administration imposed "light" penal sanctions. Additionally, however, the coolies won the right to commute their *prestations* after the mandatory sixteen days had been worked. They were offered $3.40 for the extraction of a cubic meter of laterite and $2 to transport it a distance of one to four kilometers (AOM Aix E25 "Situation politique general de la circonscription", Savannakhet, 2nd tri 1935). While money earned in this manner would have enabled the diligent and indigent *inscrits* to meet their tax obligation for the year, the methods adopted by the administration were not immediately successful in neutralizing discontent.

During 1937, the locus of anti-administration labor activity shifted from Khantabouli to Kengkok in Champassak. Lao as well as Kha coolies delegated to work-sites on RC 13 in this *muong* were notorious for late arrival, low productivity, desertions and "arrogance" towards the *cai*. Several were arrested and given prison sentences. Even the *Chaomuong* of Kengkok was threatened with disciplinary action. The breakdown of administrative procedures in the *muong* was attributed by a colonial observer to the resident Swiss pastor whose "humanitarian sermons" had evidently been taken by heart by the population (AOM Aix E27, Savannakhet, 1 tri 1937). During the course of the year desertions by corvee laborers and other instances of non-compliance with administrative rulings on matters relating to the exercise of corvee labor multiplied in Champassak and spread to Atsaphangthong and back to Khantabouli. However, on this occasion the rules of the game changed considerably. Unprecedentedly, the administration decreed a new level of surveillance over the recalcitrant corvee laborers. Whereas the corvee system had already been phased out in other parts of Indochina, in Laos a detachment of the military was delegated to the work sites to "remind recalcitrant corvee laborers of their duty" and to bring back deserters should the occasion arise (AOM Aix E27, Savannakhet, 2nd and 3rd tri 1937).

In 1938, the "dreaded period" of corvee labor was reduced to six days. Rather than greeting this example of "administrative beneficence" with "joy", as described by the *Résident* of Savannakhet, further instances of disaffection by Lao conscripts and Lao notables alike were recorded (AOM Aix E27, Savannakhet, 1st tri 1938 and 1st tri 1939). The system, involving elements of coercion as well as appeals to obligation and order, continued in this form down until the period of the Japanese intervention. What can be said about Lao attitudes towards the corvee is that while never popular and while involving numerous obvious injustices and abuses, antipathy to the system was traditionally expressed in a spontaneous manner and not invariably as part of an organized anti-colonial or nationalist demonstration. At the same time, however, the claim of the communist opposition in Laos to stewardship of the labor movement, particularly during the Popular Front period, cannot be ignored.

However, if the economic crisis proved manageable for the Lao peasant as much owing to communitarian village support systems as to the colonial State's management of the crisis, the subsidiary fiscal crisis which affected the population of Laos reached tragi-comic proportions. The first sign of the impending crisis occurred in 1932 following the decree obliging the population to redeem the old 20 gram metal piasters in favor of replacement piasters, albeit devalued.[1] Clearly, tax recovery in new converted piasters was central to the success of the annual tax-collection campaign, in any case designed to be more rigorously enforced during the depression years, owing to a diminution of the subvention allocated for Laos by the Federal budget. The contrary effect transpired. As it happened, the population of Laos proved totally refractory to surrendering the old piasters, thereby sabotaging the fiscal campaign of 1932 (AOM A2 328 2649, 15 September 1932). This is not to say that the State abandoned the claim on tax arrears, a particularly unpopular measure as it usually transpired.

During 1933, bankruptcies were frequent and tax collection was difficult. The difficulty in implementing the demonetization project only aggravated a situation rendered "precarious" by a total cessation of exports (AOM Aix E23, May-August 1933). Indeed, the exchange operation was only effective in the main towns. The montagnards, in particular, distrusted the new piaster and insisted on paying their tax in the old currency. In certain regions of Laos, namely Luang Prabang, Sam

Neua and Xieng Khouang, the collection of tax monies could not be realized at all (AOM Indo NF 328 2649 May 1933). In view of the collective refusal of the population to comply with the tax and fiscal system, the administration dispatched the Inspectorate General of Laos, Prince Phetsarath, on mission to aid in the recovery of a massive shortfall of 600,000 piasters for 1933. A rigorous attempt at the recovery of tax money, however, was viewed as potentially counterproductive in 1) risking the non-recovery of money, in any case, and 2) provoking the displeasure of the population or even a rebellion or exodus of the population — most notably the Lao — towards Burma, Siam or the Bolovens plateau. In view of the dubious tax worthiness of the population and in admission of failure in the general colonial project of monetizing the economy as a whole, the only option open to the administration in order to recover outstanding "debts" was, as with the case of the Hmong, to permit redemption of labor dues *en nature* (AOM Paris A2 NF 328 2649, February 1934).

Particularly damaging to the administration, as much in terms of prestige as in loss of revenue, was the "invasion" of Laos by near perfect counterfeit metallic piasters in early 1934. The inability of the bank tellers and the population to distinguish an authentic piaster from a false one in a country that was still not fully monetized, had the effect, in the words of a colonial observer, of "killing credit, ruining commercial exchanges and drying up the source of tax". The demonetization disaster, he noted, had been regrettably carried out at a time, not only when the population was starved of cash, but at a point in Laos' history when it had no choice but to raise revenue from local sources. Again the conclusion was that there was no choice but to redeem *prestations* in kind (AOM Indo A2 NF 328 2649, June 1934, report by Eckert). The arrest of a gang of Sino-Thai counterfeiters in Pakse and the confiscation of their forges and machines in April 1934 did not, however, immediately translate into a sense of restored confidence in the piaster on the part of the population (see Indo NF 328 2649, April-May 1934). Even during 1934, when there were signs of economic recovery in Cochinchina, there was no indication of revival in Laos (AOM Aix E24, Vientiane, 4th tri 1934).

Whatever the long-term benefits to the Lao economy of improved communications systems — either as a means to facilitate exchange and the general process of monetization of the country or through expediting exports — the extension of the road network in Laos during the 1930s was seen as critical to the success of the colonial pacification project, especially in northern Laos and in the Bolovens plateau. Quite clearly the ability of the colonial power to deploy military forces over increasingly large parts of the country was a demonstrable negative stimulus to rebellion.

THE COLONIAL STATE AND RELIGIOUS HEGEMONY IN LAOS

Writing in 1966, Moore noted that the inhibiting role of religion apropos peasant revolt could be explained by some organic cosmology that conferred legitimacy on the role of the ruling classes in combination with some acceptance of the harmony of the universe and the acceptance of fate. Yet he finds the more usual situation in peasant societies is that of an "underground tradition" often in opposition to the priestly classes, even if this seldom finds its way into the historical record (Moore 1966:456). Building upon this general understanding, Scott has sought in a 1987 study to rethink the notion of hegemony or ideological domination, indeed seeking to turn Gramsci and Althusser on their heads. He finds that based on the results of his research in a Malaysian village that the notion of hegemony and the related concepts of false consciousness, mystification, symbolic production and ideological state apparatuses fail to make sense and seriously mislead the understanding of class conflicts in most situations. He argues, contrary to Gramsci that the "imaginative capacity of subordinate groups to reverse and/or negate dominant ideologies" is widespread. Thus at the level of behavior this is matched by footdragging, dissimulation, evasion, etc. (Scott 1987:331). In view of the variance between colonial Vietnam, Burma or Laos and late twentieth century Malaysia it would be apposite to bear in mind Moore's contention that "there are forms of solidarity that promote peasant insurrection and those that oppose it" (Moore 1966).

In his 1977 study Scott raised the valid question of to what extent the process of hegemony — linked with the question of central State power and with its attendant mystification, applies to the peasantry? (Scott 1977:273-275). The other side of the coin is to determine whether peasant passivity is linked with coercion or fear of repression. This is not an analytical cul de sac, Scott concludes, for "It can be resolved by asking how much coercion it takes to maintain the agrarian order and what happens when the balance of forces changes". Elsewhere he maintains that this can be answered in terms of "whether the values embodied in peasant culture do in fact accord with the dominant myths of the social order" (Scott 1976:240). One way of addressing the question, he continues, is by asking to what extent the institutions of ruling class elites penetrate the ruling sector and organize the experience of the peasantry (Scott 1977:273- 275).[2]

As we have seen, the system of the protectorate in Laos depended upon buttressing traditional social hierarchies where they coincided with French interests, and eliminating or modifying them where they were at odds. A major point of convergence in this arrangement was over religion. The French displayed a studied unwillingness to interfere in the Buddhist *sangha*, whether viewed as a parallel hierarchy to the native administration or as the quintessential expression of Lao village solidarity. Clearly cognizant of the centrality of religion to social mores and order in Laos, the French moved quickly to proscribe Protestant missionary activity in the country, a position endorsed by the King of Laos. Following a report in 1905 that the Presbyterian mission in Chiang Mai was circulating information concerning the Russo-Japanese war and which "we have no interest in spreading", the Governor General, acting with the assent of the Minister of Colonies seized the pretext to instruct the *Résident Supérieur* that he resist all missionary activity in upper Laos. Both Presbyterian missions as well as French Catholic missions were instructed to "conform with local belief" (AOM Aix E8, Governor General to Minister of France, 12 December 1908). While western missionaries eventually made some inroads into Laos, especially among the Hmong and certain other sections of the minority population, converts could probably be measured in terms of hundreds only during the colonial period.[3]

In 1933 the French made some attempts to reinvigorate Buddhism in Laos — otherwise seen to be in decline — by reorganizing the clergy and by creating a Buddhist Institute as they had done three years previously in Phnom Penh. While this met with only limited success, temple schools, however, flourished under colonial patronage, especially during the depression years and for reasons perhaps not unrelated to the economic malaise in the country. As one official noted:

> In spite of budgetary restrictions during the period of economic crisis, they permit a continuation of efforts commenced in Laos to diffuse education while giving the children of the villages in the interior, an education particularly well adapted to their mentality and traditions.
>
> (AOM Paris A2 NF 328 2649, March 1933).

Even an earlier attempt by a Lao official to gain approval from the colonial authorities to suppress the cult of the *phi* (spirits) in a Thai Neua area was met with disapproval. While acknowledging that Buddhism was preferable to the heterodox "*phi*" cult, the Commissioner of the government commented that questions on "morals, religion and politics" could not be arbitrated on by a *chaomuong* (AOM Aix E10 "Suppression du culte des "Phi" chez les Thai Neua, proposition formulee par le Chaomuong de Vangvieng", Commissioner of the Government to the Résident Supérieur in Laos, Vientiane, 14 February 1923).

A more unlikely threat to the traditional religious order in Laos (and Cambodia), however, came from a different quarter, that of the Cao Dai faith. Founded in Cochinchina in 1926, Cao Dai rapidly fanned out into other parts of Indochina. Hierarchical in organization and syncretic in theology, Cao Dai was perceived as a rival to the communist party in view of the threat it posed to both traditional hierarchies and the colonial order. At stake in Laos and (Cambodia) was the *sangha* (the religious community and hierarchy), on the one hand, and the French prestige, on the other. Fearful of Gandhian-like passive resistance to the colonial order, the French were moved to outlaw the activities of Cao Dai in Tonkin, Cambodia and Laos.

As Scott points out, the Cao Dai was from the outset an alternative to rebellion. Through a number of local self-help and communal ventures, it met many of the most urgent, tangible needs of its adherents (Scott 1976.221). But Werner, in a major study on the question, reminds us that Cao Dai dignitaries were themselves products of new social forces generated by colonialism (Werner 1981:63). The remarkable but short-lived success of Cao Dai in Laos would not contradict this assessment. Such was the degree of acceptance of the new faith that one Cao Dai priest, Dang Trung Thu, managed to win over 300 converts in Laos in the three months since his arrival in that country from Cambodia. Skilled at hypnotic suggestion and with a reputation as a healer, his proselytary activity found fertile ground among the Lao peasantry and even among members of the aristocracy, at which point in time the authorities became alarmed (SHM 7F66 Vientiane, 6 September 1934). At least eighty Lao had earlier been observed in attendance at Cao Dai ceremonies at their religious capital in Tay Ninh during 1932 (SMH 7F66 February 1932).

The chief mover of Cao Dai activities in Laos, Dang, had first come to the attention of the authorities in late 1931, when he attempted to send protest notes to the minister of Colonies, the Governor General and the King of Laos, evidently concerning efforts to hamper his activities. Consistent with other actions taken to preserve the religious and social hegemony of the Theravada Buddhist State order in Laos, the French outlawed Cao Dai in Laos by an *arrête* of 17 February 1932. In 1934 Dang was arrested and deported (SHM 7F66 6 September 1934 and AOM Paris Slotfom 111, 49) Such vigilance was borne out by events. In 1940, Phan Van Ky, a Vientiane based member of the *Garde Indigène* — and evidently a Cao Dai adept — was found to be in possession of Vietnamese language pamphlets extolling both Hitler and Mussolini and predicting the defeat of France (in Indochina) (SHM 7F66, 23 January 1940).

While extreme manifestations of religious fatalism were viewed by many colonial observers in Laos as a "natural" impediment to the popular acceptance of the French *mission civilisatrice* and while such manifestations of superstitious behavior on the part of the population as adherence to heterodox faiths as Cao Dai reinforced the belief of the authorities in the irrationality of their charges, it was nevertheless the case that on balance a susceptibility to "mystification" on the part of the Lao worked to allay their acceptance of "progressive" western ideas and, as a consequence, made them easier to govern than, say, the Vietnamese. Clearly, however, the situation had to be carefully managed. The religious fatalism that served the status quo — especially in consideration of the majority Lao — also carried the danger or potential of developing an antagonistic dimension as revealed below by the shaman or millenarian inspired rebellions that recurred with some frequency in the ethnic minority milieu during the colonial period.[4]

It follows too, unlike China (and Vietnam), Laos lacked what Moore called the prerequisites of totalitarian control, the *pao chia* system, Confucianism, welfare policies, class and patrilineal lineage (Moore 1966:200). Marx's well known observation on the peasantry in the *The Eighteenth Brumaire of Louis Bonaparte* might well apply here:

> The small holding peasants (of France) form a vast mass, the members of which live in similar conditions but without entering into manifold relations with one another. Their mode of production isolates them from one another instead of bringing them into mutual intercourse..... Each individual peasant family is almost self- sufficient; it itself directly produces the major part of its consumption and thus acquires its means of life more through exchange with nature than in intercourse with society. In this way, the great mass of the French (Lao?) nation is formed by simple addition of homologous magnitudes, much as potatoes in a sack form a sack of potatoes......Insofar as there is merely a local interconnection among these small-holding peasants, and the identity of their interests begets no community, no national bond and no political organization among them, they do not form a class. They are consequently incapable of enforcing their class interest in their own name, whether through a parliament or through a convention....
>
> (Marx)

The argument that the Lao upheld a more sober view of the formidable instruments of colonial state repression — the police, the army, the courts — than the less culturally advanced and less colonially penetrated ethnic minorities also bears consideration. As shown below, the demonstration effect of successful pacification campaigns against rebellious ethnic minorities clearly held out a salutary lesson to other advanced groups. The fact that, chronologically speaking, the last of the ethnic rebels to sustain armed revolt to the colonial power were also the most primitive of the rebels seems to bear this thesis out. But even given the characteristic "irrational" dimension of the ethnic minority revolts, including those of the *phu mi boun* among the Lao of the *Isan*, and which occurred in spite of the demonstratively overwhelming superior fire-power of the central state, it is perhaps significant that even during adversary times, no single

Lao messiah arose in this tradition and whom may have become a central rallying figure of the Lao peasantry against colonial power.

CONCLUSION

We have seen, then, that on balance direct intervention by the colonial State in the economic sphere was successful in mitigating the worst effects of the fiscal crisis in Laos, thus preempting a major subsistence crisis and neutralizing rebellion. We have seen that despite an unfavorable reaction by the Lao peasantry to State intervention, weak social class formation in Laos did not prefigure in that country the most hopeful expectations of the communist opposition in Indochina that class conflict would emerge as an internalist development or as an externally engendered consequence of the metropolitan economic crisis. Likewise the lack of absolute poverty in the Lao peasant milieu relative to Annam or Tonkin and the ability of the Lao peasant to fall back upon strong communitarian structures in a favorable ecological setting eased the burden of the State in managing the crisis.

As a general comment on the handling of the 1931-1935 fiscal crisis in Laos, it can be said that initiative as well as imagination was used by local authorities to meet chronic budget shortfalls. These authorities, however, reacted tardily to correct the more obvious abuses of the system, both in response to internal criticism from the colonial inspectorate and the external criticism from the Vietnamese press and the Lao people themselves. It is clear, however, that despite certain rectifications to the system, the corvee laborer shouldered the burden of the local fiscal rescue operation. While relatively better off Lao or Vietnamese could afford to redeem their corvee obligation in cash, the only option for the impecunious masses was default.

NOTES

1. According to Robequain, the trade piaster was withdrawn from circulation on 31 December 1931 and the bank notes of the Banque de l'Indochine became the means of exchange within Indochina. With some understatement he notes that "at first the natives were undoubtedly annoyed at the appearance of a currency unsuited to a country where climate, insects and the impermanence of buildings all render the preservation of money very difficult" (Robequain 1944:145).

2. For discussion of this problematic in an Indonesian context see Gunn 1979.

3. One Vietnamese source notes that to back up preparations for conquest of Laos, Bishop Puginies sent more than twenty Catholic missionaries to northeast

Laos in early 1873, followed by thirty others in 1883. The result of this activity was an estimated 5,000 Catholic converts in eastern Laos (anon 1982:35). In any case Catholic sources present an even less rosy picture of early missionary activity: "As group after group of courageous young missionaries entered Laos, the number of martyrs increased."

Of 14 Catholic priests who entered Laos in 1878, by the end of that year, 6 had been murdered, 7 died of malaria and the sole survivor died back in Tonkin. Of 62 catechists in the party (no doubt Vietnamese) 47 were murdered by "bandits" and 15 died of malaria (Menger 1969:9).

4. The adversary attitude of the population was also reflected in popular entertainment. The following jingle sung during the colonial era demonstrates this point:

"Le francais au grand pif, dans sa voiture Peugeot,
s'en va percuter un banian,
paf, son grand pif eclate en deux!"
(*Bulletin de l'Association d'Amitie et de Solidarite*, No. 5, 3 tri, 1978).

PART THREE

The Political Economy of Peasant Rebellion in Laos

Développant sa tradition de patriotisme, le peuple Lao de toutes ethnies ést dressé par vagues successives contre les colonialistes: les mouvement de lutte les plus remarquables furent ceux de la population de Savannakhet (de 1901 à 1903) sous la direction de Pho Kadouat, ceux de la population du Sud-Laos (de 1911 à 1936) par Ong Keo et Ong Kommadan, ceux de la population au nord-Est du Laos déclenché depuis 1918 jusqu'à 1922 sous la direction de Tiaofa Patchay. Ces soulèvements, bien que réprimés dans la sang, faisant fiasco, n'en avaient pas moins contribué au développement de la tradition de patriotisme et de lutte héroique du peuple Lao.

(*Les 30 Annees de la révolution Lao*,
Rédaction Générale de l'Agence
Khao San Pathet Lao (KPL),
12 Octobre 1975).

5

The Political Economy of the Kha Peasant Rebellions of Southern Laos

PEASANT REBELLION IN LAOS

While conventional scholarship has portrayed the colonial era as "peaceful" (Toye 1968:48), in reality, rebellion stirred all the major ethnic groups in Laos at various points between 1893 and 1954. But such outbursts, or what E.J. Hobsbawm has termed "archaic social movements" (Hobsbawm 1965), were not limited to Laos, and in fact knew no boundaries locally.

As a general statement, the administrative reforms ushered in by metropolitan powers in their colonial peripheries masked hidden tensions. Almost typically economic and political incorporation gave way to the flight of the subject peoples and their revolt. Peasant resistance typically took multiple forms in response to local conditions and the degree of economic and political coercion. Often the need on the part of the colonizing power to raise primitive capital conflicted with the pacification mission. Thus the imposition upon peasantry of systems of taxes and corvees as much as the introduction of commodity relations met with unpredictable results. Forms of resistance ran the gamut from tax evasion, to armed revolt, to inter-tribal warfare to flight. Such subordinate peasant eruptions may have been of heroic character or may have taken more prosaic form or what Scott has termed "everyday forms of peasant resistance" (Scott 1985).[1] Aside from active and passive resistance, peasant victims of a modern world restructuring were also want to reinvoke or restore a pre-capitalist past by way of the magical invocation of traditional deities. As pre-modern forms of protest, such "millennial" outbursts seldom took on a national character but — arguably — assumed the form of proto-nationalist responses to the intervention of outsiders.

The case of Laos in the early incorporation phase in the late nineteenth century and during the opening decades of the twentieth century is replete with such instances. The following chronology of revolts by the majority Lao (*Lao Loum* in Lao communist nomenclature) and particularly the minorities of polyethnic Laos during the period of western colonial impact is eloquent.

1820	— revolt of the Blao of Sekong under the Lao monk Ya Pu
1876	— revolt of the Kha of Muong Ngoy
1895	— revolt in Houa Phan led by Bang Thuoc
	— incidents in the Kingdom of Nan Nghi
	— resistance of chief Sene Lovang Anakhete of Louang Phou Kha
1895-1907	— revolt of the Kha of the Bolovens led by *Phou Mi Boun* (lit. men with merit)
1896	— rebel atack on the Xieng Khouang post
	— pursuit of "Annamite" rebels on Lao territory
	— various acts of "piracy"
1898-1899	— rebellion in Khammouane
1901	— rebel attack on Psi post in Attopeu
1902	— incidents in Bassac and Savannakhet (Phocaduot)
1910-1936	— revolt of the Kha of southern Laos under Ong Keo and Kommandan
1910	— rebel attack on Pak Hin Boun post
1914	— incidents in Sam Neua
1916	— Tai uprising in Sam Neua
1914-1923	— revolt of the Lu of Muong Sing led by Chao Fa Pha Ong Kham
1918-1922	— revolt of the Hmong (Meo) under Chao Batchai
1920	— Khou Kham movement at Vientiane
1945-9	— Lao Issara revolt

While the origins and dimensions of certain of these incidents remain obscure what is clear is that the adversary relationship of central power — whether dynastic or colonial — and local power, fundamentally challenged the myth of a *paix francais* in colonial Laos.[2]

Pathet Lao historiography dates the nationalist movement in Laos from a popular armed insurrection led by the Lao "patriot", Phcaduot in 1901,[3] eight years after the French conquest. Other ethnic rebels deemed sufficiently important and "patriotic" to rate mention are Ong Keo and Ong Kommadan, the leaders of armed insurrection on the Bolovens plateau which lasted from 1901 to 1936, the armed resistance of the Lu minority under the leadership of the *Chao Fa* of Muong Sing (1914-1918), the resistance of the Tai in Sam Neua (1916) and the Hmong rebellion of

1918-1922 led by Tiao Fa Patchay [Batchai] (see Phoumi Vongvichit 1968:40-41 and Kaysone 1980:9). One such movement which failed to win recognition in patriotic Lao history was that of Sambran, the White Python.

Clearly, resistance to central power in Laos did not commence in colonial times and not all rebellions in Laos during colonial times were purely anti-French. For instance, in 1875 the Kha chief, Nhi, at the head of his fellow tribesmen rose in revolt in Houa Phan (Sam Neua), burning and killing all in his path and inflicting a complete defeat upon a Lao army dispatched from Luang Prabang to capture him. Only with Nhi's death did peace return to the mountain province (anon. August 1927). The Khamu of northern Laos were themselves victims of the Hmong at the time of the migration of the latter from Vietnam in the early nineteenth century. Khamu crossbows were no match for Hmong blunderbusses (Mottin 1980:47).

Equally, some rebellions in the pre-colonial period conjoined montagnard followers with Lao messianic leadership. Such was the case of the revolt of the Blau, a montagnard sub-group residing in the Sekong River region who in 1820 rose up to attack Attopeu. They were inspired in this action by a Lao monk, Ya Pu. Before being captured and beheaded by the Lao authorities, Ya Pu had distributed miraculous waters to his willing adepts in return for provisions (Bourette 1951:58). As will be seen, this pattern of revolt under Lao leader and montagnard followers was repeated during the colonial epoch. As one student of the question, Ishii, has noted, otherwise religiously oriented rebellions among the Thai-Lao have a recorded history that go back to the seventeenth century (Ishii 1977:6), and, as will be seen, continues — to degrees — up to the present time!

Neither was all anti-authority activity recorded by colonial observers construed as "rebellion". In many cases the activities of bandits, labelled "pirates", existed in the grey area between social banditry and anti-authority rebellion. In common with the more notorious rebel groups the favored "bandit" terrain included inaccessible mountain redoubts and the less accessible sites of the trans Mekong region, the Laos-Yunnan border, the Laos-Vietnam border and the Laos-Cambodia borderlands.

The presence of these rebel-bandits was revealed during the opening years of the colonial administration. Among the first recorded were Sene Louang Anakete, the rebel Lao chief of Muong Phou Kha, arrested in 1895. In the same year, an uprising by the *"pirate"* chief, Bang Thuoc, was suppressed by the Lao population as he was leading a march upon Muong Het. Various other acts under the general rubric of "piracy" were reported in Cammon and Tran Ninh in 1896, certain of them committed by Vietnamese on Lao territory. Isolated acts of "banditry" were also recorded in Khone in 1918 (the assassination of a French family) and at Muong in

1924 (Mogenet 1973:75-85). Again in June 1933, the arrests in Siam of two infamous bandit leaders, Nai Sai and Nai Chau, were recorded. Having eluded the Siamese and French authorities for years, their incarceration was seen as a major defeat and loss of prestige for bandit emulators (AOM Paris Indochine A2 NF 328/2649 June 1933). To be sure, the phenomenon of social banditry was not confined to Laos but was prevalent in Siam, Cambodia, Vietnam and in other colonies or semi-colonies, and indeed in other epochs, preceding and succeeding the era of European colonial intervention (cf. Hobsbawm 1965, Cheah 1988).

The following insight offered in the Saigon press by a Cambodian informant as to why people in this colony turn to banditry is instructive:

> Why do people become *pirates*?
>
> Cambodians are very gentle and very often submit to authority because of ignorance and religion. Buddhism teaches them to be resigned and wise. If they become pirates it is because they are at the end of their means and because they have no alternative, it is because they have nothing to eat or to wear and pay and because personal and property tax is too heavy for them. Moreover, the *douane* is insupportable for them. Customs officers threaten them severely, make them pay dues, carry off the products of their cultivation, wagons, buffaloes. These activities discourage them, reduce them to nothing, prevent them from devoting themselves to cultivation and incite them to become *pirates*....
>
> ("Reflections d'un Cambodgien au sujèt des actes de piraterie au Cambodge", *La Presse Indochinoise*, 11 July 1936).

The analogies with the subject peoples of Laos are apposite.

One of the few instances of non-minority resistance to colonial rule in Laos, obviously aside from the Lao Issara revolt, was that of the revolt of Phocaduot.

In March 1901, according to a Vietnamese source, the inhabitants of Savannakhet province rose up under the leadership of Phocaduot, a *Lao Loum* peasant of Kham Thac Ken village. In late March and early April 1902, the insurgents siezed a post office and the following month besieged the French garrison and attacked the French *Résident's* office. Telegraphic and telephonic links between Savannakhet and Vientiane were disrupted. The insurrection, however, was "drowned in blood" as regular troops from south Vietnam were unleashed on the crudely armed rebels. Leaving 200 massacred in the town of Savannakhet, the rebels fell back to the Tchepone region on Route Coloniale 9, near the Vietnam border. Still under Phocaduot's command the band then moved to Kengkok. Although Phocaduot was eventually killed by colonial forces in 1903, the movement continued another three years at which time the remaining rebel leaders either surrendered or were taken prisoner (anon, *Laos: An Outline* 1982:47-8). While an instance of a majority *Lao Loum* participation in resistance to colonial incorporation, the Phocaduot revolt should, nevertheless, be considered alongside contemporaneous instances of rebellion by the southern montagnards, as taken up below.

As a foil to the analysis which tends to objectify capitalist relations in the periphery, such as that entertained in Chapter One and Two, it is worthwhile considering the peasant studies tradition, that which expresses a peasant eye view of market penetration. The perspective is encapsulated by James Scott in his study *The Moral Economy of the Peasant: Rebellion and Subsistence in Southeast Asia* and by Samuel Popkin, in his study of rural society in colonial and post colonial Vietnam entitled, *The Rational Peasant: The Political Economy of Rural Peasantry in Vietnam.*

Drawing upon the example of the Nghe-Tinh rebellions of 1930-31 in colonial Annam, Scott cautions us that the causes of peasant revolt are complex and do not reduce themselves to single or deterministic explanations. The structural context, the paths of survival and the anatomy of repression all merit attention. At the center of his study of rebellion in colonial Southeast Asia, Scott places the question of peasant subsistence, arguing that threats to subsistence agriculture increase the volatility of peasant grievances. The explosive quality of the agrarian situation he attributes to the combination of demographic change, production for the market and the growth of the State (Scott 1976:196).

Popkin labels this approach the "Moral Economy" school, finding common ground in the work of, inter alia, Scott (1976), Polyani (1957) and Wolf (1969). "Moral Economists", Popkin writes, assume that the peasant is anti-market, that peasant welfare depends upon close corporate villages so common in pre-capitalist society. In Popkin's interpretation, the "Moral Economists" argue that the intrusion of the cash nexus destroys the peasant's moral community. The colonial State thus only increases social stratification at the expense of peasant welfare and generally destroys the peasant "little tradition" and the patron-client networks that anchor it to the wider community. The violence that accompanies these structural dislocations is thus matched on the part of the peasantry by "defensive reactions" to maintain subsistence arrangements (Popkin 1979:5-8).

In his own study, Popkin sets out to find evidence to counter Scott's basic interpretation of peasant response to political change. His challenge is based on three arguments. First, he found that peasant movements in colonial Vietnam were anti-feudal and not tending to restore traditional practices. Second, he found no clear relationship between subsistence threats and collective responses. Third, he found no "class" threat. Instead, he argues that peasant protests are a "rational" and individual response and not the result of collective decision making. Against this view that peasant protests are "conservative", Popkin argues that peasant liberation movements are anti-feudal, directed at the reshaping of traditional practices as well as the taming of capitalism through the improvement of working conditions, facilitating new options, new skills, whereupon long-standing practices come to be viewed as "arbitrary caprices and intolerable". Although Popkin found that collective peasant protest occurred in Cochinchina in 1913 and 1916 against corvee labour during harvest time and against military conscription, and in Annam during the Great Depression, he maintains that the experience of Tonkin validates his thesis. Here a large number of people lost their land but no subsistence crisis or uprisings occurred. This, Popkin would put down to the application by peasants to investment logic (Popkin 1979:5-8 and Colburn 1982:441-442).

In a discussion on the relative validity of Moral Economy versus Political Economy approaches to peasant behavior in Vietnam, the French historian Pierre Brocheux reminds us that the social movements discussed respectively by Scott and Popkin are "complex, ambiguous and contradictory" and which, moreover, "should not be ignored when they are used for political purposes. Further, he counsels, if we ignore the narrow link between social and political spheres "we run the risk of missing the originality of the peasant movements (after all Scott lost sight of the ICP in his discussion of the Nghe Tinh revolts). Brocheux concludes that both Moral Economy and Political Economy approaches have their rationality and provide no inherent opposition. "We must use both explanatory approaches in competition with each other to produce an analysis that conforms with history". The political economy approach, he contends, is not necessarily associated with a "triumphant modernization" and the latter is not necessarily "tied to a post that has ended or is about to end" (Brocheux 1983:798). But what epitomizes the peasant study tradition, as Chovanes has pointed out, is the emphasis it gives to the normative nature of peasant expectations and the regulatory functions of moral norms and values. After all, both Scott and Popkin are decision-making models based on the expression of individual rationality (Chovanes 1986:207-9).

In our case study of peasant rebellion in colonial Laos we will seek to view the relationship between the threat to subsistence crisis and political activity with reference to peasant studies examples. The problematic — in terms of the hypotheses outlined above — rests on determining whether the rebellions were backward looking — messianic appeals for the restoration of a traditional order — or forward looking, anti-feudal and/or anti-colonial rebellions but seeking to accommodate to new political structures by taming the excesses of colonial capitalism or a combination of both. While in this chapter we are, in Scott's phrase, seeking to determine the "social dynamite" of colonial confrontation with the peasantry, we will reserve for the conclusion remarks on the revolutionary detonation.

A major question sidestepped in the peasant studies tradition and which has to be addressed, however, is whether the activity of bandit/rebels can in any sense be considered as evidence of "proto-nationalist" stirrings? The question has been raised, however, by certain observers, namely Moppert (1978) with respect to Laos, and Hickey (1982) with respect to Vietnam, albeit at a pre-theoretical level. Woodside (1983:749) for one, has raised the valid question as to whether the montagnards really have a sense of belonging to a single embryonic nation or whether that identity flows from resistance to outsiders per se? In other words, does the search for ethnic identity by minority rebels create, as Woodside suggests, feelings of separateness as well as identity?

KHA POLITICAL ECONOMY

> Les Khas Bolovens sont plus évolues et relativement civilisées. C'est une race solide, energique, travailleuse âpre au gain, mais fourbe, anarchiste, hargneuse, extraordinairement fourbe, rancunière et vindictive.
>
> (J.J. Dauplay, *Rapport sur l'hinterland Moi*, 1929).

The first occupants of Indochina in a proto-historic period, known derogatively as "Kha" (slave) in Laos, "Moi" in Vietnam, Phnong in Cambodia (collectively termed proto-Indochinese by some ethnologists) have been attributed with a civilization analogous with the Dong Son age, as testified by bronze work (bronze drums), the management of hydraulic systems and the construction of megaliths (stone jars). Geographically dispersed throughout Indochina and southwest China, they include numerous groups and sub-groups usually differentiated by dialect. According to the categories outlined by Condominas, they exist in a "confined social space", lacking supra-village organization in normal circumstances (1980:53). As we described in Chapter Three, the Kha subsisted in colonial times and still today in a primitive-communal mode of production, although in pre-colonial times themselves became commodities as slaves or debtors. As emphasized, while key targets of the colonial program to realize primitive capital, the Kha were the most unwitting conscripts to the broader market.

Although at the margins of society since the advent of the tributary Lao State, Kha beliefs and rituals have nevertheless been absorbed by the ruling Lao. For instance, as the original proprietors of the land, the Kha have traditionally participated in court ceremonies — albeit in the way of ritually confirming their subordination — at Luang Prabang, Vientiane, Bassac or Phnom Penh (Zago 1972:11). While some would date the retreat of the Kha to the mountain hinterland of Indochina to the period of invasion by the Cham (Dufosse 1934), other accounts date it from the time of the arrival of the southward migrating and infiltrating Tai-Lao (AOM Aix F12, "Rapport sur la politique Moi", Résident to the Résident Supérieur of Laos, Savannakhet, 17 January 1942).

In view of the apparent disinterest of the court of Vientiane in making closer contact with the Kha, the court of Annam, from the fifteenth century onwards undertook to administer their highland dwelling subjects by organizing them into nine *chau* (divisions) forming what they called "Ai Lao Dinh". Indeed, the Kha of the Laos-Annam borderland still delivered tribute in the form of honey, pheasants and other forest products to the mandarins of Annam up until the 1945 revolution. According to a semi-mythical but not factually groundless version of the first major confrontation between the Lao (Phuthai) and the Kha, around the fifteenth century one hundred Phuthai families received permission from Phetisarath, the monarch in Vientiane, to settle the lands of the Se Soi river. Although they initially swore fealty to the Kha "*sadet*" or ruler, the Phong Si Phong Jang, they schemed against him and, in the course of a tribute delivering expedition, assassinated him at his capital in Ban Dong. According to this account, from that time on the Kha of southern Laos became tributary to the Phuthai and entered into a master-slave relationship (AOM Aix F12, "Rapport sur la politique Moi", Résident to the Résident Supérieur of Laos, Savannakhet, 17 January 1942).

In the political sense no single Kha leader existed, although the authority of one village chief could be exercised over another village. These collectivities rarely exceeded six or seven villages, although the basic social unit is the village. The village itself is constituted of family cells, the family elder being the chief of the cell. The "democratic" structure of Kha society (as opposed to the hierarchical structure of Tai society) was expressed in the election of a village chief. Although an individual could guarantee his victory in a village "election" by winning a simple majority expression of support, candidates were usually drawn from among the descendants of the elders or from among relatives of the elders of the wealthier villages. The village chief was also the guardian of the spirits of the village, which in Kha animist belief conferred upon him great moral authority. Among certain Kha groups, at least, the role of the sorcerer had no political connotations and was generally limited to curing illnesses and to fortune telling. Generally, animist in religious orientation, as expressed by the worship of both village and house deities and forest and river deities, some groups upheld an embryonic cult of ancestors (AOM Aix F12, "Rapport sur la politique Moi", Résident to the Résident Supérieur of Laos, Savannakhet, 17 January 1942).

While the village council only met on such occasions as feast days — buffalo sacrifice being the quintessential ceremonial expression of village solidarity and Kha animist practice — it was also a time when the advice of elders was taken into account. Should disputes arise between groups in the same village, the dissenting faction would abandon their village and go elsewhere. Traditionally, there was no adjudication outside of the group and no outside authority exercised jurisdiction over the group. However, the act of paying taxes and the recognition of externally derived justice was tantamount to the acknowledgement of the sovereignty of an outside power. In colonial times in Laos, the only authority recognised by the Kha was the *Tasseng* — whose influence varied according to his personality — and the *Phoban*. The latter, insofar as he was authorized by village elders, acted at the same time as intermediary between the administration and the Kha population, particularly in matters of adjudication of disputes. In general terms, then, the most important point concerning Kha social organization was that the village spirit took precedence of the tribal spirit (AOM Aix F12, "Rapport sur la politique Moi", Résident to the Résident Supérieur of Laos, Savannakhet, 17 January 1942).

THE "HOLY MAN'S UPRISING" OR THE REVOLT OF BAC MY (1901-1902)

The "Holy Man's Uprising" or the rebellion of the "*Phu Mi Boun*" (lit. men with merit) which stirred the Lao and minority populations of northeast Thailand and southern Laos between 1901-1902 has not only become the object of speculation on the part of modern historians but was equally the subject of controversy in the local press of the day. Without seeking to duplicate Murdoch's exemplary study on the historical setting of the rebellion — notably the events surrounding the replacement of Thai hegemony over the east bank of the Mekong by French colonial power in the late nineteenth and early twentieth centuries — and Moppert's fine archival-based longitudinal study of the entire rebellion, I will seek here, firstly, to throw new light on the revolt as an anti-colonial phenomenon — as revealed by the colonial record and the colonial press — and, secondly, to reopen the inquest into a barely suppressed scandal which ensued in the context of the revolt, namely, that surrounding the death of Bac My, one of the principals of the "Holy Man's Uprising" and the wounding of his more celebrated accomplice, Kommadan, an erstwhile national hero in Laos (cf. Moppert 1981 and Murdoch 1974).

While it is well documented that the "Holy Man's Uprising" began in 1901, Bac My, also known as Ong Keo, the individual most closely identified with the *Phu Mi Boun*, had hitherto attracted official attention as early as January 1895.[4]

According to Jean Jacques Dauplay, the leading colonial protagonist in the repression of the ethnic minority rebellions in southern Laos and who took up official appointment as the French Administrator of Saravane in January 1906.[5] Bac My, a Kha Alack by ethnicity, was son of a *pho ban* (village chief) of the little village of Chakam, tributary to the Lao "mandarins" of Saravane. Not of the mandarin class and holding no position higher than that of village chief, Bac My was nevertheless considered "more intelligent than his fellows". Proficient not only in Lao but in Pali, he had prior experience of the study of Buddhist texts and had even made a pilgrimage to Bangkok, all of which lent him a certain prestige in the eyes of his fellow Kha Alack tribesmen. Having proclaimed himself *Phu Mi Boun* in the opening months of 1901, Bac My then assumed the appellation, *Pha Ong Keo* (*Pha* meaning "sacred saint", *Ong* meaning "king, prince or divine person of high rank" and *Keo* meaning "diamond or precious stone"). Similarly, he employed a title otherwise reserved for the king of Luang Prabang, namely, "*Chao Som Det Phali Pha Nhoc Thong Phou Zhong Pha Sat Na Khong Thoï*" (Supreme Chief of the religion or *Pontifus Maximus*) (AOM Aix F6, "Administrator-Commissioner of the Government to the Résident Supérieur of Laos, Saravane 1910).

Significant preludes to the *Phu Mi Boun* rebellions of 1901-1902 should not, however, be ignored and, as mentioned, other uprisings labelled millenarian have been recorded in Thailand from the seventeenth century onwards (Ishii 1977:6). With respect to Laos, according to one colonial observer, the Kha of the Bolovens plateau (the geographic locus of the revolt) had risen up twice before during the nineteenth century. On the first occasion, a a certain Asa Thiet Guon and his rebel forces pushed onto the Bolovens to free it from Lao domination. The revolt lasted two years and terminated with the capture of Asa Thiet Guon and his subsequent decapitation in Bangkok. Around 1850 a "sorcerer or shaman known as Mo Ha, a native of Sisakhet (Thailand) fomented a similar uprising to that of the first. In an analogous manner, this movement came to an end with the capture and death of its leader (AOM Aix E6, "Rapport du 24 October 1907 de M. Dauplay, Commissaire du Gouvernement à Saravane").

Archival sources reveal that within two years of the establishment of the French protectorate in Laos in 1893, agents of the colonial State were successful in collecting taxes from the various Kha "tribes" inhabiting the Bolovens plateau. Erroneously, as it transpired, the prospect of rebellion on the plateau was then viewed as a distant prospect. As elsewhere in the periphery at the point of incorporation, a certain social, political and economic restructuring of local society was involved. In tandem with the imposition of taxation and corvee demands over the subject peoples (paid or requited in cash in lieu of payment in kind) and with the redrawing by the colonial administration of the local *muong* or province boundaries came the appointment of an indigenous class of collaborators in replacement of uncompliant or "independent" indigenous authorities. Thus by 1895 the Kha of the Bolovens had been administratively removed from the jurisdiction of the local province of Bassac, to which they traditionally existed in tributary relationship and, according to geographic location, were reassigned under the jurisdiction of a number of provincial mandarins. These new French appointed or approved indigenous authorities included the Phaya Ma Ha Tilat and the Phaya Mong Hoa of Saravane and Kamtong (AOM Aix E6, "Rapport sur la reconnaissance du plateau des Bolovens", January 1895).

By 1901, then, the province of Saravane had been subdivided into eight *muong* englobing 183 Lao and 194 Kha villages and included 4,853 registered Lao tax-payers versus 2,971 Kha. A total of 24,934 Lao were deemed to have "submitted" to colonial authority, versus 12,084 Kha. That left a balance of some 30,000 "independent" or unpacified and hence non-taxpaying Kha in the province. Among the "submitted" Kha were such sub-groups as the Kha Bolovens, the Kha Hin, the Khatong, the Kha Nie and the Kha Alack. The "independent" Kha included a section of the Kha Alack as well as the Kha Pou Kao, the Kha Khou Tou and the Kha Ta Hoi sub-groups. The province of Saravane then hosted a European population of three only (*Indochine Francaise Annuaire de l'Indochine: 1901*).

Early in 1901, Bac My withdrew to Phu Tatun, a local mountain redoubt. Meanwhile the rebel chief's portrait was displayed in numerous temples throughout the province. By March the movement had taken a more threatening turn, the prelude to a general insurrection. The following month, in response to the burning by the Commissioner of Saravane of a temple erected in Bac My's honor on the Nong Het plateau, the rebels murdered a Frenchman named Menard (Murdoch 1974: 55-61). Apprised of the deteriorating security situation in southern Laos in June of the same year, the *Résident Supérieur* immediately set about organizing the machinery for the suppression of the rebellion. The "pacification" operation involved the dispatch of military reinforcements to the Bolovens plateau from Tonkin, Annam and Cochinchina. During the rainy season the rebels divided into two groups; while Bac My's group refuged in the mountains at the source of the Sedone, a second group based itself in the upper reaches of the Sepion river. Both resisted the French with impunity. Although the French themselves suffered heavy losses in operations against the rebels, their tactics of starving the latter of rice and depriving them of outside supplies of powder, lead, sulphur, saltpetre, salt and opium proved to be efficacious in the long run (AOM Paris A30 (106) carton 21, "Rapport special sur les evénéments survenus sur la plateau des Bolovens et sur l'incident sur la Poste de Psi", Saigon, 26 September 1901).

Aside from Bac My — clearly only primus inter pares in the revolt at this stage — other chiefs included Ong Luong, Luong Sakda and Vong Tasseng, a Kha Bolovens chief from Nong Bok. The presence from June onwards of Lao mandarins among the rebel population must have been particularly damaging to the French cause, however. Prominent among the latter were the *Chaomuong* of Khamtong Niai, the *Oupahat* of Kamtong Moi, the *Ratsavang* of Saravane, the *Oupahat* Luong of Attopeu. Among the montagnard adherents to the rebel cause were found, Kha Boloven, Alack, Nhaheun, Kha Phou Thong, Loven and Souk Kha. Thus by November 1901, as a consequence of armed actions by the rebels and armed repression by the colonial military, one third of the local population of the greater Bolovens region had been annihilated with 28 *Garde Principal* and 100 militia killed. Only after two years of military operations was the western part of the Bolovens considered pacified (AOM Paris A30(106) carton 21, "Rapport special sur les événements survenus sur la plateau des Bolovens et sur l'incident sur la Poste de Psi", Saigon, 26 September 1901 and cf. Moppert 1981).

ONG MAN'S REVOLT (1901-1902)

Continuing through 1901, a parallel non-violent movement emerged in northeast Thailand. In March 1902, this rebellion had been joined by Ong Man — a so-called *Phu Wiset* or "wise man" — and his followers in a confrontation against a Thai army dispatched to crush the movement. Driven back into Laos, Ong Man joined forces with the followers of Bac My in a mass attack on the French Commissariat before escaping to *Phou* Louang in the Bolovens in league with other Loven rebels including Kommadan (Murdoch 1974:59, Tambiah 1984:310-314 and Ishii 1986:174-179).

Following an attack by Ong Man's 1000 strong band on the provincial Thai town of Kemmarat on 28 March 1902, the *Résident Supérieur* of Laos took precautions that events in Thailand did not ramify in Laos. The French record reveals that the original request to suppress the rebellion in the 24 kilometer "neutral zone" along the Mekong came from the Thai side. The French Minister in Bangkok was of the view that the authorization be given to the Thai to intervene militarily in the zone provided that "cooperation" would be entered into. The ensuing French response was to immediately dispatch a company of 200 Vietnamese riflemen reinforced by 30 Europeans to Bassac from where, according to circumstances, they would assist the Thai in suppressing the revolt by way of a march on Udon (AOM Aix F16, Governor General to Minister of Colonies, Hanoi, 10 April 1902). In the event, the Thai authorities forbade the French to cross onto the Thai side of the Mekong (Murdoch 1974:59). Reservations over allowing the Thai authorities a free hand in suppressing the revolt in the neutral zone were in turn expressed by the Minister of France in Bangkok. Observing, inter alia, that Japanese agents circulating in the Mekong valley were encouraging anti-French sentiment at Korat, Ubon and Battambang, he argued that Thai military actions would have the unfortunate results for the prestige of France in what he clearly implied was a French sphere of influence (AOM Aix F16, "Governor General to Commander-in-chief of the Forces", Hanoi, 5 May 1902).

As a response to the success of the Thai military operation, Ong Man and his followers, 15,000 strong and armed with 300 rifles, departed Thailand for the region between Savannakhet, Muong Phine and Song Khone where they set about cutting telephone communications between Hanoi and southern Laos. On 24 April 1902, the band led by *Phu Mi Boun* attacked Savannakhet on three occasions in the same day. Driven back by the colonial *Garde Indigène*, the rebels suffered 100 dead. Further detachments of military were directed towards rebel headquarters in Song Khone. Despite the manifest religious coloration of the revolt, the Governor General of Indochina, Brévié — with some degree of understatement — declared it is a "rebellion against French authority" (AOM Aix F16, Governor General of Indochina, Broni, to the Commander-in-chief of Division, Hanoi, 5 May 1902).

The Thai scholar, Chatthip, in a study of the Holy Man revolts of northeast Thailand from 1699 down, finds a common dimension, namely liberation from state power or negation of the State. This ideology, he argues, had its origins in primitive communal society where villages were "autonomous, pre-existing the state". Chatthip therefore argues that the primitive communal mode of production has persisted up to modern times in the consciousness of the northeastern (and Lao) peasantry. Reference to Vientiane in a number of the northeastern revolts was not necessarily a manifestation of ethnic consciousness. Rather, Vientiane stood as a symbol not as a concrete attempt to establish an administration modelled on the dynastic State (Chatthip Nartsupha 1984:111-134).

Additionally Luther has observed that the *Phu Mi Boun* rebels of the *Isan* or northeast region of Siam during the late nineteenth century had never really been defeated but resurfaced as "social bandits" (peasants who had lost their land and had no reliable source of income) especially during times of economic crisis. These albeit localized revolts, he argues, served as important social indicators of how the tax burden levied to finance western modernization affected the local peasantry. He also advances a version of the "subsistence ethic" thesis, pointing out that, already beset with low productivity and low standards of living, the additional tax burden drove a substantial part of the population to the brink of poverty. These resistance movements, he argues, can only be understood in terms of the peculiar economic situation and the respective role of the State. He submits, moreover, that the question of ethnic identity and separateness further adds an element of cohesion to marginalized economic groups (Luther 1978:57). While the process of the integration of the *Isan* into the modern Siamese State and the *Phu Mi Boun* phenomenon in this region is a separate question and has in any case been the subject of some enquiry (Bunnag 1977, Ishii 1986). Luther's restatement of our central problematic serves as a useful point of departure for a discussion of the *Phu Mi Boun* phenomenon in southern Laos.

KOMMADAN'S REVOLT (1901-1937)

Along with his relative Kommasang, Kommadan (sometimes Khommadan) was originally a constituent member of the *bao* or entourage of the leader of the 1901-02 "*Phu Mi Boun*" or "Holy Man's rebellion", Ong Keo (Bac My) (cf. Colanna 1938, Murdoch 1974 and Bunnag 1977). The entire *bao* drew together Lao, Cambodians, Burmese as well as Souie, Phou Thai, Kha Loven, Kha Alack and Kha Nge minorities. Until his surrender on 13 October 1907, this group was but one of four rebel bands operating in southern Laos. Held together by little more than their shared anti-colonial dispositions, the other three were those of Ka Duc, who died in prison following his capture in April 1906, the Ong Xit-Ong Veun band, which surrendered in December 1906, and the Bac Preuil (Ong Thong) band which fled under pressure to Siam in 1907-8. Bac Preuil was captured and executed in Pakse in November 1909 (AOM Aix F6 "Mort de Bac My et capture de ses lieutenants", Dauplay to the Résident Supérieur, Saravane, 19 September 1910). (See Map III)

Kommadan, who ethnically belonged to the Nha Huen (Nya Hon) Kha sub-group was unknown to the French until an attack by his partisans on Nong Bao in 1905 (Moppert 1981:53). Several weeks before the surrender of a Latsavang member of the band, Kommadan and Kommasang separated from Bac My and led the majority of the Kha Loven rebels into the maquis in Attopeu. In 1907 he mounted a raid on Nong Bok and in February of the following year attacked Pak Bong. Described by the colonial official, Dauplay, as "elephant and cattle smugglers" and as "rebels before the rebellion", the pair attained an early notoriety although Kommasang's name does not recur in the colonial reports (AOM Aix F6 "Dauplay, Administrator-Commissioner of the Government to the Résident Supérieur", Saravane, 15 September 1910).

On 2 December 1908, Kommadan initiated the first of his many written communications with the world outside his mountain redoubt on the Bolovens plateau in the way of a letter to the *Chaomoung* of Nong Bok stating his refusal to surrender. Although he had previously evinced the greatest deference to Bac My by addressing him as *Chao Som Det Phali Pha Thong Phou Zhong Pha Sat Na Maha Khong Them* (a Lao-Pali version of *Pontifex Maximus*) three days later he sent him a letter strongly protesting at his surrender and the state of "indifference" of his *bao* (AOM Aix F6, "Mort de Bac My et capture de ses lieutenants", Dauplay to the Résident Supérieur, Saravane, 19 September 1910).

On 14 November 1910, Kommadan invited the local French commissioner, Dauplay, to his *sala* in Phou Loung mountain for discussions. The events of the meeting which ensued merit elaboration not only as history but as confession. In Dauplay's words:

> The reception of the envoys of the Great Turk by Louis XIV was certainly not less remote or haughty as Kommadan when he deigned to take my hand at the moment when I entered the *sala*.

After an interval of ten minutes, Dauplay records, he decided to take the initiative:

> Deftly removing my pith-helmet, I took hold of the Browning and delivered from two meters, two shots, striking him (Kommadan) under the armpit and in line with his liver; the points of impact were clearly indicated by the little red spots on his white vest. Three shots hit Loung Visa at the moment when he rushed to the aid of his brother. In an instant all of the rebels leapt out of the *sala* including Kommadan as the rifles of the partisans started to crackle"

With scant attention to the consequences of his actions or indeed the ramifications of his own report, Dauplay wrote with supreme irony that although Kommadan possessed considerable strength, it appeared "impossible" that he would have survived his wounds (AOM Aix F6 "Mort de Bac My et capture de ses lieutenants", Dauplay to the Résident Supérieur, Saravane, 19 September 1910).

Ong Keo was less fortunate; even under house arrest he was a thorn in the side of the French. Following the cancellation of a visit by the Governor General to Pakse in January 1909, the local population staged two enormous *boun* in honour of Bac My at Pakse and Dong Kho. He was offered flowers, candles and mats to sit on in all of the villages through which he passed (AOM Aix F6, "Dauplay to the Résident Supérieur Saravane, 15 September 1910). Invited into Dauplay's house under the pretext of examining photographs, Bak My and his companions were ordered to sit down. "Attempting to escape", Bac My was bayonetted to death. His head was preserved in formaldehyde (AOM Aix F6 "Mort de Bak My et capture de ses lieutenants", Dauplay to Résident Supérieur", Saravane, 19 September 1910).

A remarkably accurate corroboration of the confidential memo on the wounding of Kommadan was published in the Cochinchinese newspaper, *L'Impartial* of 20 February, 1918. The author, Lefevre, drew his account from information supplied by a French doctor who witnessed the incident. Nervous of the prospect of further public exposure of the two events, an official enquiry into the wounding of Kommadan and the killing of Bac My was opened (see AOM Aix E7, "official telegram", Résident Supérieur of Laos to Councillor Juriste on mission, Xieng Khouang, Vientiane, 2 March 1918). Judged by his colleagues as a faithful servant of colonial policy, Dauplay was shamelessly exonerated from blame (AOM Aix E7 "Governor General to Dauplay", Hanoi, 9 July 1918). Not even transferred out of the colony, he continued his career in administration in northern Laos, published his version of the revolt in the Bolovens (Dauplay 1929) he acted as a local savant on minority questions.[6]

Kommadan's Political Program

The most opprobrious burden for the Kha of the Bolovens was the system of corvees. From the opening years of the French era in Laos, the Kha had been press-ganged into labor corps to work on such tasks as rock breaking in projects connected with road-building and improving the navigation course on the Mekong. The rapidity and violence with which the French sought to accumulate primitive capital from among the Kha is conveyed in the following inter-governmental memo:

> (The Tahois, Kattang, Alak and Nges) have the most real difficulties in requitting their $5.10 (capitation tax) as well as their *prestations en nature*, they do not even wish to have the matter mentioned. They prefer — speak less of the Tahois and the Kattang — to rent (their labor) for three months on the *ray* of the Bolovens plateau and to derive from it the several *piastres* necessary than to undertake twenty days supervised corvee. It is incontestable that, while certain Kha villages are as rich as some Lao villages, the small amount of trade in which they engage in is as barter. Practically everywhere money is lacking and every time one arrives to collect the tax, payment is never complete.

> It is not unusual, after four visits at month intervals, to be unable to collect one half to two-thirds of the total amount registered in the village tax-rolls.

While the same observer urged his superiors to reduce the tax rate for the Kha by one half, humanitarian gestures were seldom compatible with colonial objectives (AOM Aix E9 "Rapport sur la Situation de la Province au 31 May 1912", Saravane). The extreme sense of pathos at which the Kha found themselves during the colonial occupation is conveyed in Kommadan's words:

> When the French came to the plateau to disturb or oppress the Khomes, was it necessary for me to give them the rotan, put them in prison, inflict penalties upon them?
>
> (AOM Aix F6 "Mort de Bac My et capture de ses Lieutenants", Dauplay to the Résident Supérieur of Laos, Saravane 19 September 1919).

It is in this context that one should seek to locate Kommadan's political program.[7] The rebel chief's first set of political demands transmitted to the French were by way of his *homme de confiance*, Vang Na. These were, first; the revocation of the authority of the *Chaomuong* and all the *muong* authorities on the Bolovens, second; the nomination of a Phya Khome or chief of the Bolovens including the region spanned by Pakse, Saravane and Attopeu, third; the removal of such (non-Loven) races from the plateau as the Nha Eun, the Souei and the Phouthai and fourth; the reduction of the capitation for the "Khomes" to 1.50 piastres per annum (AOM Aix F6, "Mort de Bac My"). As this programme suggests, the notion of paying taxes was not questioned by Kommadan; after all the Kha had been paying tribute to one or other overlords for centuries. It is apparent that what mattered more for them was to attain assurances from the governing authority over their place in history and their destiny in the new order of values. But while the Kha of the Bolovens had in the past reached a modus vivendi over that agenda with the Siamese lords and the Lao princes of Bassac, the early French administrators in Laos had proven that they were contemptuous of even entertaining dialogue with the Kha.

It is also the case that the ability of the *khabot* (traitor/rebels) to resist colonial power increased to the degree that they were able to acquire firearms. Trade in the weapons, we have seen, was the other side of the coin of the slave trade. Certain indigenous Lao authorities were evidently in complicity in the traffic. The perceived threat that this constituted to French authority might be measured by the severity of the punishment meted out to those found guilty of the crime. In 1914, for instance, a number of Lao mandarins involved in the arms trade received sentences ranging from five years imprisonment to forced labor for life (AOM Aix E16, Dauplay to the Résident Supérieur, Saravane, 5 May 1919).

After a fifteen year period of apparent inactivity, Kommadan's revolt rekindled. The first indicators of a resurgence of activity by the *khabot* was the discovery in 1924 of his "propaganda" in places as far afield as the Sekong region of Laos, the Darlac region of Vietnam and the Strung Treng region of Cambodia. This took the form of messages written in what Kommadan called "Nang Su Khom" or Khom language script, probably intelligible to monks versed in Pali.[8] In the same year it was observed that a group of six to twelve Kha emissaries were en route to *Phou* Louang, Kommadan's redoubt. While Kommadan was hopeful of receiving representatives of the Rhade chiefs of Vietnam whom had also resisted French attempts at pacification, these Kha emissaries were more likely from the Sekong region of Laos (AOM Aix F6 "Commissioner of the Republic to the Resident in Strung Treng", Saravane, 17 March 1926). During December 1925, the montagnard peoples of the Vouen Sai region of Cambodia were also subject to an "active propaganda" by Kommadan (AOM Aix F6 "telegram to Vientiane", Phnom Penh, 15 January 1927).[9] Other official communications affirm that Kommadan had made contact with a Moi chief in south Annam (AOM Aix F6, Luang Prabang to Vientiane, 6 January 1926).

Kommadan's next recorded "political" act was in June 1926 when he sent invitations to all the Commissioners of the government in lower Laos inviting them to his Thung Vai (Plain of Reeds) temple-*sala* headquarters on *Phou* Louang mountain in the southeast of the Bolovens Plateau. The occasion was to be his investiture as the *Phya* Ha Khom or chief of the ancient Khome race to which he, Kommadan or "King of the Khomes" claimed to be heir. In return for recognition, he pledged that he would pass on to the French the taxes which he collected himself (Moppert 1981:54).

Earlier in the same year Kommadan had even expressed in a letter to the *Résident Supérieur* his willingness to pay taxes to the *Chaosivit* (ruler) of Bassac. He pointed out that in precolonial times, and indeed before the Siamese administration was established over the Bolovens, the "Khomes" had paid an annual head tax of two ticals to King Anou of Vientiane collected by the agents of the Prince of Bassac. The creation of the *muong* of Saravane, Khamthong, Attopeu, Pakse and Wapi by the French administration, he indicated, was not responsive to the traditional order:

> If the *Résident Supérieur* wishes to extend his protection over we Khomes of the plain and the plateau and to make a *kong* of our region

> as part of the circumscription of Bassac, we would be grateful. The authorities of Bassac are in effect the former rulers of the Khome race.

Referring, by inference, to the dislocations caused by corvee requisitions and other forced population movements engendered by the colonial administration, Kommadan intimated that the Khomes would resist resettlement. Further, in the way of claiming acknowledgement and respect for the particularity of the "khome" people, Kommadan drafted a code of their rites and customs:

> I bring to your knowledge, Monsieur, the *Résident Supérieur*, that I have written down the rites and customs of the Kha Khome race and I beg you to come and examine it and question the people as to the correctness of this writing. If you find that these customs do not correspond to the sayings of the people then I ask you to throw it out.
>
> (AOM Aix F5, "Kommadan to the *Résident Supérieur* of Laos", Thongvay, Phou Luong, 22 February 1926).

This submission was not answered.

Precisely one year later — numerology must have counted for something with Kommadan — he reiterated the plea in a letter to the *Résident Supérieur* but now included *Tiao* Phetsarath (to whom we owe the translation into French), the Governor of Bassac and the Lao, Siamese and French authorities in general. In his letter he indicated that he would pay taxes to whichever authority administered the Kha Khomes as a single undivided unit "under a single tutelage", whether they be Lao, Siamese or French. What was important, however, was that the administering authority draw up a statute of administration with the Kha Khomes. Kommadan observed that neither the Lao tax-collectors of King Anou, nor the Lao tax agents of the Siamese or the French had ever bothered themselves to observe such a convention. Failing in this matter:

> We do not see ourselves in any obligation to any authority which does not draw up a written statute with us.... we deign not to remit taxes to an authority which refuses to accord us a statute fearing misfortune for our descendants in the way that we have encountered difficulties with the administration as in the past.
>
> (AOM Aix F5, "Kommadan to the *Résident Supérieur* of Laos, Tiao Phetsarath, the Governor of Bassac, Tiao Bounlieng, the Lao, Siamese and French", Thongvay, Phou Loung, Vientiane, 22 February 1927).[10]

He also delivered, by way of emissary, nineteen letters addressed to officials of France, Siam, China and "urban Indochina" as well as to the *chef de poste* of Nongmet. In one of these letters he revealed — not unreasonably — that he refused surrender to the French for fear of punishment and imprisonment for life. In yet another letter, he requested aid for the Kha Khomes (AOM Aix F5 "official telegram").

While Kommadan may have been casting his net far and wide, for an erstwhile outlaw and social pariah his letters weigh up as sound political statements. In requesting a legal statute of administration for the Kha "race", Kommadan was at least abreast with the King of Luang Prabang who was contemporaneously expressing his own anxieties as to the juridicial standing of his kingdom. In presenting what amounted to a charter of Kha minority rights, Kommadan was decades ahead of Lao or even French thinking on the subject. As a literate, thinking and charismatic Kha, Kommadan clearly had qualities which distinguished him from his fellow tribesmen.

In any case, the administration had no intention of entering into negotiations with the *khabot*. As the *Résident Supérieur* pointed out in a dispatch to the *Résident* of Saravane:

> The absolute preservation of our prestige is the overriding question. No engagement should be taken or accepted by you which would incur the smallest slight to our authority in the Kha country of lower Laos. It should be well understood that you should not reply to any invitation from Kommadan to meet with him or his delegates at any designated places which would authorize him to dictate the conditions of his surrender to us.

Indeed, no letter of his outlining the conditions of his surrender was even to be forwarded on to Vientiane. Unconditional surrender and repentance would be the only tolerated behaviour of Kommadan and, in the interim, he was to be hunted relentlessly like a wild animal (see AOM Aix F6 "telegram from Résident Supérieur to Résident of Saravane, Pakse and Attopeu", 3 July 1926).

With a reputation among his subjects as "the master who exercises no corvees", Kommadan then dropped out of the colonial records for another five years (Moppert 1981:55).[11] When he emerged from this period of withdrawal — quite clearly with accumulated merit and prestige in the eyes of the Kha Loven and the Nhahuen — it was with some *éclat*. A *boun* staged by Kommadan at Thong Vai was attended by 139 Kha Loven from surrounding villages, including some headmen. Thirty partisans armed with flint-lock rifles took care of security. Nevertheless, seventy-eight villagers were apprehended and arrested by the authorities under article 83 of the Lao penal code (AOM Indochine Paris A2 NF 328 2649 Le Boulanger, Bulletin Politique, Vientiane 6 May 1931). This was the first of a series of *boun* staged by Kommadan at Thong Vay, symbolic of the expanded influence and prestige he had over both the Kha Loven and the Nhaheun who traditionally existed in a tributary relationship to the former. Indeed, both Nhaheun as well as Loven were among those who paid tax to Kommadan while attending the *boun* (AOM Aix E25 Attopeu, 2nd tri 1931).[12]

Continuing through 1931, Kommadan attempted to rally as many Kha to his side as possible. This involved delivering *"epistles"* against those Kha who paid tax to the French. During September of that year armed emissaries of Kommadan "lured" some 38 more Kha to join him at Thong Vai promising them relief from tax and corvee. The French were always careful to note the loss of taxpayers — in this case twelve — as every shortfall in budget receipts had to be accounted for and made up in some other way (AOM Indochine Paris A2 NF 328 2649, September 1931). Occasionally Kommadan took the offensive, notably in staging armed raids on the work zones of RC 9 then under construction by corvee labour (AOM Indochine Paris A2 NF 328 2649, October 1931).

During the same year a Cambodian named Chane Khoune was arrested in a Kha village in an "unspecified" region west of the Sekong, ostensibly on a charge of holding an out of date *carte d'impot*. The examining magistrate at Saravane determined that he had been living with the rebels for two years but had broken away to create a new civil administration. To this end he had declared himself the Phaya Khom of Muong Pachim Phnom (chief of the *muong* of the high region called Pachim), appointed administrative officers and collected tax, actually paid in the form of woven materials. In defense, Chane Khoune pleaded that he had suffered one of his periodical "crises of sanity" (*crise de folie*). The consensus of the French authorities was that the facts of the case justified his arrest. It was speculated that Chane Khoune had been invested by Kommadan to make propaganda on his account in more distant parts of lower Laos. In fact he had been active in the Muong of Phone Thong from 1928. The only sequel to this incident was the seizure of rifles in a village whose population was known to be sympathetic to Kommadan. As will be seen, Kommadan was *primus inter pares* among the *phu mi boun* and had numerous emulators and competitors. Chane Khouan may well have been seeking to cultivate his own clientele among the Kha (AOM Aix E22, "Situation Politique", Saravane, 4th tri 1931).

In the late 1920s a new spectre appeared in Indochina, the airplane. First perceived by the Kha as a *phi,* they were soon disabused of this notion. In June 1931, French airplanes bombed armed groups of "unpacified" tribesmen near Dou Chang in the Sre Kthum region of Cambodia in retaliation against their assassination on 26 May of Gatille, the district chief of Snoul, who had been mustering corvee labor from among the highlanders. Speculating whether this was the beginning of a general uprising of the tribes, the pro-administration *L'Impartial* of Cochinchina editorialised:

> We should not *a priori* deplore the intensity and inexorability of the military operations of 6-7 June against a collectivity which would undoubtedly have inflicted heavy losses.
>
> (*L'Impartial*, 12 June 1931 and see Hickey 1982:327)

Although an isolated incident, the French took no chances against the occurrence of a general uprising in the Moi hinterland. The direct consequences of these "serious" incidents in the Cambodian province of Kratie was the establishment of the first permanent *Garde Indigène* post on the Bolovens and a general heightened preoccupation with security in the Moi hinterland (AOM Indochine Paris A2 NF 328 2649, Vientiane, 1 July 1931).

While it is likely that at least some montagnards were, willy-nilly, caught up in the events of Nghe Tinh, there is no evidence that the montagnard revolts of the 1930s in either Laos, Cambodia or Vietnam were inspired by communist propaganda. What was common between the revolts of the montagnards and the Nghe Tinh rebels was their shared experience of repression by military columns and bombs. Indeed, the psychological dimension of shared oppression at the hands of the French by both montagnard and lowland peasantry during the 1930s was an important factor in shaping the "tactical" alliances between the communists and the minorities during the 1940s.[13]

Likewise, perceived relative deprivation served to harden anti-colonial attitudes. While the discrepancy between tax rates for the Kha in Annam versus Laos would figure as a major grievance of the Kha during the late 1930s and early 1940s, the only defection from administrative control of the tax-payers of Attopeu during 1933 was attributed to the more rigorous rates which applied in Laos versus Cambodia (AOM Aix E23, Attopeu, 3rd tri 1933).

By 1932, the exodus of Kha tax payers from the French controlled zones to Kommadan's retreat was stemmed, partly because of famine which became more severe as the year progressed (AOM Indochine Paris A2 NF 328 2649, September 1931). In the following year, bad harvests and the deepening famine thrust the rebels back on the defensive. Paradoxically, Kommadan had brought upon himself the economic crisis in *Phou* Louang. The more recruits he won, the less his ability to support them on the barren land of the Plain of Reeds. There was, however, a safety valve to this subsistence crisis to which he did not hesitate to resort. He raided the rice stores of those Kha villages who paid taxes to the French (AOM Aix E23, Saravane, 3rd tri 1933).

The phenomenon of flight by victimised minorities during the colonial period was not limited to the Kha of the south, but reached dramatic proportions in the north of Laos as well. In early 1933, a large scale migration of Khamu from Luang Prabang to Siam occurred. Dauplay, an official investigator singularly blind to the social consequences of colonial policies, laid the blame entirely upon the Lao mandarins. He recalled that one of the contributing causes of the rebellion on the Bolovens — an affair, moreover, which his own maladministration had managed to magnify — was the extraordinary "indifference" of local French Commissioners to the activities of the Lao *Lam Kha* from 1895 to 1902. Thus the afflux of Khamu taxpayers to Siam he attributed to the excesses of the *Nai Khoueng* and the *Lam Kha* (tax intermediaries) in dishonestly withholding, for their personal gain, up to one third of the tax revenue collected from the Khamu (AOM Aix E23 "Dauplay", Luang Prabang 1st tri 1933). The Lu and Nhuon population, generally considered as "impermeable" to French influence, also expressed their contempt for the colonial tax order by migrating to Siam (AOM Aix E25 2nd tri 1935).

Kommadan's Revolt as a Millenarian Movement?

While the distinction might be viewed as arbitrary, commencing in 1933 Kommadan's revolt took on a decidedly religious coloration or what one French rapporteur described as the "moral preoccupation of the old Kha chief in his declining years". In a series of letters intended for the King in Luang Prabang and the local administrative chiefs, he invited them to pay homage to the new *Maitreya* (AOM Indochine Paris A2 NF 318 2649, 1933) or bodhisattva in the form of the future Buddha. This phenomenon has been widely observed in the Thai-Lao milieu, especially in association with *phu mi boun* insurrections. According to Yoneo Ishii, in an essay on Buddhist millenarian revolts in north-east Thailand, millenarianism is "essentially a pre-political phenomenon" appearing in regions where relevant political institutions are lacking or underdeveloped or inaccessible "so that the distressed could find no institutionalised way of expressing their grievance and pressing their claim" (Ishii 1977:74).[14] Such, we would submit, is a common dimension of Kommadan's revolt.

The religious phase of Kommadan's revolt, then, was manifested by *boun* giving, the distribution of amulets, the rallying of followers to the new faith and other epiphenomena characteristic of the extension of the *phu mi boun* cult. It was reckoned that during this phase of "religious fanaticism", Kommadan attracted more than a thousand adepts to his redoubt. As far as the colonial State was concerned, he was responsible for the loss of 271 taxpayers from fifteen Kha villages (AOM Aix E25 Savannakhet 3rd 1934 and Saravane 2nd and 3rd tri 1934). Presumably to protect his "subjects", he constructed several corrugated iron barracks as his administrative headquarters on the *Phou* Louang (AOM Aix E25 Attopeu 4th 1933).

On 18 March 1935, Kommadan launched what was probably his greatest *boun* over a period of seven days and seven nights in order to inaugurate his new religion. Numerous local people attended in spite of the counter *boun* staged by the local French authorities in Saravane in honor of the arrival of the Governor General (AOM Aix E25 Saravane 1st tri 1935). While the content of Kommadan's propaganda throughout 1935 was said to be deeply religiously inspired, the anti-tax dimension of the revolt in no way diminished. For instance, the Kha tribes of Tahoi and Lamanan on the perimeter of the rebel zone openly resisted the Nai Kong who came to collect taxes (AOM Aix E25 Saravane 3rd tri 1935).

The more general administrative response to the Kha rebellion was the yearly convocation of the "Ceremony of the Grand Oath" at which various elements of the local population — Kha, Lao, Phuthai, French, the Buddhist clergy, and so on — were ceremoniously united. Essentially, the ceremony sought a ritual confirmation of the established hierarchical social order. With respect to the Kha, their social subordination was ritually confirmed by Buddhist prayers and ritual demonstrations of the Kha fealty to the local Lao mandarins. In French times the ceremony was viewed as an affirmation of their prestige and, through it, they sought to massage their sense of superiority over both Kha and Lao. To the pomp of the occasion was added a miniature display of military might by the *Garde Indigène*. It was also the occasion on which rewards were made to loyal elements of the population, as in the conferring of ranks upon the mandarins. Contrariwise, it was an occasion for the administration to make an accounting to the population. For instance, on the occasion of the "Ceremony of the Grand Oath" in Attopeu in 1929, the population was advised that the rates for commutations of *prestations* were to be raised. Not surprisingly, this communication was "coldly received" by the population and the dignitaries whose numbers were in any case diminished by the "flagrant absence" of several Kha chiefs (AOM Aix E21 "Rapport General", Attopeu, 1 December 1929). At the "Ceremony of the Grand Oath" in Saravane in 1935, *collaborateurs* were reminded that the *mission civilitrice* could only be effective to the degree that the taxes were efficiently collected (AOM Aix E25, Rapport General, Saravane, 4th tri, 1935).[15]

One student of millenial Buddhism, Stanley Tambiah, describes millenial Buddhism as the "antimony of the established Buddhist polity wherever it is seen to be corrupt and debased, or to require restoration and resurrection in the face of social decline or alien intrusion". To this end, millenial claims and rebellions are integral to the processes of "galactic polities" in Southeast Asia (Tambiah 1984:319). The French colonial officials who oversaw the "Ceremony of the Oath" would probably not have disagreed with such a "functionalist" interpretation, especially given state-directed efforts in Laos and Cambodia alike to resanctify the relationship between State, *sangha* and social order. Thus for Tambiah, the quest for "totality" is in opposition to the "treacherous search for underlying sociological condition that generates millenial movements". This barb is directed at Keyes's concern with the equation between millenial movements, crisis and power. Our bias, however, *contra* Tambiah, has been to read out of ideological forms of peasant and local ruling class opposition, the deeper structural causes. Stated another way, our central concern has been to look to the capitalist engendered disruptions in the pre-modern economic, social and moral orders of colonial subordinates. While we cannot deny the millenial ingredients of Kommadan's revolt, as with the earlier *phi mi boun* rebellions, we should not ignore the epiphenomenal quality of their varieties of religious" protest either.

Repression

To crush for once and for all the festering revolt on the Bolovens, the Governor General requested the participation of the army (see AOM Indochine Paris NF 271 2398 (1) "The General Director of Military Services, 20 January 1936). During the first quarter of 1936, two important decisions bearing on this matter were decided. These were the twin strategies of armed penetration of *Phou* Louang massif and the "pacification" of the Kha zones of the Upper Sekong, west of the Annamite chain. Director of the operation in the field was Colonel Nyo. He had at his disposal two companies, one composed of Vietnamese *tirailleurs* and the other composed of Rhade and Jarai minority forces (AOM Aix E25 Saravane, 1st tri 1936), a classic divide and rule situation. In the opening days of 1936 the police action was mounted on *Phou* Louang. In the Sekong valley alone, some 4000 Kha submitted to the French authority (AOM Indochine Paris NF 329 2657, February 1936). While the police operation did not immediately permit the capture of Kommadan, official reports reveal that it had the effect of swelling the number of new taxpayers from among such disparate tribes as the Thalien, the Alak, the Kantou and the Kha Nge, or all those minorities living between the Bolovens, the Upper Sekong and the Pogo on the frontier with Annam (AOM Indochine Paris NF 329 2657, March 1936).

Kommadan himself was killed in the course of an engagement with the military in *Phou* Deng near the village of Nong Ke. This operation, aimed at definitively cleaning the rebels out of *Phou* Louang, involved moving military supplies and reinforcements by elephant to Nong Met. Kommadan's correspondence, seal and weapons were seized. Certain of his female camp followers were captured (AOM Indochine Paris NF 329 2657 September 1936). By April 1936, the first Kha corvee laborers were at work, a new delegation englobing the Kha Nge, Kantou, Pakho and Tao tribes was created and placed, under the military command and; an unspecified number of Kommadan's partisans were deported to the town of Lao Ngam in the *terre rouge* country of Cochinchina, where they were kept under strict surveillance (AOM Aix E25 Saravane, 1st Tri 1936).

In the course of his thirty-five year struggle for tax justice for the Kha Loven, Kommadan had himself assassinated two *Garde Indigène*, one French *Garde Principal* and one Lao mandarin (AOM Indochine Paris NF 27 23 98 "Governor General to the Minister of Colonies", 26 December 1936). At the time of the military operation on the Bolovens, he had successfully rallied to his side some 5000 partisans or "*grévistes de l'impôt*", as the French called them, from some 200 villages. For the entire period Kommadan dealt a severe blow to French prestige in Indochina. Not only had Kommadan succeeded by moral force and religious charisma in persuading his partisans to withhold their tax or tribute to French tax agents, but his "guerrilla" tactics had rendered the Bolovens unsafe for colonization. In the light of the foregoing it is not surprising that in Lao communist historiography, his name is synonymous with revolutionary heroism.

While the news of Kommadan's death spread from village to village, survivors of his band kept roaming the forests, tracked relentlessly by the *Garde Indigène*. Among them were two of his wives and his sons, Khamphan and Nhu Song. With the capture of Khamphan on 27 July 1937, the "Kommadan question" was declared settled (AOM Aix E27 Bassac 1937). However, along with another son, Sithon, Khamphan again took up the banner of anti-colonial struggle, when released from detention by the Japanese occupier at some point in 1945.

SAMBRAN (THE WHITE PYTHON): THE KHA REVOLT OF 1936-1939

Drawing attention to a single colonial report on a rebellion by montagnard devotees of a "Python God", one authority on the ethnohistory of the highlands, Hickey, goes on to argue that belief in this new "religion", accompanied by a collective refusal to perform corvee, symbolized for the highlanders the beginning of a golden age in which they would be rid of all outsiders including the French.[16] He also notes that the influx of colonialists in Kontum province in Annam during the 1920s provoked a strong reaction by the highlanders in the area. In March 1929, the first known aerial attack on dissident villages in the highlands was recorded. Montagnard response to the "fire in the sky" was predictable and took the form of both flight and armed resistance. At the same time, armed resistance to road building activities in the Sedang country was met by an exhibition of counter-violence on the part of the *Garde Indigène*. In neighboring regions of Cambodia, pacification preceded road-building. Similar waves of repression and unrest followed, the most significant being the attack on a French military *poste* by 500 Mnong warriors.[17] In 1936, following armed attacks by Katu warriors on Vietnamese settlements near An Diem, the French decided to establish a military presence in the region extending from the Lao border south to Kontum (Hickey 1982:326-329).

While acknowledging that the ferment associated with the "Python God" cult swept up diverse montagnard tribes in the highlands of Annam, Cochinchina and Cambodia as part of the generalized tendency of these peoples towards collective expressions of "ethno-nationalism", shaped by interactions with outsiders, Hickey reveals no knowledge that the cult took root in Laos.

The first repercussions in Laos, then, of the activities of the devotees of the sorcerer Sambran (the White Python) was recorded in Attopeu in the region of the Upper Sakamone river (an affluent of the Sekong) during 1938 (AOM Aix E27 Bassac 2nd tri 1938). The influence of Sambran was particularly pervasive over the Kha tribe of Tamang. Altogether, then, thirteen Kha villages were subject to Sambran's "indoctrination". It follows, of course, that by declaring their loyalty for Sambran these villages withheld payment of tax from the French appointed tax collectors. Originating in Annam, the "White Python" movement penetrated into Lao territory, notably the Dac R Bay and the Dac Plong valleys of Attopeu. In lieu of paying taxes to the colonial authorities, those Kha under the influence of Sambran redirected their tribute towards him. D'Jao, a Sambran "emulator", issued a subscription to the Kha population for 100 traditional jars, gongs, woven covers and shirts to the value of $2000. Winning back the loyalty of these Kha was seen to be a delicate question. The act of taking the "oath of blood" was conceived as the only reliable indicator of submission of the Kha to the local Lao mandarins (AOM Aix E27, Bassac, 4th tri. 1938 and Attopeu, 4th October 1938).

At first perceived as a local religiously inspired movement, the colonial authorities noted with alarm that within a few months it had developed into a generalized uprising of the Kha population of Saravane and of the western side of the Annamite Cordillera tributary to Annam. The major foci of the revolt in Laos was the upper Sekong. The movement of dissidence had in fact been simmering in the region over the previous two to three years and may have had more than one focus centered on more than one sorcerer or shaman.

For instance, in 1936, one such sorcerer named "Phi Noi" (little spirit or man possessing a malevolent spirit) sought to provoke a rebellion of taxpayers in the region south of the Pakse-Saravane frontier. Under hot pursuit of the authorities, he fled leaving behind him several members of his entourage, his weapons and his belongings (AOM Indochine Paris 329 2657, February 1936). As recounted by Wall, memory of Phi Noi lives on in oral history of the Nya Hon. In seeking an explanation for the non-appointment of a Nya Hon *naikong* between 1937 and 1942, Wall learnt that the appointee had gone in pursuit of a Nya Hon called Phi Noi who had broken a tribal taboo. The *naikong*, Noun, having reported Phi Noi's "activities" to the French in Attopeu, was encouraged to track down the rebel. Duly rewarded by the French he killed Phi Noi and resumed his office as *naikong* (Wall 1975:8).

Sambran's rebellion, however, came to a head in late 1938. In November of that year, eight formerly pacified villages refused to execute labor dues. These villages which had the capability of mustering 500 to 600 warriors refused all attempts at pacification. The armed revolt erupted on 23 December with an ambush by Kha warriors on fifty *tirailleurs* and *gardes*. In what was described as "open armed rebellion", one *garde* was struck by a poison arrow. The French responded with a new innovation on the pacification theme in Laos. Surveillance of the rebels was kept up by aircraft.

The military then entered the region in a joint "search and destroy" operation involving the local Administration of both Annam and Laos. As a continuation of the broader pacification of the Moi hinterland, the troops moved on the village of Mang Ha in a pincer movement from Saravane and Annam. The objective was to create new administrative posts, to show the flag and to bring those Kha who had escaped the tax umbrella of the administration back into the fold. The response of the "submitted" Kha to the advance of these military columns was predictable; flight to the forest to join their "unsubmitted" brethren. The presumed author of the Kha uprising, Nai Djien, was arrested on 27 February and put in prison in Saravane along with several of the chiefs of the "rebel" villages, and charged with "outrage against the public peace" (AOM Aix E27 2nd tri 1939 and 1st tri 1939, Saravane). The submission of the rebel villages was declared in the early summer of 1939.

As the *Résident Supérieur* commented on this rebellion, it would have only begun when the French claimed tax and *prestations*. Formerly the country could be crossed without arms, he noted. Deprecating the heavy-handedness of the *Garde Indigène*, he submitted that the underlying principle should be to "domesticate primitives, not to bring savages to submission by force". Doubtless with an eye to the Vietnamese press, he remarked that the situation could be exploited by "enemy propagandists". Yet he did not view this uprising as a "revolt" against the authorities per se, but rather a return to "dissidence".

A more convincing explanation of the affair is provided by Provost, the Inspector of Colonies, who pointed to the widely observed condition of the heavier tax and *prestation* burden in Laos vis-à-vis Annam. He noted that while in Annam the generalized Kha uprising was seen more as a reaction against the tutelage of the French administration, in Laos the uprising was viewed as owing most to the sorcerer Sambran (AOM Paris Indochine NF 290 2502 2505, "Politique de contact dans la province de Saravane: Rebellion de Groupements Khas dans la Delegation de la Haute Sekong, Rapport par Provost", Mission 1938-39).

In summing up the significance of the Python God rebellion, Hickey notes that the movement did not seem to make any significant changes in the existing tribal leadership. Shamans, in any case, it might be pointed out, typically functioned in the montagnard milieu without any particular hierarchy. It is more difficult to agree with Hickey — in the light of the experience of Kommadan and other anti-authority millenarian rebels in Laos — that even despite the arrest of rebel leaders by the French, their roles appear not to have taken on political tones (Hickey 1982:327). Likewise the analogy he draws between the shared experience of the Python God devotees and the Viet Minh (whom emerged as actors in the montagnard milieu in the mid-1940s or earlier) on collective highland identity may prove under examination to be fictitious, especially in view of the retreat by the communist party from promises of unqualified ethnic autonomy (cf. Hickey 1982:327).

To be sure, as Scott has written, a bias of the historical record and the archives has been with peasants only when they have been menacing. State centered concerns, moreover, have been abetted by "a now fading left-wing, academic romance with wars of national liberation". Scott reminds us that elements of the subordinate classes beyond the middle-class, organized and heroic should also be considered. This is laudable but unduly dismissive. This essay has also reminded us that the heroic imbricates with the foredoomed. Or, in Scott's memorable metaphor, polyp-like the peasants make their presence felt by aggregations of political acts (Scott 1985: xvii). But to be relevant, it is argued here, we cannot neglect the large scale and heroic (Kommadan's revolt), nor the yet to be made heroic and patriotic (the White Python revolt) or, for that matter, the Phi Nois, the minor and forgotten irruptions of peasant anger (no easy task if the written record is wanting). The social historian's task is to tease out the connecting links at the interstices; whether they be mythic, remembered or imagined, symbolic or recorded. To be relevant — and political — we should also look out and upwards from the individual to the community to the tribal-pan tribal, national or even trans-national horizons, such as that achieved, albeit unconsciously, by Sambran and his adepts. Clearly oral history as well as the written record has its part to play here.

SEQUELS TO PACIFICATION: THE SCANDAL OF SARAVANE (1937)

One incident which throws light on the penetration ethos of the colonial regime in the highlands bears retelling. In January 1937, 180 corvee laborers (for the most part Kha) working on RC 9 near Kengkok in Saravane province in southern Laos, deserted the job site in protest of a local requirement to work beyond the sixteen days of annual labor service as stipulated under colonial law. More than eighty were imprisoned, and order was established with the help of the military. A short time later, nine Kha villages in Muong Nong in Saravane were deliberately burnt by the military in a retaliatory raid directly connected with Kha intransigence over the labor-due requirement. A press report of the time described "atrocious scenes, men at work surprised and caught up in the flames, women charred with babes in arms...." (*La Lutte*, 3 October 1937). Echoes of the affair were heard as far afield as the French Chamber of Deputies, where it was reported that the inhabitants who fled the burning villages were shot at like "wild game". Others were taken prisoner. "Abominable" acts occurred. the *mot d'ordre* given to Lao officials was "dont say anything about it". The *Résident Supérieur* of Laos who arranged the expedition — "the results of which exceeded his expectation" — was rewarded with promotion to the rank of second class administrator (AOM Paris Indochine 272 2399 "Chamber of Deputies", nd.).

Abuses of power and administrative excesses had been frequent enough in the opening decades of the French occupation of Laos, but the absence of a local press in Indochina virtually precluded external exposure of contentious issues. As might be expected, with the surfacing of a lively press in Cochinchina, Annam and Tonkin during the Popular Front days (1936-39), colonial excesses even in distant Laos could hardly escape outside scrutiny. Such was the case of the 1937 "Scandal of Saravane", as it was then dubbed by the colonial press. Indeed, that the Minister of Colonies in Paris was drawn into the affair could largely be attributed to press coverage of the events in *L'Alerte* and *La Lutte* of Saigon (see also Mogenet 1980:80-92).

What, then, were the reasons for Kha intransigence over the tax *prestation* issue? The correspondent for *L'Alerte* suggests that it was a combination of structural injustices in the corvee system exacerbated by abuses at the hands of those delegated to implement policy. He explains:

> Normally, the *prestation* time is sixteen days, less the time of travel for every twenty-five kilometres... but it is not always so.... Precise examples have been given to us of corvee laborers who are obliged to do fifteen days work on the job-site, no matter the season and even though their village may be more than sixty kilometers from the job site. These corvee laborers, who, moreover, do not receive any pay must feed themselves and before leaving their villages must provision themselves with all the necessities for sixteen to twenty two or twenty four days taking into account travel time. It often happens that provisions are exhausted at the end of ten to twelve days. In this case they must buy provisions from the Vietnamese merchants and the women of military and others who live like parasites along the roads. Often the corvee laborers have only a clump of bamboo for shelter and even sleep on the ground.
>
> (*L'Alerte*, 2 July 1937).

As the correspondent of *La Lutte* discovered at first hand, the place was one of "extreme insalubrity", a "veritable mosquito and leech ridden hell" where malaria, bronchitis and Tuberculosis were endemic. It also happened to be the region in which the notorious Lao Bao penitentiary was located, from which nine out of ten political prisoners reportedly never returned alive (*La Lutte*, 3 October 1937). To this he added, not without pathos:

> My people then gave me some names of these recalcitrant taxpayers and corvee laborers, at first thrown in prison, then obliged to work for nothing on public works, that is to say pulling carts, breaking rocks to bank up the roads and finally dead from suffering buried anonymously without any formality: Sak Nouk, Miu-Ka, O-Brac, Ma-San, Bau-Cuc, etc., etc....
>
> ("Plus de cent etre humains ont peri dans un incendie allume par ordre", *La Lutte*, 3 October, 1937).

Small consolation, indeed, for these victims to have their names recorded for posterity by journalists of the day.

Another vexing question was that of the corvee tax differential between that required of Kha residing in Annam and those residing in Laos, an arrangement which led to frequent abuses by Lao tax collectors as well as by mandarins in Annam. As reported in the Chamber of Deputies, a typical exchange between a tax collector in Laos and a Kha of the Laos-Annam border region went like this:

Tax collector:	"Pay your taxes".
Kha peasant:	"We have already paid, here are our receipts".
Tax collector:	"They are for Annam. Pay your debts to Laos".
Kha peasant:	"We see no inconvenience that the sums that we have already paid be made over to Laos".
Tax collector:	"Your previous payments are nil. Pay!"
Kha peasant:	"But you know we have no money".

Thus the recalcitrant villages who formerly paid their taxes to Quang Tri at the rate of $3 to $3.50 were required to pay 6$30 to Laos, and in this particular year were requested to pay an iniquitous double tax (AOM Paris Indochine 272 2399 "Chamber of Deputies", nd.).

By this stage the affair had all the makings of a scandal. As the Minister of Colonies in Paris insinuated in a dispatch to the Governor General of Indochina, the practice of issuing exemplary lessons to the natives by *force majeure* would not wash with the French public:

> The information that you have sent me appears to have sought to minimize as much as possible the gravity of the facts and to transform into rebels men who were in difficulties in effecting the *prestations* demanded and then at a time when their presence in the rice-fields was indispensable.
>
> I am told that the repressions were all the less justified when in a total of forty years we have not exactly brought great things to the Lao population. A perusal of the budget permits us to establish that the existing services; Native Justice, Ordinance Survey, Agricultural Services, Forests and Irrigation — only figure as memorials or as insignificant sums.
>
> Is it the case that the *arrêtes* permit the *Chef de Province* or the *Résidents* to demand from the population sixty days work in zones one hundred kilometers distant from the localities inhabited by the laborers? One understands that the abuses of the *Cai* (labor bosses) are real and that journalists — more or less suspect to be sure — are given to exaggerate the incidents that I have pointed out to you.
>
> (AOM Paris Indochine NF 2722399 "Minister of Colonies to the Governor General of Indochina" Paris 2 August 1937).

The Governor General, Jules Brévié, responded to this challenge to his sense of administrative probity:

> The facts have been grossly exaggerated in the local press at the instigation of the Vietnamese concessionary mandarins... the damage

> to property was minimal, some twenty to twenty-five empty houses were burnt.... I am in accord with the Résident Supérieur of Laos that these measures of repression are inadmissable.
>
> (AOM Paris Indochine, NF 27222399 Brévié, Governor General of Indochina to Inspector of Colonies Barquez concerning measures of repression against several Kha villages in the province of Savannakhet, 14 September 1937).

The "scandal" had its sequel in the administrative shakedown undertaken in the Lao province of Saravane. The *Résident Supérieur* attempted with the best intentions to remove the casus belli of Kha discontent, primarily perceived as abuses caused by the mandarins of Annam or their agents who crossed the border into Laos to collect tax and tribute which did not necessarily end up in the local Annam treasury. Accordingly, a Committee of Enquiry was constituted and a Vietnamese mandarin, Nguyen Van Chinh, the Tri-Huyen (sub-provincial chief) of Huong Hoa (Quang Tri), to whom tax abuses in villages in Laos had been imputed, was prosecuted. He was retrograded one rank. All in all there was little stimulus for reform emanating from the authorities in Hue and a great deal of vested interest in not tampering with a system that had for generations supplied prebends or other non-monetary benefits to local officials. An *Arrête* of 8 September 1937 issued by the *Résident Supérieur* of Laos did, however, offer some relief to the overtaxed and overworked Kha in Laos. This lowered the number of days of corvee to be furnished to the Kha from twenty to fifteen. A second text reduced the per capita personal tax for Kha in Laos from $2 to $1.50. While the *prestation* requirement for Kha in Laos was still more than stipulated in Annam (five days), the Kha in Laos were, initially at least, to be offered the option of commuting *prestations en nature*. It was pointed out that because of these measures the local treasury would lose some 25,000 piasters in revenues.

In the interests of administrative rationalization, those Kha formerly administered by three different provinces of Laos — Pakse, Savannakhet and Saravane — were to be absorbed by a new delegation called Upper Sekong (*arrête* of the Governor General of 26 March 1938). To preempt misunderstandings between local authorities in Annam and Laos over the administration of the Kha, joint tours were to be mounted in Kha territory. Medical and teaching services were for the first time placed on the administrative agenda. The services of the Salt *Régie* were solicited to reward compliant Kha with salt — a rare commodity in the highlands — and to withhold it from the intransigent (AOM Paris Indochine NF 2722399 "Governor General of Indochina to Inspector General of the Colonies, Chief of the Mission of Mobile Inspection in Indochina" and "*Résident Supérieur* to the Governor General of Indochina", Vientiane, 25 April 1938).

A COLONIAL MONTAGNARD POLICY

As Hickey, has written, the French "penetration" of Kontum, Ban Me Thuot, and Dalat had achieved a certain success by the beginning of the First World War. Central to the viability of the French project of economic exploitation in the highlands was the need for road construction and other public works, including labor for privately owned French plantations. Not only did the subject peoples of the remote villages of the interior — broadly designated montagnards in this work — find themselves obliged to pay taxes, but they were also expected by the French to provide corvee labor or labor dues. Colonialism indubitably demands the services of local collaborators, and such was the case in the highlands where local chiefs were vested with new authority by the French administration (Hickey 1982:291 and 321). While by the third decade of the century the French "pacification" of the interior had reduced armed opposition to the nuisance level, pacification's twin imperative of administrative penetration of the conquered zones and peoples posed equally serious ethical questions.

A number of questions are raised by the foregoing. How did the colonial administration set about formulating a minority policy in a polyethnic environment where traditional boundaries were arbitrarily interrupted and disposed of in the course of the French conquest? Short of revolt, how did the montagnards adapt to the colonial taxation policy and concomitant monetization of their traditional economies?

To venture answers to these questions this section will focus attention upon the montagnards of the Laos-Annam frontier. Annam was the central region of Vietnam under the French, and the Laos-Annam frontier was a major cultural divide in Indochina and one of the last interior backwaters to be targeted by the French policy of "contact". While it is not the leading issue under discussion here, the Laos-Vietnam boundary question is clearly still of contemporary interest as the matter remained unsettled in 1975 when the communist regimes in Laos and Vietnam consolidated control over the interzone. Again, while not an issue of discussion here, it would not be surprising if the present governments in Indochina were not faced with some of the same problems in the administration of the highlanders as those encountered earlier.

In 1922 the French Governor General of Indochina, Francois Baudoin, described the highlands as a "truly offensive anachronism" and a "black mark" (*tache sombre*) on the entire tableau which made up the French empire in the Far East. Writing twenty years later, the French *Résident* of Savannakhet added that while the Moi of Cochinchina as well as in Kontum, Darlac, Upper Donnai and Pleiku in Annam and the Kha of the Bolovens in southern Laos had responded to French pacification and were open for "colonization", the Kha of the interior of Savannakhet and those living in the region bordering Annam remained singularly refractory to French colonial goals (AOM Aix F14, Extract from the report of Inspector of the Colonies, Barquez).[15] Indeed, as noted in a Vietnamese account, as late as 1945 there were still regions outside French control such as the tri-border area and the region around Ngoc Lina inhabited by the Jehtrieng and Sedang (Dang Nghiem Van 1972:20).

According to colonial observers, the Kha Leu — a Kha sub-group located athwart the Laos-Annam border region in an area which, in 1946-49, became a major Viet Minh staging area — had, historically speaking, played a "double game" with remarkable "hypocracy". Since the fifteenth century, although inhabiting territory under the theoretical sway of the King of Vientiane, the Kha Leu had paid tribute to the Emperor of Annam. When, a century later, the Phuthai (Lao) extended their domination over the montagnards of the region, as symbolized by their assassination of the Kha *sadet* (king) of Ban Dong, the Kha Leu sought the protection of the Court of Annam. In colonial times, when in search of new lands to cultivate, they acknowledged Lao suzerainty only to become Vietnamese when taxes and corvee were solicited by the administration in Laos. Although a tribute in pheasants and parrots paid by the Kha Leu to the authorities in Annam was kept up until modern times, certain Vietnamese mandarins took advantage of their traditional suzerain status by tracking the Kha Leu across the border into Laos to solicit taxes in kind. Finding the Vietnamese taxes less onerous than the tax duty in Laos, the Kha Leu complied, but emphatically rejected the overtures of the Lao tax-collectors (AOM Aix F12, "Rapport sur la politique Moi", Résident to the Résident Supérieur of Laos, Savannakhet, 17 January 1942 and Barthelemy Report).

Customarily the proprietors of ancestral Kha lands divided the *ray* between members of their family. In a process that became exacerbated during the late 1930s and again during the 1940s, population pressure on ancestral land on the Annam side of the border and a concomitant fear of famine left the Kha with only one solution, emigration to the Lao side of the Annamite Cordillera. The migration process began with the exclusion of young married couples from their natal villages and ended with the re-establishment of *ray*, villages and the family *phi* on Lao territory. The process of "invasion" occurred all along the Savannakhet-Quang Tri border which, as the authors of a delineation carried out in 1916 acknowledged, followed no natural divide, certainly not the watershed, the more obvious line of demarcation (Barthelemy Report).

By the mid-1930s, as Hickey explains, the French felt need for better coordination of their administrative policies in the highlands, confident as they were of their fundamental control. In three successive conferences held in Dalat between July 1935 and May 1937 the administration brought together local officials from the mountain provinces of Cochinchina, Annam, and Cambodia along with military and political officials from Saigon. Notable recurring topics on the agenda for discussion included border problems, taxation, corvée, "banditry," local highland leadership and the "politics of salt" (Hickey 1982341-3).

Viewing the delineation of the frontier as central to the resolution of the Kha Leu problem — and no doubt building upon the Dalat Conferences — the colonial authorities convened yet another conference on minority issues at Tchepone on 18 March 1940. At this conference it was decided that the border be adjusted to account for realities. Immigrant Kha Leu villages actually in Laos would be reattached to the sector of the *chef de poste* of Khe Sanh and the Tri Huyen of Huang Hoa in Annam. Although the border was redefined with more precision, problems created by unresolved questions lingered until the 1946-49 period (and indeed the border was subject to further adjudication and adjustment in 1977 by the new communist regimes in Laos and Vietnam). But despite these readjustments the Kha Leu were still in certain circumstances subject to a double taxation. In a familiar refrain, one local French administrator commented that "most of the difficulties relating to the discontent of indigenous tribes have their origins in the abuse of power committed by the authorities in Annam" (Barthelemy Report), although, to be sure, this could be read as obfuscation on the part of an official seeking to exculpate Laos from its share of the blame.

By 1942, the much touted fiscal reform for the Kha in Laos had not been implemented with any satisfaction to the subject peoples. As the *Résident* of Savannakhet wrote:

> .... the misplaced and very rigid application of the ruling texts has provoked a certain discontent among the Kha with regard to the administration in Laos and has reinforced the influence of the Vietnamese authorities.
>
> (Barthelemy Report)

If by 1942 the more assimilated Kha of the interior as well as the Phuthai acquitted their taxes without resistance, the Kha of the frontier region still manifested a "repugnance" in dealing with the Lao mandarins. The Inspector of Colonies, Barquez, who led an enquiry into the matter, offered the following explanation for the greater success of tax collectors from Annam in their dealings with the Kha:

> I am able to state that the collection of tax (among the Khas of Annam) was effected in the following fashion: a card is drawn up with the name of the tax payer and showing the amount needed to redeem *prestations* ($2.50). Although this is an individual card, a collective card

> is delivered by the village ensemble. The village pays to the collector a sum superior to that which figures on the card... various presents are added to this... honey, rice, tobacco, pheasants.

Although, as Barquez noted, this demonstrated a "doubtful administrative probity" on the part of the Vietnamese mandarins, for the Kha it presented certain advantages over the operative system in Laos. In Annam, the Kha were not compelled to work in regions distant from their villages and when they were lacking silver they could always pay the mandarins *en nature*, with gifts of forest products (AOM Aix F14, "Extract from the report of Inspector of the Colonies, Barquez").

While the broad lines of a Moi or montagnard policy were not fully fleshed out until 1942 under the Vichy administration of Admiral Jean Decoux, it is doubtful if any but the most hesitant first steps were taken towards policy implementation in the period before the Japanese *coup de force* of March 1945. Nevertheless, in recognition of past abuses and failures in their dealings with the Kha in Laos widespread reforms were envisaged. The Kha were to be rendered sedentary by way of delimiting their cultivated land and by forcing them to break with their agricultural practice of shifting cultivation. Equally radical was the projected policy of avoiding the deployment of indigenous intermediaries between the montagnards and the administration: As the *Résident* noted:

> ....nearly all of the uprisings, assassinations, wars and other incidents which have bloodied the Mois country are due to the foreign auxiliaries interposed between the French representatives and the indigenous peoples.

Such a view would tend to unjustly exculpate the French from all blame. As it happened, it was decided that French military agents would assume a tax collection role in the montagnard villages, as part of a policy termed "oil stain" and implying a limited colonial presence.

While the long term goal envisaged was greater penetration of the interior with roads and administrative posts, this was to be coupled with a more pragmatic tax policy. In the interests of attaining uniformity with the system operative in Annam, only "evolved" Kha were henceforth required to pay in cash. Under the new dispensation, only Kha corvee laborers in Laos would henceforth be required to work on local projects such as constructing intra-village tracks. In tacit admission of the excessive speed in which primitive accumulation had been foisted upon the montagnards, Kha villages in Laos were to be permitted to revert to a system of paying tribute in lieu of tax, but equal to the amount of tax forfeited (AOM Aix F14, "Extract from the report of Inspector of the Colonies, Barquez").

As a French military strategist, Barthelemy, noted of the frontier problem in 1947, it was still a source of grave difficulties between the "prickly" young "nationalist" governments in Laos and Vietnam. He urged his superiors to resolve the litigation over the territory in dispute between Laos and Annam before the area became the object of an "undeclared and bloody struggle for influence" at the cost of the population (Barthelemy Report). This was an oblique reference to the role of the Kha alongside the Lao nationalist and Vietnamese revolutionary forces in the struggle to resist the French restoration during the 1946-49 period.

As a solution to the border and security problem Barthelemy recommended to his superiors the creation of a French controlled montagnard state or buffer state (*état tampon*) in the central highlands. This would supercede the three notional border traces laid down by the colonial authorities between Laos and Annam in respectively 1916, 1938 and 1940 (Barthelemy Report). While the montagnard state concept found acceptance in the highlands of Tonkin and Cochinchina, one might surmise that it was never adopted in the central highlands because of the nationalist objections of the Lao and the Vietnamese.

Notwithstanding certain overall French successes up to around 1953 in pursuing a divide-and-rule policy in the interior, the record of achievements among the montagnards of the central highlands was less impressive. For instance, such was the reluctance of the Kha to side with the French — and such was French mistrust — that the first mixed Kha-Lao military units, namely the Seventh Company based on Ban Phone, were not formed until 1948 (AOM Aix Laos F15, Thakek, 16 December 1948). By that date the Viet Minh and the Lao Issara had achieved demonstrably greater success in striking tactical alliances with the montagnards astride the southern Annamite Cordillera (cf. Gunn 1988).

CONCLUSION

While the answer to Woodside's objection raised at the beginning of this chapter, as to whether ethnic rebels responded more to internalist or external stimuli, cannot be easily resolved — as the two aspects have revealed themselves to be closely connected — it was certainly the case in Laos that the aggravation of minority grievances by external actors, especially colonial actors, left them exposed to exploitation or manipulation by one or other parties.

Kha peasant response to market penetration was even less equivocal. We can conclude that there was a direct positive relationship between market penetration and political activity; in the case of the Kha, armed rebellion. Changes wrought by the colonial State to the Kha moral, social and political order pushed them into direct confrontation with the constituted authority, first expressed by avoidance and then withdrawal of corvee labor and tax. The outbreak of armed rebellion by the Kha in the early colonial period was fueled by colonial counter-violence. During the economic crisis, as customs duties and other sources of income fell dramatically — most notably in Laos, the loss of substantial income from the Federal budget subvention — the colonial State bore down more heavily upon its main pillar of fiscal support, the head tax (cf. Scott 1976:8). Collecting the grossly regressive head tax from the Kha during the depression years was like squeezing blood from a stone. The followers of both Kommadan and the White Python had nothing to lose by revolting, although the cost-benefit analysis of revolt versus compliance shifted in favor of the French as the means of achieving pacification became increasingly sophisticated in the late colonial period. The Kha peasant's defense of community and an equitable tax order — the Kha in general did not reject entirely the principle of paying tribute — was typically manifested by religious ideology. As one student of this phenomenon in the Thai-Lao milieu has remarked, there is a tendency for a *phu mi boun* to appear in a moment of crisis (Keyes 1972:14). So it was in the case of Kha revolt in colonial Laos. Messianism provided the irrational device to rally popular support around a charismatic figure. While dearth of cash certainly magnified the tax burden of the Kha to extremis (cf. Scott 1976:98), the preference — even willingness of the Kha — to pay tribute to the traditional mandarinal authority, whether Bassac or Hue, puts paid to the view that the notables were a primary cause of Kha peasant grievance, a view also favored in certain colonial accounts of Kommadan's rebellion (cf. Dauplay 1929).

NOTES

1. In Scott's (1985, p.xvi) turn of phrase "the prosaic but constant struggle between the peasantry and those who seek to extract labor, food, rents and interest from them", involving footdragging, dissimulation, desertion, pilfering, slander and so forth.

2. This list has been adapted, inter alia, from Mogenet (1980:73-93). For the official Lao communist version see Kaysone Phomvihane (1980:9).

3. This rebellion occurred in the area along RC 9 in southern Laos close to the Laos-Vietnam border (Ky Son 1980:11).

4. That would make Bac My (Ong Keo) as four years senior to the Thai *phu wiset* (wise man) who appeared in the northeast in 1899 rather than two years junior as stated by Keyes (1977:295n). Actually described in period colonial reports as a *Phu Mi Boun* he initially attracted the surveillance of the colonial authorities

in the context of having "concealed cult objects from the Catholic missionaries" on mission in the Bahnar country of Cochinchina. His accomplice in this affair was a certain Ong Dam (Black God) who had earlier evaded capture by agents of the King of Bassac (Rasadanai) and who had sought sanctuary in the "kha" (montagnard) villages at Ban Nasia.

5. Between 1901 and 1930, the province of Saravane was under the control of the Commissioners, Remy, Chambert, Dauplay and Vitry. Between 1930 and 1936, the *chefs de province* were successively, Grossin, Vitry, Garric, Loupy, Thierry and Colonna (Colonna 1938:87).

6. For a thinly fictionalized account of French colonial fantasies over life among the montagnards of southern Laos, see Desme 1923.

7. A popular Chru (montagnard) song expressed the sentiments of the population towards the corvee obligation thus:

"I wept under the heavy burden I carried,
I removed my head cloth to wipe my tears,
After I passed three stations,
My heart perspired,
I used the garment to wipe my heart." (Hickey 1982:115)

8. Existing copies of his letters in the colonial records reveal that he signed his name with a lac or garuda symbol. Such symbology was also employed by anti-colonial rebels in Burma such as Hsaya (Master) San (cf. Herbert 1982:5).

9. Chandler notes that the assassination of Resident Bardez in April 1925 in Kompong Chang province of Cambodia by irate villagers offers a watershed of sorts and a "rare example of rural Cambodians uniting in an anti-colonial cause". As a single act, however, he doubts whether it can be treated as a prologue to nationalism even though Bardez assassins have been made heroic by nationalist historians (Chandler 1982:35-49). Neither was there any ostensible connection between revolts by lowlanders in Indochina with montagnard revolts in the period under review.

10. Some years later, the population at large in Attopeu (Lao as well as Kha) expressed discontent at an administrative rationalization which placed Attopeu under the purvey of Pakse. Assurances were given by the *Résident* of Bassac that only a change of name was at issue and that the population would not be subordinated to the Lao mandarins of Pakse (AOM Aix E25, Bassac 4th tri 1934).

11. During the period of "withdrawal", Kommadan's son, Sithon — the future Pathet Lao revolutionary hero — came to the attention of the colonial authorities in the context of litigation over the issue of an apparently unauthorized "borrowing" of a rifle and hunting lantern, ostensibly used for duck hunting (AOM Aix E6, Governor of Bassac to the Commissioner of the Government at Pakse, Bassac, 1 July 1927).

12. According to Wall, an ethnographer of the Bolovens, the Loven adopt an attitude towards the Nhaheun similar to the attitude of the Lao towards the Kha. More numerous than the Nhahuen, more acculturated to the Lao culture, the Loven considered them as inferior. While ethnically very closely related, the Nhaheun considered the Loven as lords of the plateau. The rift was perpetuated into the 1950s, the Loven in the main backing the Pathet Lao while the Nhahuen took the adversary position (Wall 1975:7).

13. According to an ICP document, "Moi agricultural workers" supported the Nghe-An Soviets (AOM Paris Slotfom 111, 54, Annex to NP 35, "Projèt de Résolution soumis au Congress du PCI au sujèt du travail parmi les minorities ethniques".

14. Tambiah, a student of millenial Buddhism, describes the phenomenon as "a totality of beliefs, expectations, practices, and actions that have as their object, the reconstitution of an existing social order in terms of an ideal order, a future utopia which at the same time is a return to an ideal and positive beginning". (Tambiah 1984:319).

According to the political scientist, Hagopian, criteria for the existence of a messianic movement are (1) a discontented or oppressed collectivity, (2) hope in the coming of a divine emissary, and (3) the belief in a simultaneously sacred and profane paradise (Hagopian 1974:25).

15. For a description of this bizarre ceremony as conducted on 1 January 1926 by Sabatier, the Governor General of Indochina, in Annam, in the context of initiating the colonization of Darlac, see Hickey 1982:306).

16. The Vietnamese ethnologist, Dang Nghiem Van, also notes that the most prominent of the uprisings by central highlanders against French rule was that by the No Trang Long and Xam Bran (Sombran) movements (1982:20).

That the Sambran revolt was no isolated incident might be seen against the following list of *phou mi boun* or "messiahs" who emerged in the interzone athwart the Annamite Cordillera from the 1890s onwards.

1890 — Kham and Khun, two Lao who claimed they could fly, attracted gifts of chickens and pigs from the "Moi". Only when a Vietnamese challenged Kham to fly onto the veranda of a house on piles was the imposture unmasked.

1901 — a *phou mi boun* instigated an attack on the Psi River post, northwest of Kontum.

1908 — a tame civet cat from the Psi River post was proclaimed a messiah. That same year, the Bahnar and Jarai paid homage to a self-styled ya (heroic demi-god) who claimed to have instigated the revolt of the short hair in the plains of Central Annam.

1910 — the people worshipped a dwarf, in 1916, a giant.

1924 — the airplanes that flew over Kontum for a land survey were seen as "white-winged heroes" destined to restore a golden age and expel the French.

1939 — a two year old child attracted faithful followers.

1941 — a European employee of the Water and Forestry Board was believed to be a magician.

(Bourotte 1951:103 citing Maitre, *Jungle Moi* p.477 notes and F. Guilleminet, "Recherches sur les croyances des tribus du Haut- pays d'Annam," BIIEH, 1941, pp.10-33).

17. According to Vietnamese press reports, during March 1935, a group of Phnong commanded by their chief, Beu Degn, attacked the French post, Le Roland. "Bloody" reprisals taken by the authorities had the counter-productive effect of driving the montagnards deeper into the forest ("Que se passe-t-il dans le Haut Chlong?", *La Lutte*, 30 March 1935 and *La Depêche*, 26 March 1935).

6

The Political Economy of Rebellion in Northern Laos

These primitives in Laos don't easily comprehend the exigencies of the fisc, the caprice of our laws, the imbroglio of our regulations, they cannot concede in their childish intelligence that they must pay for the air they breathe, the right to live at an exorbitant rate — minimal in our eyes from the monetary point of view — but which for them represents an amount a hundred times inflated, almost a fortune. That we impose our laws upon them, and moreover, enforce them, fine, but that they are liable to have their heads removed for a light infraction such as contravening a customs *arrêt* on salt or tobacco, it seems that the men who adjudicate in courts as well as the executioners have exceeded their rights and have committed the most monstrous assassinations.

(Jacques Duroit, *L'Opinion*, Saigon, 9 February 1908).

With the end of dynastic rule in China in 1911, political instability spread south through Yunnan to northern Indochina. Inside Laos, as discussed below, instability took two forms, "feudal" as in the case of the Lu and "republican" or war-lord as in the case of Chinese elements.

REVOLT OF THE LU (1914-1916)

The colonial administrator, Paul Boulanger, observed that the montagnards of upper Laos were more or less "violently agitated" during the entire period from 1914 to 1921. Up until 1914, he contends, the various races of Muong Sing, Lu as well as montagnard, had accepted French tutelage, the only major dissenter being the Lu chief and "vulgar bandit", Van Na Poum, until his death at the hands of the military in 1910 (Boulanger 1931:356-7). To be sure, as Adas has written, given the colonial rapporteur's habit of indiscriminate labeling of anyone who resisted colonial rule as a bandit, it is very difficult to determine which bandit groups were exponents of popular resistance and which were merely common bandits (Adas 1981:218). There is, however, no mistaking the anti-French and popular character of the revolt of the Lu of 1914-1916. Led by a Lu prince and centered on Muong Sing, one of the former constituent *muong* of the ancient Tai-Lu political federation of Sip Song Panna, the rebellion took on the character of a movement for the secession of the *muong* from French rule (see AOM Aix Q2, Monographie du V Territoire Militaire, May 1926).

Muong Sing had only been fully incorporated into French Laos in April 1904 following preliminary negotiations between Scott for the British in Burma and Pavie for the French side (Boulanger 1931:333). Pavie had originally secured the Lu country for France by winning over the *Chao Fa* (prince) of Muong Sing. In 1907, however, the old *Chao Fa* was succeeded in that position by his son Phra Ong Kham, who did not share his father's pro-French sentiment and, indeed, developed an implacable contempt for the French. Following his initial flight to Sip Song Panna in December 1914, the *Chao Fa* led the Lu people in rebellion against the French for the next two years. It took the French three military expeditions before they could restore order and reestablish their administration. This they achieved by stripping the principality of its vice-regal prerogatives and converting it into a simple *muong*. Although the *Chao Fa*'s family was authorized to return to *Muong* Sing, the *Chao Fa* himself eventually died in exile in China in 1923 (Boulanger 1931:375).

In theory, the principality had up to this time been governed by the *Chao Fa*, considered by the population as an emanation of Buddha. He was seconded by a *Ho Senam* or Assembly of "mandarins". Each was of the Lu race and was supposed to have been responsible for a special service such as finance, public works, police and so on, although in practice they were more often than not concerned with anything but their allotted duties. Under the colonial order, appointments to the *Senam* were made by the *Chao Fa* but subject to the approval of the French administration. Before the French occupation, the *Senam* comprised 150 members, but the numbers had been progressively reduced, to seventy-five in 1899 and twenty-five in 1905 (AOM Aix Ell, "Situation Geographique et Ethnographique de la Principaute de Muong Sing", nd.).

In tandem with the French imposed corvees and taxes, the *Chao Fa* upheld his traditional seignorial rights. The population could be called upon to exercise a variety of servile duties, eg., as *tahoi* (partisans), *malalec* (sword-bearers), *timoi* (parasol bearers), *kounan* (intendants for the preparation of fêtes), watchmen for the *Chao Fa*'s cattle, laborers for his rice-fields, huskers for his padi, watchmen and so on. According to colonial accounts, the *Chao Fa* subjected his people to "a reign of terror". As in other *muong*, the montagnards were the major victims of domination at the hands of the mandarins. Not surprisingly, the Kha and the Tai Neua desired to be rid of the yoke of the *Chao Fa* (AOM Aix E11, "Situation Geographique et Ethnographique de la Principaute de Muong Sing", nd.).

Even before his defection in 1914, the *Chao Fa* was seen to be turning his not inconsiderable talents to "evil". This became most apparent between 1905-1908 during the period when extensive public works projects were carried out in northern Laos. Village chiefs acting on the orders of the *Senam* refused to supply corvee labor for the French while requisitions required for the *Chao Fa* or the mandarins were met. According to the French rapporteur, the only possible explanation for this act of duplicity was the "natural" proclivity of the Lu to surrender themselves to pomp and pageantry as long as it gave them the "illusion of being a great people" or at least at the top of an ethnic hierarchy which placed the montagnards at the bottom (AOM Aix E11, "Situation Geographique et Ethnographique de la Principaute de Muong Sing", nd.).

The rebellion of the Lu probably commenced as an attempt by relatives of the *Chao Fa* to usurp power. In any case the Phya Kham Lu fled to Sip Song Panna in 1909 and from there mounted opposition to both the French and the *Chao Fa*. With the flight of the *Chao Fa* to Muong La in Sip Song Panna, clan rivalry and court intrigue at Muong Sing became subordinated to the war of resistance mounted by the Lu peoples against the French. While the *Chao Fa* awaited a propitious time to stage his return from Sip Song Panna, his armed bands engaged in running guerrilla actions against the French forces in Luang Nam Tha and Muong Sing. The advice tendered by the *Résident Supérieur* to his beleaguered deputies in the Lu country was to hold "blow by blow" the posts already occupied until reinforcements could arrive. The strategy was to guard the valleys of the affluents of the Nam Tha, the most likely "invasion" route of the Lu "pirates" towards Muong Sing. A major fear of the French was that the rebellion would be consummated as a true war of secession, especially if the *Chao Fa* was contacted by enemies of France in China (AOM Aix E11, "Situation Geographique et Ethnographique de la Principaute de Muong Sing", nd.).

THE CHINESE REVOLT OF 1914

In November 1914, what the French saw as a band of "Chinese pirates and opium smugglers" entered Laos from Yunnan and attacked the administrative center at Sam Neua, killed the French administrator,

Lambert, and made off with between 100,000-200,000 piasters from the local treasury along with 49 kilograms of opium and a supply of weapons. Fortified in the post, the rebels repelled attempts by the military to dislodge them. Reinforced by "turbulent elements" drawn from the local population, the band withdrew in the face of the *tirailleurs* summoned from Hanoi. From Sam Neua, the rebels marched on Sonla, successfully destroying French posts in the Black River region (AOM Paris Indochine A 50 NF (28) 3 "Note pour la presse" nd.). Before storming Sonla and occupying the office of the *Résident*, the rebels staged a procession and fête in the Black River region celebrating the *coup de main* at Sam Neua. On this occasion they brandished flags of the Chinese Republic and their own revolutionary standard, featuring a black triangle on a red background (AOM Aix Q1, "Situation Politique du Laos" 4th tri 1914, Report to Governor General, Vientiane, 11 January 1915). Pursued by the military the rebels retreated to Sip Song Panna whence they had come via Dien Bien Phu.

If the ringleaders of the rebellion were Chinese from Sip Song Panna, the rest were drawn from local Chinese residents in northern Laos, Sonla and Hoa Binh (AOM Aix E12 "General Report", Tranh Ninh, 3rd tri 1914). At the time of the attack on Sonla the rebel forces had been swollen from the original group of thirty Chinese and forty Kha and Phuthai to include 200 Chinese and 600-700 Lao and Kha mine coolies (AOM Paris Indochine A 50 NF (28) 3 "official telegram", Lai Chau, 29 December 1914). These were joined by Black Tai elements from Muong Het in the Black River region, otherwise referred to by the French as the "dregs of the population". Other Tai supporting the rebel cause were from the clientele of local functionaries whose positions had been revoked by the French for misdemeanors (AOM Paris Indochine A50 NF (28) 3 "Governor General of Indochina to the Minister of Colonies", 5 February 1915).

The chief of the rebel band went by the name of Leang San or Liang Tou Tou, in emulation of the Chinese military "governor" of the region during the Ho (Black Flag) invasion in the late nineteenth century.[1] Indeed, by assuming the name of special commander he attempted to pass himself off as King of the Ho. Allowing no allusions as to the intent or permanency of the rebellion, the rebels posted the following proclamation at the occupied post at Sam Neua:

> We Leang Tou Tou,
>
> In execution of the orders of the chief superior, Li Yuen Hong, we have seized the *poste* of Sam Neua to render good will to all. Everyone continue to cultivate your land and remain peaceful. It will be necessary to unite and obey orders received.
>
> (AOM Paris Indochine A50 NF (28) 3 "Governor General of Indochina to the Minister of Colonies", 5 February 1915).

Neither was the anti-French dimension of the rebellion ignored:

> The French army which is at Muong Boun Nua is encircled, it seeks to rescue itself but is unable.
>
> 1. If this army requests any provisions, porters or coolies, refuse to offer any services.
>
> 2. Any infraction of this order will lead to the death penalty for the guilty.
>
> 3. The French army in Muong Boun Nua will be destroyed blow by blow.
>
> 4. All the soothsayers have predicted the annihilation of the French people. Even Paris has been crushed by the German army. It is no use counting on France. Drive out the French and the country will commence a happy and prosperous era and will enjoy entire religious freedom.
>
> Authorities receiving this proclamation, make it known to all inhabitants.

Ambiguously dated the twenty-eighth day of the second month of the Chinese era, 2615, the proclamation was signed by the military chiefs, Xing Tchai and Xing Liani in the name of the newly proclaimed country of "Phu Nan Khui" (AOM Aix Q1 "Situation Politique du Laos", 4th tri 1914, "Report to the Governor General", Vientiane, 11 January 1915).

Having eliminated the French from Sam Neua the Chinese rebels sought to restructure the local administration. All in all, eight *chaomuong* were to be nominated from among those Lao *tasseng* who had joined the rebel cause. The Chinese chief pledged double salaries for all, and a generous *pia* (measure) of opium a day for the coolies. Twenty coolies conscripted from each *tasseng* were to be employed to construct a redoubt headquarters for the rebel administration at Sam Neua. In an evident departure from past administrative practice in the province, the Chinese chief paid for everything he requisitioned. (AOM Aix E12, Tran Ninh, Barthelemy, 4th tri 1914). While in fact several new *chaomuong* were nominated and installed in office on double salary, the majority of the Lao *Tasseng* remained pro-French, as did the Hmong of the province (AOM Aix Q1 "Extract from the report of the Résident Supérieur", 15 January 1915).

Following suppression of this short-lived rebellion, a War Council was convoked with a view to the restoration of the status quo ante. Six of the guilty (or at least six scapegoats) were summarily executed. These included Ba Phom, the former Lao *chaomuong* of Xieng Kho, Khamphan Ken, a Lao guilty of assassinating a French missionary and the Chinese rebels, Hy Vo Ky and Ba La. Witnessed by the mandarins and the local population, the executions were reported by the local French observer to have had a very "salutary" effect upon the population, especially the execution of Ba Phom who had held very high office for eighteen years and who was well known locally (AOM Aix Q1 "Extract from the report of Drouot, Administrator Commissioner of the Government at Sam Neua", 2 April, 1915).

The major repercussion, however, was the reorganization of the territory between the Black River and the Upper Mekong bordering Yunnan as military regions (Military Region Five in Laos and Military Region Four in Tonkin). Simultaneously, a state of siege was proclaimed in the regions. According to the Governor General, this drastic measure was justified by the continued threat posed to the French order by the Chinese rebels. In June 1915, between 1000 and 3000 rebels, 500 of whom were well armed, were still holding out at Muong Hou in upper Laos, where they were being resupplied from China, but only the Yao population of the region was reported as susceptible to rebel influence. (SHM. 10 H 73 "Etat Major de l'Armée de Terre" and AOM Paris Indochine A50 NF (28) 3 "Note pour la Presse" nd.). On the diplomatic level, although various approaches were made to the Chinese government in Yunnan, the Governor General did not consider intercession with Peking to be warranted. (AOM Paris Indochine A50 NF 28 (3) "Governor General to the Minister of Colonies", 31 May 1915).

Should, then, this rebellion be viewed as a political movement? According to the Governor General, not at all. In his view it was simply the work of opium smugglers out for "vengeance and death". According to this reasoning, Lambert had brought vengeance down upon his own head because he went about the suppression of opium smuggling with a degree of zealousness unmatched by his predecessors. That he made enemies among the local Chinese, the leading smugglers in northern Laos, was undeniable, but why did other ethnic groups and strata join in the revolt? The entire Muong population of the hill country of Than Hoa and Hoa Binh were seen as inveterate opium smokers — women included — and averse to paying an elevated price for opium sold by the *Régie*. The opium heisted by the rebels at Sam Neua included opium confiscated from smugglers. Indeed the post was attacked the night before the collection of taxes was to have been efficiently accomplished. This manifest act of "banditry", according to the Governor General, was largely a result of retribution sought by Ba Phom, the Lao functionary whose position was revoked in June 1913 and who had been fined 800 piasters by the *Douanes et Régie*. It was then that he made common cause with the Chinese and was himself responsible for rallying the Tai, the "wretched auxiliaries of the bandits". Following this argument, all the proclamations, discourses, letters and demonstrations of Leang San, the Chinese rebel chief, were just "boasting and parody" (AOM Paris

Indochine A50 NF 28 (3) and see AOM Aix Q1 "Extract from the Report of the Résident Supérieur of 27 November 1914).

Still, there is evidence of a far more careful preparation for the revolt than is suggested by a single-minded action of bandits. Although ignored by the unfortunate Lambert, a rebellion by the Chinese in northern Laos had already been brewing for some four or five months. This involved rudimentary military training of rebel units. Unlike the Lao, most Chinese in Laos were literate and were ardent readers of newspapers from their homeland. Au courant with events surrounding the 1911 revolution, the resident Chinese in Laos were able to influence the local population in many ways. Leang San reportedly even told the *Chaomuong* of Sam Neua that he was sent by the President of the Chinese Republic to conquer Annam. Indeed, after the initial *coup de force* at Sam Neua, the rebels were sufficiently well organized to sound out the entire Chinese population residing in the territory between Sam Neua and the Black River as to joining in a general uprising against the French administration (AOM Paris Indochine A50 (28) 3 "Governor General of Indochina to the Minister of Colonies, 5 February 1915).

Nor should we overlook the historical antecedents of the revolt which might also be described as a localized manifestation of Chinese republicanism fueled by a lingering memory on the part of the Chinese population of the Black Flag revolts, which swept northern Indochina in the late nineteenth century (cf. Marr 1971:46-47). By the Treaty of T'ien Tsin of June 1884, Peking had abrogated to France all rights of suzerainty in Tonkin. Local Yunnanese mandarins, Chinese troops and bandits living semi-permanently in the Black River region had never recognised this treaty, however, nor was the government in Peking — Imperial or Republican — inclined to discipline them. They lived off the local population like locusts and, on the occasion of the sacking of Luang Prabang, the Hos joined forces with troops of Deo Van Tri. Lartéguy and Yang Dao observe that while certain Hmong joined the Black Flags on this occasion, the majority fought against them to secure their independence (Lartéguy and Yang Dao 1979:86). On the other hand, by withholding support for Leang San's movement, the Hmong probably ensured its ephemeral existence.[2]

Overall, numerous Chinese residents in Vietnam rallied to Sun Yat Sen's Tung Meng Hui society and welcomed the republican leader during his visits to Vietnam in the early 1900s. Sun saw in Tonkin a safe-base from which to launch anti-Ch'ing rebellion into Kuangsi and Yunnan. But with the failure of one such rebellion in 1908, Sun was deported from Indochina by the French either at the request of or in complicity with the Chinese government. One official Ch'ing memo of the time described Sun Yat Sen as a "head of a band of robbers which had been committing depradations and disturbing the public peace in Kwangsi on the borders of Annam..." (PRO Colonial Office 273 343, "Waiwupu to his Majesty's Minister", Peking, 30 January 1908). While we have no evidence that the Tung Meng Hui took root in Laos, it would not be too fanciful to draw the inference that bolder elements among his former subordinates took matters in hand to strike a blow for northern Lao and Vietnamese independence, albeit on Chinese terms.

A probable sequel to the rebellion occurred in April 1932, when a band of 300 Yunnanese "pirates" armed with 150 weapons rallied in the Taland region with the intention of attacking Muong Le. The colonial authorities surmised that this band was in league with elements of the *Garde Indigène* who had turned their guns against the French during December of the previous year. Not usually given to cooperation, the Chinese authorities in tandem with the French suppressed the rebellion. Its origins were believed to lie in the failure of the crop, more particularly because young plants were destroyed by the rains (AOM Paris A2 NF 328 2649 "Les Rapports Politiques Mensueles", April 1932, May 1933).

Conventional histories of the Black Flags (cf. McAleavy 1968) have tended to emphasize the destructiveness of their military campaigns and their ideology of "anarchy". Accordingly, their pioneering struggles against French colonialism in Indochina have scarcely merited serious consideration from Lao or Vietnamese historians. Yet, the attempt of Leang San and his army to liquidate the French Opium *Régie* and the colonial tax system in northern Laos figured as a major prelude to armed mass revolutionary insurrection on the part of the population of this region some decades later.

THE POLITICAL ECONOMY OF HMONG PEASANT REBELLION

> Nous deux, nous nous aimons, nous voulons vous marier,
> mais nos parents ne le veulent pas,
> Je veux mourir je penserai à vous,
> A l'endroit ou je serai enterré,
> il sortira de mes siens une plante
> Cette plante portera des fleurs puis les fruits
> Si vous coupez ces fruits il en sortira une séve.
> Vous la preparerez, puis vous la fumerez.
> En fumant, vous vous consolerez de ma mort.
>
> ("Legende du Pavot, Pays Kha Kho, Extrait de l'étude du Chef de Batallion Roux", AOM Aix Q2)

The Hmong or "free" (Meo), along with the Yao, Ho, Mouseu and Lanten are known in Laos by the generic label of *Lao Soung* and currently comprise about five percent of the population. Migrating south from China, they first settled in the provinces of northern Laos from the beginning of the nineteenth century (Yang Dao 1975:7). The Hmong scholar, Gary Yia Lee, records that the first Hmong migrants to arrive in Nong Het were Green Hmong, followed by two groups of White Hmong (Lee 1987:216-7). The first Hmong (Meo Khao and Meo Lai) to settle in Muong Khamkeut in the southern province of Cammon only arrived by way of Tran Ninh and Sip Song Chau Tai in 1890-91 (AOM Aix Ell, 11 March 1907). An elderly Hmong village chief in Xieng Khouang related to the author in 1974 that he had a very clear memory of the migration of his clan from southern China into Vietnam before settling in Laos. Concentrated principally in Phong Saly, Xieng Khouang, Sam Neua, Luang Prabang and Vientiane, the Hmong in Laos belong in the main to the White Hmong group. Differentiated from them only by the color of women's clothing and dialect, the Black Hmong, Yellow Hmong, Red Hmong and Green Hmong are clustered across the border in Vietnam.

Taillard contrasts the heterogeneity and instability of the Hmong village with the cohesion and stability of the Lao village. The Hmong space of reference, he notes, is on the one hand compartmentalized because of geography and on the other hand mobile because of migration patterns, as demonstrated by the revolts of 1919-21. Drawing upon the research of Lemoine (1972) and Yang Dao (1975), Taillard describes the Hmong as responding to a "lineage power". The individual, he contends, relates to Hmong society in three ways, as a member of a clan, a lineage group and a household. The latter comprises one or two conjugal families forming a patrilocal residence group and a patrilineal descendance. This, Taillard notes, is the most stable group in Hmong society and the socio-economic unit which is maintained in spite of migrations (Taillard 1977:47). Yang Dao defines the Hmong family as persons of the same ancestor living together as much as possible and forming a real community of interests; that is to say ten to twenty people living under one pater familias (Yang Dao 1975:41). The clan, on the other hand, is an extension of the patrilineal group on the level of ethnic group and creating a "diffuse" fraternity (Taillard 1977:47). Yang Dao lists twenty-one "paternal" and consanguineous Hmong clans existing in Laos (Yang Dao 1975:43). According to Taillard, it is at the lineage level that one finds a solidarity and community of interest between members of groups claiming a common ancestor. This involves strict bonding between close relatives across three generations (Taillard 1977:47).

The Hmong village is thus a juxtaposition of lineage groups attaching themselves to different lineages. According to Taillard, one consequence of this social organization is the coexistence of two modes of the functioning of power. One follows the patriarchal and authoritarian model and the other is collectively exercised, although with a chief nominated to deal with the outside world. At the level of the lineage then, the authoritarian mode prevails. This is also the case with the clan, but as space is enlarged perceptions of common interest become more and more vague. Taillard makes the important point that by naming a representative of the Ly clan as *Chaomuong* of the Hmong population of Xieng Khouang, the French administration ignored the anthropological reality that, insofar as Hmong ethnic consciousness existed, it could only be exercised by different clan chiefs (Taillard 1977:48).

In common with other minorities in northern Laos, the Hmong typically subsisted in a primitive-communal mode of production in a tributary relationship to Yunnanese, Tai and/or Lao overlords. But unlike other minorities, the Hmong were more fully drawn into commodity networks. As will be shown, as producers of poppy the Hmong were fitted out by colonial capitalism as agro-commodity producers par excellence.

Citing the study by Yang Dao, Lee notes that by the time Laos became a protectorate in 1893, the system of Hmong paying taxes to lowland Lao had been well established. Besides a mandatory tax of two silver coins per household, *Kiatong*, *Xophia* or *Photong* — those Hmong chiefs entitled by the Lao mandarins — were also obliged to pay occasional tributes such as elephant tusks, rhino horns, deer meat, not to mention opium (Yang Dao 1975:45 cited in Lee 1987:219). But, Lee continues, with the imposition of French rule, many Hmong found themselves paying a double tax, the traditional tax now collected by the French appointed tax collectors, and an additional tax imposed by local Lao mandarins and their agents otherwise deprived of their traditional source of income from the highlanders. Various instances of conflict between the Hmong and the tax collectors, however, led the Hmong leadership to prefer Western allies (French or American) instead of Lao. Lee argues that this matter was proven by the Batchai (Hmong) revolt against the French from 1918 to 1921 which served to strengthen the bond between pro-French Hmong leaders and their colonial masters (Lee 1985:219-220). But, as shown below, the contrary was also the case of certain Hmong, victims of the double tax system, the opium monopoly and other outsider manipulations.

BATCHAI'S REBELLION (1918-1921)

Batchai's rebellion, which spanned north-west Tonkin as well as northern Laos, should be viewed, as a colonial report on the affair indicates, with reference to three interrelated aspects, firstly, the repercussions of events in China, secondly, the excesses of the Tai mandarins belonging to the family of Deo Van Tri in their dealings with the Hmong, and, thirdly, the pressure applied by Hmong sorcerers and chiefs (Saint-Chaffray Report).[3] Indeed, it might be stated that no analysis of Hmong revolt which fails to take into consideration historical, ethno-political and religious factors would be complete.

From the outset, then, Hmong migrations into Tonkin and Laos had been triggered by the repression of Han Chinese mandarins. The Hmong (Miao), in China had a long history of revolt before their migration into Indochina. Two great Miao revolts occurred on the Kweichow, Hunan and Szechuan border regions in the 1730s and again from 1795-1806. In the face of vicious repression the Miao migrated south. In 1853, a Miao rebellion enlisted support of Muslim groups in Yunnan. The Miao, who had commenced their migrations into Tonkin during the early 1800s, carried their rebellion to the plains of Tonkin in 1860 before being repulsed by Vietnamese elephant brigades (Mottin 1980:32-43).

The original Hmong settlers in Xieng Khouang, however, accepted the tutelage of the Phouan (Lao) princes who ruled the region. It appears that the Phouan granted them local administrative rights where the immigrants had formed compact settlements. Thus Hmong *kaitong* (honorific corresponding to Lao *tasseng*) were "elected" and placed at the head of the great Hmong families in the Nong Het region. The Lo, Ly, Yang, Vang and Moua clans, for instance, were each ruled by their respective Kaitong, while lesser families were ruled by "*photong*", "*chong kone*" and "*xaophay*" (titles of lower standing than *kaitong*). In return for patronage by the *Phouan* lords, the Hmong obliged them by paying tribute. Negotiations following a first Hmong uprising in Laos during 1896 — for whatever reason — led the French authorities to approve the nomination of the Moua *Kaitong* as the first Hmong *tasseng* in Xieng Khouang appointed by the colonial regime (Yang Dao 1975:45-48).

The next major recorded revolt of the Hmong occurred in 1918 in Muong La and Van Pen Tou. The catalyst of this revolt was the arrest by Yunnanese mandarins of a Hmong sorcerer and the subsequent arrest of his followers who tried to obtain his release. In retaliation, on 31 January 1918, Hmong armed with primitive rifles attacked Muong Tinh, killed the mandarins and burnt the town. With their morale and power reinforced by the capture of some modern rifles, the Hmong declared themselves "independent". One band then headed for Muong La and another to Doung Xiang, attacking it on 8 February 1918. For the rest of the month armed conflict raged between Chinese regulars, Tai partisans armed by the mandarins and the Hmong of this border region. What began as an anti-Chinese revolt had taken on an anti-Tai dimension as well. At the end of February, the Hmong were repulsed from Na Phat and Muong La by armed reinforcements. The repression of the Hmong by both the Chinese and Tai mandarins was "cruel and violent". Summary executions provoked a minor exodus of women, children and the elderly to Tonkin. While the Hmong of Tonkin had only participated in the rebellion on an individual basis, they accepted the refugees into their ranks (Saint-Chaffray Report).

News of the repression quickly travelled to the Hmong of Laokay, Lai Chau, Sonla and Yen Bay. Within months came the first signs of rebellion among the Hmong of Tonkin in the region neighboring Muong La, then Lai Chau and finally Sonla. By June 1918, the Hmong of Quynh Nhai, Lai Chau and Thuah (Sonla) were on the point of rebellion. In the Dien Bien Phu region, the rebels were energetically repressed by the local Tai mandarins. In Quynh Nhai, however, sorcerers and other "agitators" found fertile ground (Saint-Chauffay Report). It would not be the first time that a Hmong sorcerer appeared at a moment of crisis. Indeed, it might be hypothesized that typically sorcerers appeared to the Hmong at a moment of crisis, rather than the obverse, that the crisis occurred after the appearance of a sorcerer.

Rules set down by the French relating to tax collection inhibited although did not prevent the Tai mandarins from collecting illicit profits, not acknowledged as contributions to the budget but as personal tribute. The crop growing and cattle raising Hmong who populated the heights of the mountains in various localities, were the most obvious and proximate victims, although the Yao and other minorities did not escape the clutches of the Tai tax collectors. Relative to these minorities, Tai peasants paid only a small amount of tribute to their lords (Saint-Chaffray Report). According to the testimony of Tcha Pao, a Hmong rebel leader, the Tai or Hmong tax collectors sheltered behind the French administration. After harvest time, each adult Hmong had to remit to the Tai collectors, five Indochinese piasters or 200 grams of opium, two or three times that required by the French. Sanctions for non-compliance were severe (Lartéguy and Yang Dao 1979:97).

Thus while the Hmong rebellion of Quynh Nhai appeared to be attributable to the events that transpired in China and to the exactions committed by the Tai mandarins of Lai Chau, there was also a messianic element involved. This was confirmed on 11 June when the word was spread that a king had appeared, calling upon the Hmong to abandon their rice fields and to join with he who had the power to provide rice. Several Hmong families left for Quynh Nhai. Towards the end of June, a Hmong woman given to hysterics was proclaimed queen by her followers. She received adepts and homage from the local Hmong clan. The incident had further repercussions at Quynh Ninh and on the plateau of Ta Rhing. In spite of the messianic element, however, the rebellion was believed to have an underlying political dimension (Saint-Chaffray Report).

The French authorities promised the Hmong of Quynh Nhai that they would examine their grievances against the Tai notables if they returned to their abandoned fields. However, three promoters of the movement, including the Hmong chief and a sorcerer, were arrested and taken to Lai Chau. The Hmong stated that at "no price" would they continue to subordinate themselves to the Tai authorities and in particular to Deo Van Khang, the eldest son of Deo Van Tri, who had replaced his father upon his death as feudal overlord of the Tai. Rather, they wanted direct access to the French administration in order to escape from the "extortions on life and property" imposed by the Tai. Perceiving that the Hmong were to be removed from their authority and that they would lose their windfall profits, the Deo did everything possible to counteract these propositions and to prevent the implementation of a new code of inter-ethnic relations. On 15 August the Hmong complained of a raid by armed Tai, led by Deo Van Khang, in the valley of Nam Lai (Saint-Chaffray Report).

On 30 October, a group of Hmong from Dien Bien Phu rose in revolt. They threatened communication lines between Sonla and Lai Chau, repulsed a French patrol and burnt the village of Muong Phang. Led by a certain Batchai, 300 of them looted and burnt hamlets in the precincts of Dien Bien Phu. A dozen Tai were killed and the *tirailleurs* were summoned from Yen Bay. In spite of negotiations with local French officials, Batchai revealed himself as beyond redemption. On 5 December, the Delegate of Dien Bien Phu who went to continue the discussions with Batchai was killed in an ambush by partisans of the latter (Saint-Chaffray Report).

Described by the French administration as an "epileptic" and a "sorcerer", Batchai was originally from the Dien Bien Phu region. Although his family had been imprisoned during the course of the Hmong uprisings in Tonkin, Batchai had been released. At this juncture he declared himself a *Chaofa* or messiah in line with a widely held Hmong belief in a returning Hmong king or saviour. Gathering followers and attacking the French, Batchai was then driven by the military out of Tonkin and into Laos (Angeli Report). His overall pretension, however, was to bring peace and prosperity to the Hmong and to establish a "great royal, independent kingdom" of the Hmong (see Lartéguy and Yang Dao 1979:99).

With the intervention of the military, Batchai's revolt could no longer be construed as solely an anti-mandarinal affair. After rebel activity was reported among the Hmong of Long He (Chau of Thuan) bordering Dien Bien Phu, the French entered the rebellion on the side of repression. Batchai was attacked in the fortified village of Ban Nam Nghan on 12 October by the *tirailleurs*. While his group suffered heavy losses, Batchai himself managed to escape in the direction of Sonla, where he took refuge with Hmong rebels in the Chau of Thuan. On 27 December, several Tai villages were attacked by another Hmong chief, the so-called King Camxu of Long He. Although the revolt was not general in the Chau of Thuan, the rebels succeeded in terrorizing the population. While Camxu was deserted by his partisans following a fierce exchange with the *tirailleurs* in his mountain redoubt, Batchai's band of fifty went from strength to strength before retreating into Laos (Saint-Chaffray Report).

Although Hmong groups from Muong Sai and Muong Ngoi deserted their villages to join the rebels in Dien Bien Phu, the first groups in Laos to be influenced by the rumor of events in Tonkin were the Yao. In early 1919, the Yao made it known to certain Lao that within a year or two, a messiah would appear who would lead them to happier regions. They would thus leave behind for the Lao their crops, flocks and houses (AOM Aix E16 1st tri 1919).

Throughout the following year, Batchai managed to extend his revolt over a triangular section of territory covering 40,000 square kilometers. With Dien Bien Phu as the apex of the triangle, its base was an east-west line located 150 kilometers north of Vientiane, the west side of the triangle was the valley of the Nam Ou and the east side was Sam Neua Cua Rau. Repelled by the military from Xieng Khouang and Hua Phan, Batchai consolidated his position in the Phou Chom Chick Phou Chom Chang region, where he constructed his citadel in Phoi Loi, north of Muong Hiem. Seen as a "natural" fortress by the French military, Batchai's redoubt was located at 1000 meters altitude in an area where visibility was reduced to several meters by thick forest, and where the terrain clearly favored the guerrilla. One of the largest military expeditions in colonial Indochina up until that time — and certainly the largest yet assembled in Laos — was mounted to break Batchai's rebellion; four companies of *tirailleurs* were brought in from other parts of Indochina to restore order (AOM Aix E16 1st tri 1919 and Dorey Report) (see Map IV).

The White and Black Hmong of this region were very recent arrivals, all the adults having spent their childhood in China. The deeper valleys of the periphery were peopled by Black Tai in the north and Lao in the south. At around 500 to 800 meters altitude lived the Kha "shamelessly exploited" by both the Tai and Hmong for coolie service. Making common cause with the Hmong against the French were the Yao, also known as Xa and Man but more dispersed and demographically weaker than the other ethnic groups (Dorey Report).

As far as the rebels were concerned, the local population were either for the rebellion or they were against it. In the latter case, villages were burnt and the inhabitants massacred or led off into captivity. In these circumstances it was not surprising that nearly all the villages in the rebel zone joined the cause. The clan and lineage structure of Hmong society made it imperative that Batchai win over the Hmong chiefs if his rebellion was to succeed. We know little of Batchai's political program except that it was both anti-Lao (or Tai) and anti-French. Although the Hmong are not generally literate, Batchai actually disseminated propaganda tracts some of which were believed to have fallen from heaven (see Alleton 1981:33). Batchai's success in extending his rebellion so rapidly into Laos was attributed by the French to the assistance rendered by a relative, the *Soung Quan* (a Hmong title) of Hoei Thong. Likewise the *Soung Quan* of Phou Gni and the *Soung Quan* of Houei Thong joined with Batchai and his *chef de guerre*, the *Soung Quan* of Lao Vang. Notable Hmong dissenters from Batchai's cause, however, were the *Phya* Sai Hmong and *Soung Quan* Lao Meng, chiefs from the periphery of the rebel zone (AOM Aix E16 Luang Prabang 4th tri 1919).

All the Kha villages in the rebel zone either capitulated or fled in the face of rebel attack. Those who remained were reduced to slavery. While Kha women were "guarded" in their villages by Hmong warriors, the men were conscripted as coolies, either to construct defensive structures or to serve as emissaries. Rumour of impending Hmong attack served to make most Lao evacuate their villages and flee ahead of the marauding bands. Those Lao on the western perimeter of the rebel zone fled to the other side of the Nam Ou where they re-established their gardens while those Lao of the high valleys of the Nam Soung and the Nam Seng were reduced to refugees and forced to forage for food in the forest following the burning of their houses and the robbing of their harvests and cattle (AOM Aix E16 Luang Prabang 4th tri 1919).

While some of the French experts thought that only the capture of Batchai would permit the revolt to be neutralized, others surmised that even then a new sorcerer or *phu mi boun* would appear to take his place. As it happened, one emulator of Batchai sought to pass himself off as a *Chaofa*. This person went from village to village announcing that he had received a mission from heaven to deliver his compatriots from the Tai domination and that a king would come to place himself at the head of the mountain peoples. Just as his propaganda was beginning to attract followers, he was arrested by the authorities in Tran Ninh (AOM Aix E16 2nd tri 1919).

Despite Batchai's wearing guerrilla tactics and command over the mountain peaks, his movement began to fragment in the face of the French repression. Alleton describes internal dissensions between Hmong clans as a major contributing factor in Batchai's isolation. By the time of his death, practically all the Hmong had made their submission and even began to pay taxes again (Alleton 1981:36). Batchai was killed by pro-French Kha on 17 November 1922 in the Muong Ngai region in Luang

Prabang. At that point his first lieutenant Phya Chan capitulated and swore his loyalty to king and country by praying at a pagoda. Following the capture of Lao Sing, another of Batchai's lieutenants, the "pacification" of the region was seen as practically terminated and the withdrawal of occupation forces was then envisaged (AOM Aix E17 "Report to the Governor General", Vientiane 10 January 1923).

That the revolt did not take on a more general and permanent character could be attributed to the fact that not all the Hmong joined in. Clearly Batchai was unable to convince or intimidate all Hmong chiefs into believing that he was the "true" *Chaofa*. Others may have had a better estimation of French military capabilities or a different estimation of French rule. For instance, although the Hmong of Muong Sai and Hongsa were worked over by Batchai's propagandists, they proved unwilling participants in the revolt. According to information supplied by Phya Sai, a pro-French Hmong chief, the *Soung Quan* Song was a reluctant participant in the rebellion. His village had been occupied by Batchai's White Hmong guerrillas as a reprisal for not supplying conscripts to the rebels (AOM Aix E17 4th tri 1919). Supply was also a major problem for both the rebels and their adversaries although the French eventually had the capacity to cut the major trails into Batchai's redoubt. Stricken by shortages on Phoi Loi, the rebels had to be supplied by caravan from their clansmen in Dien Bien Phu (AOM Aix E17 2nd tri 1920).

Causes of the revolt

While not ignoring the political motive of the Hmong rebellion, notably the widely observed proclivity of the Hmong to seek autonomy, Savina echoes many colonial observers by giving credence to the irrational elements of Batchai's revolt or the "revolt of the mad" as it became known. With equanimity, however, he concludes that in Hmong political cosmography, religion is used as a weapon to win political freedom (Savina 1930:259). Indeed, Hmong shamanism has been the subject of one major study (see Morechand 1955 passim). According to Savina, the Hmong are waiting for a liberator or a king (*phoa thay*) — just as the Jews are waiting for a messiah. What we call revolt, he continues, they call *oa phoa thay* or king-making. It is by the shamans that a Hmong "sorcerer" is named and empowered. The shamans are the source of prayers-magic and such paraphernalia as amulets to ensure vulnerability against an enemy (Savina 1930:259).

While the actual extension of the revolt into Laos was clearly the work of Batchai, the "sorcerer", as one colonial observer remarked during the course of the revolt:

> ....it is essential to know whether the seed sown by Batchai will fall on ground prepared to receive it and favorable to its germination and development.

He continued:

> We have been twenty five years in the Meo country and we don't know a word of their language, we are unable to have interpreters, nor (Meo) schools, military (conscripts) or administrators.... no study of the Meo exists.... The Meo say, we do not see you.

The same official advocated a policy of greater contact with the Hmong as well as an attempt to understand them. The suppression of Tai and Lao trading intermediaries was viewed as the *sine qua non* of any attempt to remove abuses (Angeli Report).

On a similar theme, the administrator de Barthelemy observed, the process of centralization of administration in Laos pursued under the colonial order, merely reinforced the subordination of the non-Lao peoples to the dominant Lao:

> Laos seems to be administratively organized as if it was inhabited only by the Lao. The regulations were Lao, the mandarins were equally Lao and the Provincial Council — embryo of the future Consultative Chamber — never included a representative of the mountain races.... Unconsciously we have, through this spirit of centralization, created an aristocracy of peoples, but what unconscious misery for the races of second rank, who can only approach us with difficulty.
>
> (de Barthelemy nd:139-40).

Another administrator, Roux, put the blame at the feet of local Lao chiefs — "very lazy, very rapacious" — who treated the Hmong as "milch cows". If the warrior spirit of the Hmong sometimes welled up, he contended, then it was for very good reasons notably crushing taxes, illegal requisitions and opium (quoted in Lartéguy and Yang Dao 1979:94).

Contrary to Alleton's assertion, abuse of the opium trade was not a major cause of Batchai's revolt, at least not in the way of the Chinese rebellion of 1914 in northern Laos (cf.Alleton 1981:38-41). That was not to say that the last of the Black Flag bands which had terrorized northern Indochina at various times over the past half century were entirely uninterested in profiting from Batchai's rebellion. Firstly, the Yunnanese Chinese sought to take advantage of the turmoil in northern Laos and the Fourth Military Region in Tonkin to purchase low price opium. Secondly, the Yunnanese caravaners entered Laos with the intention of selling guns and cannons to the insurgent Hmong. At Muong Sen, 150-200

Chinese smugglers living in close contact with the Hmong were taken as common enemies of the French, all the more so as the former displayed German military pictures (Dorey Report).

As a sequel to the revolt, rebel chiefs were summarily executed by the authorities, and their lieutenants made to pay compensation to the victims of their rampage. In defence, the Hmong responded that they "were mad and possessed by the devil" and, by inference, not responsible for their actions. If there was an irrational motive for the revolt, the French did not accept a prima facie case for the diminution of culpability. Observing that the Hmong had great reserves of money and were blessed with a good opium harvest, the French established a committee for each *muong* comprising three Hmong, three Lao and one Vietnamese to determine the collective guilt of each Hmong clan and the amount of compensation to be paid (AOM Aix F6 "telegram from Vientiane" 2nd bureau, 26 August 1920). Suggested criteria for indemnity were set at fifty piasters for every Lao or Vietnamese killed, not including compensation for loss of houses, cattle and crops (AOM Aix F6, "telegram", 11 February 1920). Acting as government agents, the Banque de l'Indochine collected a total of 375 kilograms of silver from the Hmong, worth, however, only 7000 piasters due to the dubious quality of silver (AOM Aix F6 "Governor to Director of Finances", Hanoi, Vientiane, 26 August 1920).[4]

In order to preempt a recurrence of Batchai's rebellion, the French commissioned an enquiry to ascertain the abuses to which the Hmong were subject and set forth guiding principles for a more equitable Hmong administration. This task befell the French Catholic missionary and Hmong specialist, Father Savina. Duly drawn up and with the best intentions, the statute proclaimed that the Hmong should not be subordinate to any other races in the administrative hierarchy, but like Lao or Vietnamese would administer themselves, "under the surveillance of the government of the Protectorate". To this end a census was to be taken of the Hmong by tribe and habitat. A new territorial delineation of the cantons and communes was to be drawn up "with care and precision". All of the Hmong of Tonkin and Laos were to be invited to "freely" elect their own tribal chiefs, one each per province, per military territory, per canton and a mayor for each commune. Elections were to take place, not in the main towns, but in villages under the guidance of an official and according to majority vote. Taxes were to be requited to the French administration "in the presence of all the chiefs of the canton and all the assembled mayors". Subject to French approval, Hmong customary law was to be binding upon them. For the first time under the French administration, Hmong chiefs would be authorized to adjudicate intra-Hmong disputes, although fines were to be paid to the French authorities. Contrariwise, Hmong chiefs would be responsible to those they administered and were to furnish yearly political reports on their *muong* (Savina 1924:np).

Some five years after Batchai's revolt was crushed, the Hmong tribes of Luang Prabang, Tran Ninh and Sam Neua were reportedly "peaceful" and in excellent *ésprit de corps*. This felicitous state of affairs was attributed to the implementation of new administrative measures including the constitution of autonomous Hmong groups under elected chiefs, directly responsible to French Commissioners (AOM Aix D6, "Rapport au Conseil de Gouvernment", 1926). But because of past grievances as well as continuing clan conflict, Hmong discontent was always simmering and barely constrained throughout the entire colonial period.

HMONG CLAN RIVALRY AND OPIUM TAX POLICIES (1931-1937)

McCoy has argued that by choosing Touby Lyfoung as opium broker in Xieng Khouang province and Deo Van Long for the Tai country, the French made political commitments with unforseen consequences for the future of their colonial rule. Specifically, the refusal by the French to recognize the hereditary rights of Touby's rival clansmen, Faydang Lobliyao (later a vice-president in the future communist government) served to drive the latter into an alliance with the former's enemies (McCoy 1972:78-85). While both men are White Hmong and, indeed, related by marriage, it has also been said that "whatever Touby's people do, Faydang's do opposite" (Barney 1967:275).

The most important Hmong political center in Laos during this period was the Nong Het region of Xieng Khouang contiguous with Son La in Vietnam. The two most prominent clans in the Nong Het region, since their migration from southern China in the late nineteenth century, were the Lobliyao and the Lyfoung (McCoy 1972:80 and Lee 1982:191-219). Not having joined in Batchai's revolt, the French had entrusted Lobliyao with control of the district of Nong Het, reorganized as a *tasseng* in 1921. When a dispute broke out within the Ly clan the French divided the district into two, naming Song Tou, son of Lobliyao, as head of the district of Keng Khui and Touby Lyfoung's eldest brother as head of Phac Boun. Song Tou, however, turned out to be an "incapable" chief, meaning that he did not faithfully deliver his taxes to the French (Mottin 1980:48).

Deep seated differences between the Lo and Li clans came to a head in late 1931. On 30 October, the French *Résident* in Tran Ninh visited the village of Phaklack in Nong Het, mountain fief of *Caitong* Lobliyao, with a view to adjudicating a dispute between the latter and Lyfoung. Accused of not paying the salaries of his Hmong coolies, he was taken to court.

Even though Lobliyao was Lyfong's ex son-in-law, they were widely observed to have nourished mutual sentiments of "implacable hatred" (AOM Aix E22 Tran Ninh, 4th tri 1931 and see Lartéguy and Yang Dao 1979:98). While the rift between the two clan leaders was in no way healed by the court proceedings, at least the pair had foresworn setting their partisans against each other.

Not unrelated to the Hmong clan conflict question was the matter of direct representation of the Hmong to the French administration. Ever since Batchai's revolt, the French had promised to allow the Hmong direct representation, yet some ten years later the Hmong were still beholden to the Lao intermediaries and the mandarins. As a way of defusing barely contained Hmong discontent over this issue, the *Résident* in Tran Ninh requested the Hmong *Caitong* to assist in the debates at the next meeting of the *Conseil Consultative Indigène.* Not permitted to become a full member of the *Conseil*, the *Caitong* was still to be invested with a consultative capacity in order to "illuminate" members on questions concerning the Hmong of the region (AOM Aix E22 Tranninh 4th tri 1932).[5]

If there was any lingering doubt as to the loyalty of the Hmong to the administration, then it was confirmed negatively in January 1933. On that date, at an assembly of the various Hmong *tasseng* of Muong Khoune, the *Caitong* Lobliyao urged them not to deliver their opium to the *Régie.* Sentiments between the French and the *Caitong* Lobliyao were evidently reciprocal. The rapporteur of the affair held that the illogicality of such an action could only be explained by his opium and alcohol addiction. Neither was his death in 1935 lamented by the French. It was estimated that the presence of the *Caitong* at Nong Het at any time required a permanent garrison of *Garde Indigène* and a detachment of militia (AOM Aix E23 Tranninh, 2nd 1935), the implication being that revolt would break out if the French presence was removed from the region.

Upon the death of his father, Song Tou was replaced as district chief by Touby Lyfoung's father, a more reliable conduit for the collection of taxes. Thus the entire district passed from the hands of the Lo clan to the Ly (Mottin 1980:48). With the death of the old *Caitong*, his considerable fortune in gold, silver, opium and cattle was fiercely disputed. One of the disputants was Faydang (Lartéguy and Yang Dao 1979:103). Faydang, younger brother of Song Tou, resented this loss of prestige very deeply. He had expected at least that he would be able to take up the administration of Keng Khuai, but when the elder Lyfoung died, it was the ardently pro-French Touby who succeeded him (Mottin 1980:48). According to Lee, Faydang had previously appealed unsuccessfully to the Chaomuong of Muong Kham as well as to the French commissioner in Xieng Khouang (Lee 1982:200). He had also petitioned Phetsarath in Luang Prabang, the act of which was interpreted by the French as insubordination. Henceforth, the French were unwilling to entrust Faydang with any authority in the region. In turn, when Phetsarath eventually fled Laos in 1946, he left Faydang behind as his representative among the Hmong (McCoy 1972:82-83).

Opium Apart from the well documented evidence of Hmong clan rivalry, a fundamental crisis beset the Hmong peasant cultivator; this was expressed by the contradiction engendered between the demands of the State opium procurement system and economic hardship. In the Hmong peasant economy, the opium and tax questions were inter-related. A poor opium harvest meant an inability to generate income to pay taxes or commute corvee demands in cash. The reverse was not always the case. A good opium harvest did not necessarily translate into rewards for the Hmong peasant farmer or good will on the part of the Hmong to the French. The real beneficiaries were the opium brokers. In good or bad seasons, the Hmong peasant still had to pay the grossly regressive personal tax and to supply corvee labor on demand.

One student of the Hmong, Westermeyer, sees opium as the ideal cash crop in the local "agroeconomy". Firstly, it is highly portable over rough mountain terrain. Secondly, it is grown at a time when rice and corn are not raised. Thirdly, poppy does not deplete the soil of its nutrients as rapidly as rice, corn or vegetables and, finally, unlike a number of other cash crop alternatives, poppy produces income in the first year it is produced. Within the Hmong economy, Westermeyer continues, opium is essential for the acquisition of two key metals, iron and silver. Iron is used for the manufacture of certain essential implements like hoe and axe heads, machetes and flintlocks. Silver is important to the Hmong as both a medium for adornment, status or for use as currency (Westermeyer 1982:44-5).

Touby, who himself was the only Hmong member of the Opium Purchasing Commission (McCoy 1972:83), has explained how this system of purchasing opium direct from the producer failed in a way which suggested untoward consequences.

> ...In each province the French set up buying offices where the opium was bought. But first they tried to deal direct with the producers, which didn't work out. They couldn't pay the producers until they knew the morphine content of their opium, and analyses took several weeks. The unfortunate growers were so poor they couldn't wait that long. So the French had to use middle-men who had some capital and were able to advance money. There were Vietnamese, Lao and a few Meo who had grown rich. These "brokers" paid for the crop in cash, making

> sure that there was a handsome margin between the price they paid the peasants and the price they received from the French authorities. They paid the growers in silver bullion from the Bank of Indo-China or else with goods of various kinds, costed on full price. So they made a double profit. They were the people who grew rich on opium for, believe me, the Meo were well and truly exploited! Some of those merchants would deliver up to a tonne and a half a time to a buying office, and they made a real packet.
>
> (Lamour and Lamberti 1974:117).

In the following pages we will show how this opium collection system worked in practice.

1931 was a year of a poor opium harvest and a marked increase in the sale price of opium; in June the price of raw opium increased from $36 to $40. The *Douanes et Régies* only offered $26 a kilogram and began their buying campaign too late to have much success. Responding to market forces, the Hmong had already sold their crop to Chinese and Vietnamese dealers who travelled right to their villages and bought up the reserves. Anticipating to purchase 300 kilograms for one purchasing expedition, the *Régie* collected only one hundred (AOM Aix E22 Tran Ninh, 2nd tri 1931). Stated another way, despite the penalties for abuse of the system, the Hmong only requited one third of their opium surplus to the State. Thus for the entire season the *Régie* collected 1400 kilograms at an average price of $29 a kilogram. This sale would have realized $40,000 for the 50,000 odd Hmong. It was observed, however, that after the *lam* took their share, the Hmong still had enough surplus to pay their taxes and to purchase horses, buffaloes and ploughs (AOM Aix E22 3rd tri 1931).

Rumors of revolt by the Hmong of the village of Samto were circulated during December 1932. The discontent of the inhabitants was attributed to a running dispute between the Hmong of that village and a Lao notable who otherwise exercised the functions of *Chaomuong* of Samto. Taking no chances, the French rushed brigades of *Garde Indigène* to the region. At the same time, the chiefs of the provinces of Xieng Khouang and Sam Neua were instructed to open an enquiry to determine the source of Hmong discontent. While the revolt was defused, Hmong grievances were in no way addressed (AOM Paris Indochine A2 NF 328 2549, Bulletin Politique, December 1932). A particular surveillance was kept over the Hmong chiefs during the same year. Not only were they observed to be suffering hardships owing to a bad opium crop, but they were viewed as susceptible to be influenced by emigre's from the peasant revolts of Nghe Tinh (AOM Aix E23, Xieng Khouang, 1st tri 1932), an ominous portent, indeed.

The combination of the prospects for fortune in opium farming in northern Laos and the prohibition of the cultivation of poppy in Siam led, during 1930, to a reverse migration of Hmong from Siam to Luang Prabang province (AOM Aix E12 Luang Prabang, 2nd tri 1930). Likewise, in breach of the regulations, certain Kha groups were drawn into opium cash cropping in that year (AOM Aix E22 "Independent Inspectorate of the *Douanes et Régie* in Laos to the Résident Supérieur, Vientiane, 12 January 1932). By 1933, however, poor opium harvests and a shortage of cash caused by the demonetization of the piaster again threw the Hmong back onto the subsistence economy. Their "malaise", it was believed, could easily be exploited by trouble makers (AOM Indochine Paris A2 NF 328 2649 "Rapports Politiques Mensuels", February 1933).

Indeed, it was feared that the economic crisis would provoke a revival of the revolt of 1919. A number of solutions were proposed by the chiefs of the northern provinces of Laos to facilitate the recovery of tax. These were a) the partial acceptance of the old piasters as tax payment, b) the expanded execution of public works which would permit the population to procure itself the cash otherwise not generated by free market activities, c) the more efficient purchases of otherwise contraband opium produced by the Hmong on the border regions. By February 1933 it was conceded that a large part of the Hmong population was "materially incapable" of acquitting tax (AOM Indochine Paris A2 NF 328 2649, "Rapports Politiques Mensuels", February 1933).

In a break with the past, the administration permitted the commutation of Hmong personal tax in opium; this was not only a de facto breach of colonial tax ethics but a reversal of the drive for primitive accumulation which, we have seen, undergirded the colonial state project. To be viable, the *Régie* had to offer a price for Hmong opium competitive with the going free market price, the idea of course being to neutralize Hmong discontent (AOM Indochine Paris NF 329 2657 "Bulletin Politique", May 1935). Politically the policy paid off. An opium collection campaign undertaken in March 1936 by the *Douanes et Régie,* assisted by customs agents, a chemist and Lao mandarins realized nearly 5000 kilograms of high quality opium at an average (although reduced) price of $12 a kilogram. Not only was the fight against the smugglers being won but the impoverished population had gained the wherewithal to pay their taxes in silver (AOM Indochine Paris NF 329 2657 Bulletin Politique, March 1936).

1937 was described by the *Résident* of Xieng Khouang as a particularly bad year for the Hmong peasant farmer, so bad that poppy seeds had to be purchased from outside. One measure of the scale of operations might be viewed by the quantity of seed required, 2000 kilograms at a price of 0$10 to 0$20 a kilogram (AOM Aix F9 Xieng Khouang, 19 January 1937).

As was often the case, a dearth of opium was paralleled by a dearth of rice. 1937 was no exception (AOM Aix E26 Tranninh 1937). As a test of the good will of the Hmong and to raise money for the cash starved budget, those Hmong who could not commute their *prestations* in cash were to be employed on road maintenance work on RC 4, to which special funding had been allocated. With the approach of the opium harvest they would be released from these duties to return to their fields (AOM Aix F9 Xieng Khouang, 19 January 1937).

Paradoxically, for one of the more geographically sequestered and clannish of the ethnic groups in Indochina, the Hmong had emerged under colonialism in the 1930s as more fully drawn into the money economy than many lowland Lao peasants. Forced into dependence upon opium poppy monoculture, the Hmong peasant farmer was with regularity thrown back upon the subsistence economy by seasonal vagaries and crop failure. The cycle of exploitation, economic crisis, messianic appeals, clan conflict, rebellion or near rebellion, and military coercion or containment, was repeated throughout the colonial epoch. While the rising price of opium and the overall expansion of poppy cultivation benefited certain Hmong chiefs and intermediaries — and no doubt staved off revolt — the Hmong peasant farmer adapted only uncomfortably to the boom and bust opium market economy.

CONCLUSION

The revolt of the Lu under the *Chao Fa*, as we have seen, illustrated the phenomenon of the rebel aristocrat. The *Chao Fa* provided not only leadership but was simply the most prestigious personage in the Lu world. "Feudal" in the way he treated his subjects, he was, nevertheless, the symbol of Lu separateness and identity (see Moerman 1967). The impulse to rid themselves of the corvee and the colonial tax burden was undoubtedly a major factor in facilitating popular support for the *Chao Fa*'s rebellion. For the man himself, his rebellion may have been as much a war of secession for the restoration of traditional boundaries and traditional prerogatives. The revolt therefore has a dual anti-colonial and "feudal" quality. Above all, however, the revolt illustrates the particularly Lao-Lu quality of the importance of a clientele to a rebel leader as much as the importance of a meritorious leader to a clientele.

Distinguished by its political program and its foreign element, the revolt of the Chinese in 1914 is a more complex phenomenon. Although anti-fiscal and anti-French and while attracting a limited participation of the local population, it would be hard to conceive that had the rebels established their republic, they would have removed all local abuses.

Clearly, however, the Opium *Régie* had alienated not only the local merchant cum opium smugglers cum Black Flags but had driven a number of the lesser Lao nobility into social banditry. The Kha, as was usually the case, had nothing to lose by joining the rebels. Singing the praise of Chinese Republicanism, while acting out the role of opium warlords, the rebel leadership were motivated less out of crisis than out of relative deprivation. By attempting to replace one protectorate by another, the Chinese rebels have emphatically not won a place for themselves in patriotic Lao history.

The Hmong revolt, as we have seen, developed from a collective attempt to remove themselves from the tyranny of the Yunnanese warlords and the Tai overlords into a war against the French. While Vietnamese and communist historians have glorified this revolt as a patriotic anti-colonial episode, the French as guardians of the status quo became the logical targets of Hmong anger. Known to French writers as the "revolt of the mad", it certainly had its share of irrational elements. Batchai's version of the *phu mi boun* repelled the non-Hmong peoples and, indeed, did not attract all Hmong chiefs. The irrational and backward looking elements of the revolt should not obscure the rational, however. While the retreat to messianism by Batchai's Hmong at a moment of crisis expresses Scott's notion of rebellion as a "defensive rebellion", their demands for direct representation to the colonial administration, tax justice (meaning an equitable price for opium purchased by the *Régie*) and elimination of the Tai-Lao intermediaries was a direct challenge to the local Tai-Lao mandarins. The years of non-revolt or passive resistance by the Hmong are just as telling. Malingering officialdom and continued abuses by local Lao mandarins throughout the entire colonial epoch threw the Hmong as a community back upon the cultural defensive. In a boom and bust economy based upon poppy cultivation, the Hmong hill peasant more than once was driven to the threshold of subsistence by official tax collectors and opium buyers. The enrichment of certain Hmong chiefs and local intermediaries only increased social stratification in the Hmong country. We might therefore conclude that Hmong rebellion has always revealed an ambiguous quality, defensive and backward looking as well as progressive and anti-authority, whether feudal or colonial. The Hmong case, therefore points to a positive link between subsistence crisis and political activity as a group or class phenomenon. Of course it might be objected that the special product of Hmong peasant farmer monoculture — opium — attracted the attention of outsiders and evoked political responses in a way that exceeded the "normal" market penetration process.

NOTES

1. A previous instance of Ho invasion of Laos occurred in 1895 by a band of 200 under the leadership of Phan Dinh Phung (Mogenet 1973:77).

2. For an eyewitness account of the brutal operation mounted by the *Garde Indigène* to crush the rebels, still led by Leang (Luong) Tou Tou and holding out in northern Laos, see Guillemet, *Sur les Sentiers Laotiens*, 1924. While the rebels were found to be in possession of tax documents and while they had constructed sophisticated military defense systems, they were treated by the military as common criminals and shown little mercy, during the course of the military operations leading to their liquidation.

3. In June 1887, Deo Van Tri and his Yunnanese allies, known in Laos as the Ho, had attacked and sacked Luang Prabang. It was on this occasion that Auguste Pavie rendered support to the King of Laos and thus gained himself an ally. In June 1888, Pavie arrived in Sip Song Chau Tai and negotiated an alliance with Deo Van Tri, thus securing de facto sovereignty for France over a particularly strategic region (McCoy 1970:74). Originally from a family of Chinese origin which had declared itself Tai, Deo Van Tri was now the undisputed master of the Tai country. Nearly all of his mandarins were relatives whose influence extended not only to the Tai of northwest Tonkin, but also to the Chinese on the Yunnanese side of the Border. Allowing the Tai considerable autonomy under their traditional rulers, the Deo's role was viewed by the French as an indispensable "administrative compromise" during the transitional period until their hegemony could be firmly established. Considerable tact on the part of the French was required in dealing with the Deo if they were not to completely alienate the Tai (Saint-Chaffray Report).

4. Gary Yia Lee has commented on my observation that the French were not the only financial beneficiaries of the rebellion. Most notable was Lo Blia Yao, a French collaborator in putting down the revolt. However his progeny squandered his wealth thus leading, with French assistance, to the eventual succession of leadership in Nong Het to his son-in-law Lyfoung and eventually to the French educated Touby. The loser in this "struggle" was Faydang and his family who even took their protest to the Lao nationalist leader and hero, Prince Phetsarath (Lee 1985:222-3).

5. According to Yang Dao, up until World War II, there were 17 Hmong *tasseng* appointed by the colonial authorities in Laos (Yang Dao 1985:45-48).

7

Revolution and Counter-Revolution in Laos

While a fraction of the Hmong eventually rallied to Faydang's "Anti-Japanese Meo Resistance League" and subsequently to the Lao Issara and the Pathet Lao during and after the period of Japanese rule in Laos and the French reconquest, another albeit larger fraction of this minority remained loyal to Touby Lyfong, a French-appointed clan chief, and his heir apparent on the battlefield, Vang Pao. As developed in a first section of this chapter, the division within the Hmong was not only perpetuated through decades of civil and revolutionary warfare but has persisted into the post-revolutionary era as well. As we shall see in a second section, the montagnards of the southern highlands were also allotted a special role in the counter-revolution alongside US agencies inside Laos in the 1960s and early 1970s. Finally, as shown, the 1980s saw the montagnards recaste in a more than symbolic role as "freedom fighters" along the lines of the Reagan Doctrine.

That the Hmong have been victims is undisputed, but whether their confrontation with central power under the Lao People's Democratic Republic since 1975 could also be explained as a throwback to a traditional variant of shaman-inspired revolt merits attention. Scott's argument that rebellion from disaffected minority groups continues into the post-revolutionary period for reasons other than the satisfaction of standing grievances otherwise solved by "national liberation" (cf. Scott 1979) can be inferred from the admission by Hmong maquisards operating in the Phou Bia region in the latter part of 1978 that they followed a "messiah". Clearly, the proclivity of the Hmong to fight to the finish, as certain of them did in the past when under CIA/Special Forces patronage, takes on an especially tragic quality at the present time in the light of their one-sided duel against an enemy as implacable as the combined Lao People's (Liberation) Army/Vietnamese People's Army (cf.Gunn 1983).

Indeed, in a conversation with the author in 1988, Vang Pao indicated that he was in communication with fighting units of his loyalists operating on missions as remote as the Lao-Vietnamese border area.

REVOLUTION AND COUNTER-REVOLUTION: THE MONTAGNARD OF LAOS IN THE SECOND INDOCHINA WAR

McCoy has shown, in a now well known study, that the French move to do away with the opium monopoly beginning in 1946 never had a chance of success. Rather, French intelligence and paramilitary agents took over the opium traffic in order to finance their covert operations during the First Indochina War (1946-1954). He shows that the Mixed Airborne Command Group (MACG) was inextricably interwoven with the opium traffic and the most successful MACG was that operated by the Hmong macquis of Xieng Khouang around Touby Lyfoung. The US would have been apprised of the nature of this operation (Operation X) during a tour of Indochina including the Plain of Jars by US CIA operative Edward G. Landsdale in June-July 1953 (McCoy 1973:102).

Any doubts about the morality of this operation either on the part of Landsdale or the concerned US agencies were evidently caste aside. As reported by Landsdale to the then Secretary of Defence, Robert S. Macnamara, Secretary of State Dean Rusk, and Director of Central Intelligence, Allan W. Rusk, in a July 1961 memo and as revealed in the *Pentagon Papers:*

> About 9,000 Meo [Hmong] tribesmen have been equipped for guerrilla operations, which they are now conducting with considerable effectiveness in Communist-dominated territory in Laos. They have been organized into Auto-Defense Choc units of the FAL [Royal Lao Army Forces] of varying sizes. Estimates of how many more of these splendid fighting men could be recruited vary, but a realistic figure would be around 4,000 more, although the total manpower pool is larger.
>
> Political leadership of the Meos [Hmong] is in the hands of Touby Lyfoung who now operates mostly out of Vientiane. The military leader is Lt.Col Vang Pao, who is the field commander. Command control of Meo operations is exercised by the Chief CIA Vientiane with the advice of Chief MAAG Laos. The same CIA paramilitary and US military team-work is in existence for advisory activities (9 CIA operations officers, 9 LTAG [Lao Training Advisory Group]/ Army Special Forces personnel, in addition to the 99 Thai PARU [Police Aerial Resupply Unit] under CIA control and aerial resupply"
>
> (*Pentagon Papers*, Vol II, p. 646 cited in David 1973:144).

During the unsettled times of the late fifties and early sixties, a messianic movement swept through the Hmong population of Xieng Khouang. In line with Hmong folklore belief that an ancient king will return and establish a Hmong kingdom, the modern expectation — eventually lent credence by US support for Vang Pao — was that Christ would arrive in a jeep. David, in a major study of the montagnards of Laos in the Second Indochina War, has written that such "syncretic merging of elements of Christianity with a desire for modern technology and military power is indicative of the degree to which the Meo's [Hmong] traditional cognitive patterns had been disturbed". He goes on to explain how such myths served to reconcile their expectations with the realities of living in a war zone. David also notes that owing to his close contacts with the CIA as well as local prestige, Vang Pao was well suited to leading such a "revivalistic" movement (David 1973:126 and cf. Halpern and Kundstadner 1967:240 and cf. Evans 1983:18-19).

As Evans explains, the US ability to rechannel the traditional revolt of the Hmong was inordinately enhanced by the role of a certain US Agency for International Development personality, Edgar "Pop" Buell. His "ability" to call up air-borne supplies in the highlands created a veritable cargo cult. By the 1960s a full blown millenarian movement developed among Hmong refugees giving rise to the usage of an esoteric script (Evans 1983:31 and cf. David 1973:152).

While Hmong messianism was rechanneled along anti-communist lines the secret army was modelled along a version of the then counter-insurgency strategy being implemented in South Vietnam including population control and a version of strategic hamletting. By 1961 Xieng Khouang and the Hmong people became the vortex of the civil war in Laos. By the end of the decade following the partitioning of Laos by the 1962 Geneva Accords, the Plain of Jars emerged as the most heavily bombed area of Indochina suffering between 300 and 400 daily bombing missions daily (cf.Evans 1983:17).

David observes how many of the recommendations of Lansdale of July 1961 were incorporated into operational format in Laos. Accordingly, the emphasis of the US was redirected away from elitist politics in Vientiane and the build up of the Royal Lao Government to a "comprehensive military and political program on the village level". Deliberate US refugee creation from the Plain of Jars provided a pool of some 200,000 from which recruits were drawn. In the space of one year Vang Pao's irregular forces grew from 9,000 in July 1961 to 14-18,000. Between 1961 until 1967 Vang Pao's influence allowed the CIA to consolidate its military position in the northeast, although this involved a "tactical equilibrium" with the enemy according to season. Generally the Hmong irregulars tended to predominate in northeast Laos during the wet season (May to November) while the communists took the initiative between December to April, the dry season. The key to US success, he observes, was the employment of Air America, the CIA supported airline and its subsidiaries. Overall this airline kept up food, weapons — and non the less opium deliveries — via a network of more than 200 airfields and landing strips (cf. David 1973:152-3).

The period 1969-70 David describes as one involving massive population relocation. Between 5-11 February 1970 some 15,000 mountain dwellers were removed via Air America to the lowlands. David explains this as a dual strategy 1) denying population resources to the Pathet Lao and winning them over to the government. 2) facilitating — in the absence of natives — the "totally free" bombing of the Plain of Jars area (David 1973: 179).

Evans writes that in its heyday Vang Pao's CIA-backed "Secret Army" numbered close to 40,000 of whom half were Hmong. By 1972 owing to casualties and desertions its strength had fallen to below 30,000 men. By this point the Hmong component accounted for only twenty percent of his forces, the balance formed by other hill tribes, Lao and Thai mercenaries (Evans 1983:18-19).

As declassified US documents reveal, while northern Laos was of greater importance to the security of the Royal Lao Government, the primary interest of the US in Laos by 1966 was to interdict the various branches of the "Ho Chi Minh Trail" which coursed through the southern panhandle region. The operational picture in southern Laos was termed in US military jargon as the "Steel Tiger" area linked with infiltration routes in the southern part of north Vietnam.

In his major study on the montagnards in the Second Indochina War in Laos, David explains that the US was less successful in rallying indigenous support from the 250,000 southern Laos montagnards relative to their success in gathering the Hmong around Vang Pao. This he attributed to first, diverse patterns of social organization of the *Lao Theung* relative to the Hmong and second, the fact that the southern highlands had been effectively under the control of the North Vietnamese since 1956. The Americans thus operated not only among a "disinterested" population but in "hostile territory" (David 1973).

But clearly if lessons had been learnt by the French in their dealings with local communities in the highlands, they were conveniently forgotten by the US forces in their turn. Thus to compound a miserable encounter with outsiders during the colonial epoch, the montagnards of the southern highlands had the ill fortune to emerge as major targets of US bombing in attempts to interdict the "Ho Chi Minh-Sihanouk Trail" complex in the late sixties and early seventies. The trail which entered Laos across the Annamite Cordillera via such routes as Nape Pass and Mu Gia Pass — the traditional mountain crossing between Laos and Annam — crisscrossed southeast Laos before debauching into northeast Cambodia and Vietnam south of the seventeenth parallel.

As revealed in a top-secret briefing paper issued by the headquarters of the US 7/13th Air Force based in Udorn airbase in Thailand the bombing of such targets inside Laos as trucks, bulldozers and other vehicular traffic was critical to the US project. Visual reconnaisance was carried out by the 7th Air Force based at Nakhon Phanom in Thailand and using 0-1 and A-26A aircraft, A1E's from Udorn and AC-47 aircraft from Ubon. Forward Air Controllers on daily patrol provided targets for strike aircraft. They were in turn in radio contact with CIA trained "indigenous road watch teams". The Mu Gia pass linking Laos and Vietnam across the Annamite Cordillera, however, was observed in late 1966 to be still open despite "many missions — including two B-52 missions" (working paper HQ 7/13 AF, Udorn, 7 Nov 1966 cited in Pratt 1984).

According to statistics compiled by the Cornell Air War Study Group, interdiction of the trail began in 1964, peaking at an average of over 200 fighter-bomber sorties a day in mid-1967 to mid-1969. In calendar year 1971 the rate was 250 sorties per day over all Laos with 70-80 percent directed against the trail. In that year alone 296,000 tons of bombs were dropped over the trail, making it the most heavily bombed zone in the entire Indochina War theatre. But clearly, as the authors of the study laconically record, the trail did not run entirely through deserted landscapes. Refugee generation was only one deliberate consequence of the bombing of the 250,000 people who then inhabited the provinces through which the trail ran. Fatalities — impossible to estimate — most certainly increased as the bombing spread westward over even more populated zones in both Laos and Cambodia (Littauer and Uphoff 1972:69-75).

It should not be forgotten that the air activity over the trail in southern Laos, as with the bombing of the Plain of Jars in the north, was linked with ground conflict. For instance, Khe Sanh, described in colonial literature as the main commercial center for the Kha Leu in the central highlands, attracted in 1967 the sobriquet "Rockpile" at the time of its fortification by US forces. In January 1968 some 6,000 US Marines were squared off against an even larger number of North Vietnamese attackers in a devastating battle to defend the Khe Sanh firebase. Montagnard survivors of the enveloping conflict on the Vietnamese side of the frontier would almost certainly have been swept up in Operation Lam Son 719, as the US-ARVN invasion of southern Laos in February 1971 was codenamed. This unsuccessful operation pushed as far west as Tchepone linked with Khe Sanh across the Cordillera by Route 9. Indeed, as Shawcross notes of the Lam Son failure, the US reliance on bombing actually increased (Shawcross 1979:217).[1]

Owing to certain strategic factors, the coffee growing Bolovens, site of the Kommadan rebellion, largely remained in Royal Lao Government hands through to the early 1970s although a combined Pathet Lao/North Vietnamese force attacked and occupied the town of Paksong on the Bolovens on 15 May 1971. Wall notes that the Nya Hon of the Bolovens could not but avoid being involved in successively the French and American wars. Nya Hon males in particular were obliged to partake in certain military activities alongside the RLG. Military discipline, the requirement to speak Lao, and obligatory separation from families all worked to break with tradition. By 1967 each *tasseng* on the plateau was provided with a primary school, although overall literacy could not have exceeded a low 8%. Besides a higher profile Lao administration, US agencies also made their presence felt by 1963. In that year teams of International Voluntary Service workers along with US Military Advisory Assistance Team "White Star" units involved themselves in such civic action programmes as road construction, bridge building, hospitals and irrigated rice schemes (Wall 1975:186-191).

One legacy of history remaining to be resolved by the victorious governments in Indochina in 1975 was that of boundaries. On 18 July 1977 Laos and Vietnam signed a treaty of delineation as part of a broader formalization of relations, the most important document of which was the Treaty of Friendship and Cooperation. A joint committee was set up on 25 July to further implement the treaty. This was followed on 24 July 1978 with the signing of a border delineation protocol between the two countries and the planting of border markers in the otherwise unmarked sector. While an official source summarized the matter as, "Delicate cases left by history....settled on the basis of complete agreement and the spirit of mutual respect" (Vinh Nguyen 1986), sources critical of the agreement alleged that the unpublished border agreement gave Vietnam control of Lao territory including part of Savannakhet province, although this has been denied by Lao authorities (cf. Thayer 1982:254). In the de jure sense, at least, Vietnam has declared its fidelity to the international legal principle of *uti posseditis* (as you possess) or in other words respect for the demarcation lines inherited at the time of independence from the colonial power. This may be less than perfect from the point of view of montagnard autonomy and even minority rights, but realistically in such cases where existing political demarcation lines between successor states do not exactly coincide with geographical divides, the adjudication-mutual respect formula is the best that can be expected in the circumstances.

THE REAGAN DOCTRINE, RAMBO AND THE RIGHT-WING RESISTANCE IN LAOS

While, as seen, the right-wing resistance to the new communist order in Laos emerged prior to proclamation of the People's Republic in 1975, it would be instructive to situate the interventionist phenomenon within the broad ambit of the Reagan Doctrine. Otherwise enunciated during the American President's 1985 State of the Union address, the doctrine locked the US into support for anti-communist insurgencies wherever they occurred. As the logic went, "Support for freedom fighters is self-defence". Citing a *Christian Science Monitor* report, Vientiane radio in 1987 described the Reagan Doctrine as the successor of the Truman Doctrine. Whereas the former assumed an extravagant expenditure of money and weapons in support of allied countries, such as that described with respect to the US role alongside the Royal Lao Government, the latter doctrine was intended to isolate and restrict communist activities in the communist world making use of intervention and subversion. This broadcast identified White House Bathroom No. 302 [*hongnam beu sam hoi song*] as the headquarters of the organization charged to implement the doctrine with a room No.208 as the place where assistance to the "freedom fighters" was drawn up! (Vientiane Domestic Radio FBIS EAS 87 163, 24 August 1987).

Paradoxically, however, while certain official spokespersons identified the resistance in Afghanistan and Cambodia as "insurgencies with merit" (Solarz 1986:24-5), the right-wing resistance in Laos had not been analogously endorsed. This can be explained by the fact that Laos alone among the Indochinese countries hosted a US diplomatic presence (a *Charge d'Affaires*). But while the existence of diplomatic ties inhibited overt endorsement of anti-LPDR elements, in fact US agencies have not stood back from engaging in covert acts of hostility designed to exert leverage over the land-locked, war-ravaged and aid-dependent country.

In point of fact Laos still remains on Washington's list of "enemy countries" thus making it a logical target for the President's rhetoric. Moves in 1987 by the US Administration to remove Laos from its hit list have in fact only been initiated in response to what has been seen as a "cooperative attitude" on the part of the regime to the Missing-in-Action issue. In fact, given the cruel and barbaric record of the US during the Second Indochina War in literally bombing Laos back to the stone age, the shoe is on the other foot. Today it behoves the US and the Western community to cooperate unconditionally with the LPDR in restituting the war damaged economy and compensating for the appalling human and ecological losses suffered as a direct consequence of the bombing.

The first American involvement in anti-regime activities, then, appears to have been the province of individuals in the style of the celluloid anti-hero, Rambo. Indeed, their activities may well have provided the role model for the Rambo cult. For example, the "spaghetti western" actor, Clint Eastwood, has been linked with at least one expedition into Laos in search of MIA's. While official US spokespersons in conversation with the author in Vientiane in late 1980 dismissed such acts as the work of "adventurers', by early 1981 the official US link with covert anti-regime activities had taken a more sinister turn. At this juncture reports were circulating in the American mass media that CIA agents of Asian descent were at the head of between 20 and 30 mercenaries in at least two attempts to rescue what were believed to be American MIA's held in captivity in southern Laos (Fineman and Lord 1981). After the event, the then US Defense Secretary, Caspar Weinberger, went on record as stating that appropriate action would be taken if reports proved to be true. While CIA intelligence turned out to be incorrect and the raid aborted, yet another Agency-led sortie into Laos was reported later in the same year. Thus if not Clint Eastwood, then the most likely candidate for the Rambo mantle would be James "Bo" Gritz, an ex-lieutenant-colonel with the US Green Berets and whose group was ambushed inside Laos in 1982. An embarrassment to the Thai state, he was declared persona non gratia after attempting to enter Laos in February 1983 and again in December 1986.

What are the origins of the anti-LPDR resistance? From where is its leadership drawn and who are its backers? More importantly, from the perspective of this essay, what is its ethnic constituency and what echoes does the anti-communist resistance today carry from the past in terms of the tradition in Laos of local resistance to central power?

While it is true that the first organized armed resistance to the newly proclaimed communist regime in Vientiane emerged from the ethnic quarter essentially as a flow on from the CIA/Special Forces/Thai mercenary support for the largely Hmong battalions of General Vang Pao in the pre-1975 period (cf. Evans and Rowley 1984:274), one should not lose sight of international factors complicated by the LPDR's siding with Vietnam in its conflict with China over Cambodia, especially post 1978.

In the account of Jean Lartéguy and Yang Dao, his Sorbonne-educated Hmong collaborator, the evacuation of the CIA/Special Forces camp at Long Chen near the Plain of Jars by Vang Pao and the majority of his officers and families (altogether around 3,000), during the period before the proclamation of the LPDR, left the Hmong in the region in great disarray. In the precipitous retreat of their patriarch-chief, certain of Vang Pao's officers were "forgotten". Those like Colonels Ly Ndjouana and Ly Pao and commanding officers Jong Joua and Vakai Vu took up the banner of resistance to the Pathet Lao, who were in the process of consolidating their power over the demoralized Royalists. The main concentration of armed resistance by anti-communist Hmong was the Phu Bia redoubt, south of the Plain of Jars. The suppression of this rebellion, according to Lartéguy and Yang Dao, commenced in August 1977 with aerial reconnaissance by T-28's, followed by the deployment of chemical defoliants, napalm, and gas rockets. By the end of 1978, Pathet Lao battalions encadred by Vietnamese began their attack, resulting in the systematic destruction of villages and the massacre of the inhabitants (Lartéguy and Yang Dao 1979:236-255). The "genocide" argument is echoed by Hamel, who contends that the Vietnamese seek to "exterminate" the Hmong, "purely and simply" (Hamel 1980).

Only after the major centers of armed Hmong resistance from within Laos were crushed by 1978 did Ban Vinai, a refugee camp across the Mekong in northern Thailand, emerge as the major external base for ethnic minority resistance acrtivities. This encampment was in effect a transplant of Long Chen, the former CIA headquarters on the Plain of Jars and where, as mentioned, the US waged its "secret war" in the late 1960s and early 1970s in tandem with bombing activities.

Aside from attention as refugees from communism, the Hmong again emerged in the international spotlight in the early eighties, this time as victims of alleged Vietnamese use of toxic gas in Laos. While the US State Department both sowed and fervently endorsed these allegations as part of its then anti-Vietnamese, anti-Soviet propaganda line, the arguments of Evans (*Yellow Rainmakers*, 1983) as to the story making propensity of the Hmong backed by a sifting of the scientific evidence have tipped informed opinion towards skepticism. Indeed Evan's specific refutations of the "Yellow Rain" arguments have been accepted as "plausible" by such leading US Laos experts as Zasloff and Brown (1986:189).

If military measures were the chosen expedient to deal with the Hmong problem during the period of consolidation of power, and which cannot (by 1982) be presumed to be totally realized, then upon the achievement of total security and regime legitimacy the matter should have passed entirely onto the administrative plane. Questions such as encouraging the Hmong to give up slash and burn agriculture and to take up a sedentary life, to give up "superstitious" practices, and to pay taxes on cattle would attain priority. At the same time, passive as opposed to active resistance by the Hmong to fulfill these objectives would put the onus on the Lao government to make good their promises to uphold equality for all minorities, especially in the way of affording protection for the celebration of festivals, basic cultural practices, linguistic rights, etc. The following statement drawn from a recent official Lao report on the Hmong is suggestive of administrative success in dealing with this minority: "Based on the lessons acquired after carrying out nationality work in the Hmong nationality areas, the Politburo will assess the implementation of Party and state policies towards other nationalities and tribes throughout the country". In the light of the foregoing, and bearing in mind that a substantial section of the Hmong have been an integral component of the Pathet Lao movement, it must be admitted that the regime has also been competing for the loyalty of the Hmong, among other minorities, but means other than coercive (Gunn 1983:326).

Although peasants from the old liberated zones in the highlands had been required to furnish part of their rice as "patriotic duty', it was not until September 1976 that agricultural taxes were universally imposed by the new communist order. For the majority of the lowland peasantry the new taxes would have been the first such imposts since the end of the colonial era, as public expenditure had hitherto been subsidized by American aid (cf. Dufumier 1981:23-4). It is also true that certain peasants living in the Vientiane zone had been subject to tenancy rates at least as high or higher than the new taxes (cf. Luther 1983:13-4). The new tax, then, involved 8-30 percent of family production in paddy after a deduction of 100 kilograms per person for subsistence. A number of observers have commented that the progressive scale of the taxes penalized those who produced more and did not encourage intensification of production. Moreover, the system of computation and collection was open to errors and abuses by over-zealous cadres (cf. Dufumier 1981:23-4 and for details see Kahn and Lee 1980:29-30).

But, as Luther notes, political conflicts arose almost immediately when the government tried to impose taxes in tribal areas notably on animal production. Hmong, especially, responded by slaughtering their cattle and chose to either migrate deeper into the mountains or to escape to Thailand: "Hence the net result of the new agricultural tax was that the rural economy stagnated even further and local opposition arose against the regime" (Luther 1983:13-14). Paradoxically, however, it was the non-enforcement of the new tax regime that undermined the socialist government's overall project to raise primitive capital in a way confronted by the colonial state decades before. Indeed, as ILO consultants, Kahn and Lee argue, in view of the "dismal budget deficit and the overwhelming aid dependence" a radical improvement in agricultural tax collection is of the highest priority (Kahn and Lee 1980:29-30).

As "tribal" and minoritarian, the particularistic rebellion of Vang Pao's Hmong was bound to be crushed if the momentum of the revolution was to be continued. More problematical and intractable from the perspective of the regime was the right-wing resistance with its broad international links. The political right, notably members of the routed Royalist armed forces — themselves weakened and divided in fierce intramural struggles for control over USAID spoils and narcotics — drew their strength in the post 1975 period from both the swelling refugee agglomerations in Thailand and from Lao immigrants in France and the US. Locally they gained the sympathies and support of provincial Thai military figures.

In a 1983 article on the resistance in Laos, I identified a new emerging locus of support for the anti-LPDR anti Vietnamese cause and which crystalized in the wake of Laos' definitive siding with Vietnam in its quarrel with Cambodia under the Khmer Rouge and China. The various facets of the international support networks I dubbed a) the Yunnan-based China-directed resistance b) Hmong and Yao: the "smoking gun" and the Chinese strategy c) the southern-based Khmer Rouge supported resistance d) the French connection e) the American connection f) Thailand and the "third hand" (Gunn 1983).

Rhetorically, Vientiane identified the "enemy" as variously, "imperialist" (the US), "international reactionary" (China) and "militarist" (elements within the Thai establishment). However, of this pantheon of enemies China was the pivot on which the anti-Vietnamese resistance in Indochina turned, at least between 1979 and 1987. Next to the pressing task of development and meeting agricultural self-sufficiency, no other subject had been treated as obsessively by the regime in its propaganda statements — whether for domestic or international consumption — than the resistance question. To fail to underscore the international dimension of the resistance to the LPDR is thus to miss the point.

Thus at a time when sustained Lao and Vietnamese communist military pressure broke the back of organized Hmong resistance in Phu Bia mountain region and when the Hmong resistance was beginning to lose momentum, assistance came from a hitherto unexpected quarter — China. The separate visits by Vang Pao and his deputies to Beijing in 1979 signaled a rekindling of Chinese assistance to the Hmong nationality, far more numerous in China than in Laos or Vietnam. Even before 1979, the Chinese had been alert to the utility of employing Hmong from China in espionage activities on the Sino-Vietnamese and Sino-Lao border areas. By mid-1979 the Chinese strategy was in place. Hmong in Laos were to be brought into line opposing Vietnamese "hegemonism" in Indochina while opposing Soviet "socialist imperialism" at the backdoor. Some Hmong may perceive that they could better satisfy aspirations for autonomy, minority rights, and especially basic needs in China or in Laos but also along the lines of the Chinese model. The Hmong population of 2.8 million in China are given some dozen "autonomous" prefectures and counties. Indeed the Lao government feared that the Chinese design was precisely that, to set up a Hmong "kingdom" in Laos. That may equally be the dream of Vang Pao and his clansmen, who share the belief in a returning Hmong messiah (cf. Gunn 1983). While Evans fails to clarify the matter, a schism which emerged among the anti-communist Hmong evidently surfaced as a product of spontaneous support for a *"Chao Fa"* movement in competition with Vang Pao in the Ban Vinai camp (Evans 1973:31).[2] It was not until the resumption of ambassadorial ties between Laos and China in late 1987, and otherwise broken off in 1979 when Laos sided with Vietnam in its quarrel with China, that China pledged not to support anti-LPDR resistance groups.

Like the Hmong, the Yao are relative newcomers to Laos from China. In contrast to the shamanistic Hmong, the Yao carry some collective memories of Taoist traditions. Not surprisingly, the closely knit patrilineally organized Yao have also been sought out as objects and agents of revolutionary and counter-revolutionary warfare. In 1962, in the northeastern province of Luang Namtha, the US Green Berets sought to weld together a Yao mercenary army. As leader they chose the leading Yao chief of this province, Chao Mai. When he died in 1967, he was succeeded by his son, Chao Lao, although the latter apparently took his father's opium business more seriously than the venture of fighting the Pathet Lao.

As of 1981, Chao Lao was still deferred to by the Yao as their guerrilla chief and was then living among 6000 refugees in Chiang Kong camp in northern Thailand. The Yao have apparently not disavowed resistance activities. Chao Lao admits that 1000 Yao died fighting the LPLA/VPA before the date when the Chinese are said to have become involved. The Yao are also more numerous in China than in Vietnam, Laos, and Thailand, and in the manner of the Hmong, Dai (Thai or Tai Lu or Lao) and Hani (Akha) peoples enjoy certain guarantees of fictive administrative autonomy which holds out a powerful propaganda appeal to these minorities across the border in Laos.

Notably missing from this list of minority peoples are the proto-Indochinese *Lao Theung* or Kha tribes who, while represented in southern Yunnan and sometimes mentioned in the context of the Chinese-backed resistance in the north and especially in the south, are undoubtedly the major beneficiaries of the Pathet Lao victory, especially in terms of military opportunities afforded by participation in the LPLA. The conspicuous absence of the *Lao Theung* from the refugee camps in Thailand works to support the overarching thesis of this book, namely that the montagnards had nothing to lose by joining the rebellion turned revolution.

The French, American and Thai-based components of the resistance refers to the personality based cliques in those countries gathered around their clan leaders, largely ethnic Lao from the old aristocratic and bourgeois-militarist cliques who fled the country in the pre-1975 period. For example, the United Lao National Liberation Front founded in 1981 comprises two wings, that of the remnants of Vang Pao's Hmong (2-3000) and a battalion of guerrillas led by another former Royalist General

Thongridh. In addition a batallion operating in the Lao province of Champassak bordering Thailand and Cambodia had been led by Chao Boun-eua Na Champassak, son of the former strongman of southern Laos, Prince Boun Oum, before his death in 1981, had likewise lent his name to the France-based resistance. A major blow to the resistance on the ground was the death in Bangkok in November 1985 of Phoumi Nosavan, an ex-General in the Royalist Army, former US-backed strongman in Laos and a cousin of the former Premier of Thailand, Marshal Sarit. Phoumi's name had been linked with an explicitly anti-LPDR anti-Vietnamese front known as the Lao People's National Liberation Front announced in September 1980 as well as the United Lao National Liberation Front.

It transpires that the Lao resistance factions are as faction ridden and personality ridden as their Cambodian counterparts. Phoumi and Phaya In-paeng (from an elite family) fell out over the terms of a cooperation agreement evidently entered into with the Khmer Rouge in 1981. Personality differences also evidently beset Phoumi's and Vang Pao's factions. This fractured alliance in the field has been matched by divisions among the Lao refugee communities in France and the US, although never reaching the heights of acrimony such as that reached in Cambodian and especially Vietnamese emigre circles. As a Bangkok source stated the matter in 1986, the net result of the resistance after ten years of activity had been a failure to organizationally unite while operationally they remain separated across a huge geographical terrain between southern Laos and the northern hills. Accordingly their actions remain "uncoordinated and minimal" (*The Nation*, 18 August 1986).

The uphill struggle of the Lao resistance to find organizational coherence was perhaps well pointed up by the failure of the United Lao National Liberation Front in mid-1987 to win admission to the National Democratic Front, a loosely organized federation of ten armed Burmese minorities. NDF spokespersons explained that as their respective enemies were different, they could not accept Lao rebel groups into their body (*The Nation*, 17 July 1987).

Undoubtedly the most sensational of the resistance activities inside Laos was that perpetrated by an estimated 200 strong resistance force attempting to transit southern Laos in August 1987. Some 200 were eliminated in the course of 23 running gun battles. Although members of a Vietnamese group styled the *Que Minh* (Our Home), the rebels were guided by exiled Lao elements (FEER, 19 November 1987). Survivors were extradited to Vietnam where they were sentenced in a show-trial in Ho Chi Minh City. A replay of this events occurred in October 1989.

The vulnerability of the regime to the machinations of right-wing exiles across the Mekong in Thailand was dramatically brought home to the author in human terms in late 1975 when in residence in a riverside quarter of Vientiane distinquished by nature of its assorted building materials, eg. such detrius of a former age as bomb casings and flattened Budweisser cans. As I was reminded by less importunate neighbors, the naked light of my dwelling would but surely draw fire from across the river as a lamp would attract nocturnal moths. In general the discretion was justified as the nadir of resistance activities against the regime was surely the interruption by automatic weapon fire of a 1983 meeting of the Mekong Commission in the Vientiane Hilton, the Lan Xang.

CONCLUSION

Overall, the US-Laos theatre of the sixties and early seventies remains one of the least studied areas in western scholarship on Indochina. This is confirmed by one writer of popular military history, Christopher Robbins, who writes that the concerned US documents on Laos are still "covered by a whole gamut of the classification system" (Robbins 1989:454). While analogies between Laos and such other countries allotted a special place in the Reagan Doctrine as Nicuragua, Angola, Mozambique and Cambodia, could be overdrawn, the point is that reportage of mercenary acts against Laos — whatever official US disclaimers of involvement — have struck powerful chords in the imagination of Americans, especially via media images. *First Blood* (1982) is but one example of the intervention genre of film. In addition *Uncommon Valor* (1983), *Missing in Action* (1984) and *Rambo* (1985) served the vicarious "recovery" of Vietnam and Laos (cf. *Cultural Critique*, No. 3, Spring 1986 passim). Media myth-making and the creation via celluloid of freedom fighting heroes added substance to Reagan's plaintif call "not to break faith with those who are risking their lives — to defy Soviet-supported aggression and secure rights which have been ours from birth".

NOTES

1. For insights into the politicking behind the operational shifts in bombing patterns between Laos, Vietnam, and Cambodia post-1970, see Shawcross (1979:209-219). See also Fred R. Branfman, 1972 passim, for a sensitive study of victims of the air war in northern Laos, the results of which have clear inference for other bombing zones in Indochina. For the fate of the Brou minority as a consequence of the actions at Khe Sanh, see anon, *The Montagnards of South Vietnam*, Minority Rights Group, Report No.18, London, nd., p 16. Incredibly, in early 1968 the question of using tactical nuclear weapons or chemical agents as a way of reinforcing the American position at Khe Sanh was raised by the chairman of the US Joint Chiefs of Staff, Earle G. Wheeler. (Memorandum for the President: Subject: Khe Sanh," Earle G. Wheeler, 3 February 1968, US Department of Defense,

Carrolton Press Microfiche Collection, #79, 381 B). One earnestly hopes that in the rejection of this scenario broader humanitarian concerns prevailed over a narrow military calculus of cost effectiveness.

2. As recent as July 1989, Vientiane radio blamed recurrent Hmong rebellion on "a bad element called Chao Fa" (Summary of World Broadcasts FE/0512/B3, 19 July 1989.

Conclusion: From Rebellion to Revolution

Our thesis, then, has been to stress the radical historical disjunction opened up by the Lao and minority peasants' experience with colonialism. This we affirmed in our scrutiny of the role of capital in the pre-monopoly and monopoly stage, the State-sponsored development project, the State-initiated process of primitive capital accumulation and colonial control over the head-tax and labor process. To return to the theoretical underpinning of this study, it could be said that any description of the colonial process in the periphery which ignores identification of the prevailing configuration and articulation of modes of production within an historical world framework as well as the central question of the extraction and distribution of surplus, exploitation and class struggle and also hegemonic systems of ideological domination which permeate village, community and peasant procedure is simply to miss the richness, complexity and diversity of peasant and proto-nationalist responses to the colonial experience.

We do not find evidence in our study of minority rebellion in Laos to support all the findings of the peasant studies school apropos peasant movements in Vietnam. Minority peasant movements in Laos were, if anything, more anti-colonial-anti-capitalist than anti-feudal. Reinforced by an ethnically differentiated tax system and a tax collection system based on group responsibility, the units of minority peasant action in Laos were variously, village, clan, entourage and tribal collectivity. Thus, while the minority peasants hardly responded as a class, their rebellions were very much collective manifestations of peasant anger. Primitive peasant rebels in Laos were above all rational actors at the level of community only; individual responses to market conditions was hardly a luxury that could be afforded in a cash starved economy, and especially in a communitarian-tributary setting. There was, after Scott, a very clear relationship between a subsistence threat and collective response. Thus we cannot agree with Popkin who argues that "every part of Vietnam, political and economic abuse and increased stratification appeared before

— not after — the impact of colonialism" (1979:139). This is simply not confirmed by the experience of Laos. We are, however, closer to Scott's assumption that pre-capitalist cultures enjoyed a greater level of unity compared with capitalist societies (cf. Chovanes 1986).

It might be argued that I have only deduced that Lao minority peasants found French colonial rule especially rapacious. As the burden of my sources are archival and representing a version of history from above, they yield little insight into what people were actually thinking and doing in the villages. Nevertheless the accumulated evidence is overwhelming. While a "reasonable" degree of reciprocity existed between ruler and ruled in the pre-colonial period — Kommadan did not after all completely reject the notion of paying taxes to the appropriate authority — as ruler and ruled were vertically linked in the production and reproduction of religious enthusiasm etc., the fact of the matter is that colonial violence tipped the balance. This is not just the matter of the extension of State power into frontier regions where the writ of traditional Lao rulers had always run lightly — although this was also involved — but concerned the fundamental wrenching of peasant producers from an essentially tributary formation to capitalist-engendered networks of surplus accumulation.[1]

Generally, the peasant studies school — with their attention directed to the more "advanced" societies of Southeast Asia — have tended to underestimate the ethno-nationalist quality of peasant rebellion in Southeast Asia, just as they have, for varying reasons underestimated the anti-colonial versus anti-feudal dimension of revolt. While a common feature of the ethnic minority rebellions in Laos was their primitive organization, their use of primitive weapons, their narrow ethnic base and their esoteric religious ideology, all served as prototypes of a later generation of anti-colonial rebels. Yet in Laos the generation gap between primitive rebels and primitive revolutionaries was, atypically perhaps, telescoped. The mode of struggle of Kommadan's and Batchai's partisans small guerrilla units combined with "agit prop" sections moving "fish-like" among the civilian "ocean" — found its sequel in the particular generation of people's war fought out with the aid of professional revolutionaries in the late colonial era.

Wolf has argued that rebellion issues easily into revolution or "massive movements to transform the social structure as a whole". This arises because the peasant is a victim of forces larger than himself. In other words peasant stirrings are parochial manifestations of great social dislocations. Nevertheless Wolf does not find evidence for the view that if it were not for "outside agitators" the peasant would not be at rest (Wolf 1971:301).

Samir Amin notes of widescale revolts against the domination of capital, corvee and taxes in Africa that they were all crushed. Was this because of internal divisions among the rebels or the treachery of collaborators? No, they were crushed from outside by an organized and more powerful enemy (Amin 1977:152). The Laos experience offers qualified support to this assertion.

How important, then, was the role of leadership and outside agitators in the Laos rebellions? Did rebellion slip easily into revolution? Or did the Lao revolution succeed for reasons extraneous to the rebellions?

The rebellion of the Chinese republicans aside, there is little evidence that the rebellions of the first two decades of the century were the work of outside political forces, although our thesis has been to show that all the rebellions were in some way engendered by the social dislocations engendered by broader economic forces.

As official Lao historians have written of the ethnic minority rebellions during the colonial period:

> For want of a correct revolutionary line, for want of coordination on a national scale and notably for want of an authentic revolutionary party the movements for the most part failed.
> (*Phoumi Vongvichit* 1968:41).

However, we cannot ignore the role of outside agitators post 1930, as in that year Laos was included in the Indochinese Communist Party under Comintern auspices. Indeed, in September of that year, rebel militants established what amounted to autonomous village republics in the Vietnamese provinces of Nghe An and Ha Tinh. By early 1931, the ICP had extended its operations into Laos via the Mu Gia pass across the Annamite Cordillera. Unprecedented in Lao labor history sabotage occurred in the Phontiou-Boneng mines in the Nam Patene basin worked by several thousand Vietnamese coolies (cf.Gunn 1988).

Yet, while these outbursts of peasant anger were, in the main, pre-political and took on the character of localist jacqueries lacking ideology and organization, the revolutionary detonation of 1930-31 in Nghe-Tinh served to disabuse the French of any lingering romanticized view of the primitive. As one particularly perceptive colonial official observed:

> Like a sucking pump, the local Budget absorbs more of the meager pecuniary resources of the Lao people each month. In this small country, where in the word of the Gospels "one takes even from another who has not," the bad shepherds would make a good game of it. The day when a skilled propagandist of the Communist Party would preach to the masses a Marxist Gospel adapted to the mentality of the autochtone, then the day would have arrived when we would find

> ourselves, at a minimum, faced with a collective refusal to pay the taxes.
>
> (*AOM Aix Indochine E25,Rapport Politique, Savannakhet*, 1 tri 1935).

The question raised by this prophecy about how the Marxist gospel arrived in Laos, about whether this gospel as preached in Laos by communist propagandists fell on fertile soil, and if, indeed, the bearers of this alien doctrine succeeded in adapting or indigenizing it in tune with the particular conditions prevailing in colonial Laos is the subject of a separate study (Gunn 1988).

Suffice is to say that the main feature of communist activity in Laos during the 1930s — the depression years — was its exclusive Vietnamese character. Party exhortations aside, the Lao peasantry proved impervious to the Bolchevik doctrine and a Lao proletariat as such was non-existent. But the practice of incarcerating political prisoners in such highland outposts as Xieng Khouang, Luang Prabang, Lao Bao and Son La probably backfired on the colonial authorities. Contamination of the prison population by the politicals was the order of the day. Montagnard laborers on corvee details, likewise, became objects of outsider's attention. By this point communist propaganda was being focussed upon the plight of the ethnic minorities and lowland cadres were being urged to devote more time to minority problems and to step up recruitment of minorities accordingly.

Thus by 1935 official observers registered that for the first time communist propaganda was making inroads into the (southern) highlands, winning over Lao, Khmer and montagnard alike. Such concern was misdirected, however, as even party documents reveal that Lao, much less montagnards, were impervious to Party directed activities, especially those led by Vietnamese.

If the anti-colonial-anti-imperialist program of the ICP had little impact in Laos, the Japanese interregnum was important in many ways. First it revealed to members of the Lao elite that the course of history could be altered, that the foreign occupier was not invincible. It also opened up a parenthesis with the past. Laos experienced under Japanese domination its first modern administration; new opportunities were afforded for certain Lao in Japanese fostered military formations, a new self confidence seized Lao youth. Thus the Lao rebellion, when it came, was under the banner of the Lao Issara movement — a movement of Lao to resist the restoration of French colonial rule. The origins of the movement are complex enough but, from a cadre group of educated and patrician Lao gathered around Prince Phetsarath, blossomed a mass movement of armed Lao. In the wake of the Japanese surrender they sought by arms to resist a colonial restoration.

But with the Viet Minh victory in the August Revolution of 1945, Ho Chi Minh sought to succor the revolutionary wing within the Lao Issara. The figurehead leader of this wing, was Prince Souphanouvong. Working from a rear-base in the central highlands athwart the Lao-Vietnamese border, the Viet Minh took in hand the Pathet Lao.

Thus the minorities once again found themselves the object of outsiders attention, this time in a tug of war between the French and their local collaborators and the Pathet Lao-Viet Minh. Both sought to draw upon the traditional rebellions of the minorities and their age old grievances against inter-ethnic rivals. Thus Sithon Kommadan, son of Ong Kommadan, became a powerful symbol for the Pathet Lao for Kha minority participation while a similar role was reserved for Faydang on the part of the Hmong. For the first time in Lao history a broad-based movement conjoining Lao and ethnic minorities and based in the heartland of the minorities emerged on center stage.

The Lao case is perhaps striking in the way that "traditional" leaders — the "proto-nationalists" — joined league with less patrician anti-colonial revolutionaries or those who were the former subjects of traditional rulers (cf. Ishii 1986:174-9).

By the late 1940s, however, the burden of colonial violence and accumulated peasant grievance tipped the scales against the colonial restoration. As White has shown, it was in the nature of the coalition that rebels struck with Leninists that distinguished the traditional genre of uprising — implying no fundamental change to the social, political or economic system — from revolution (White 1974:77).[2]

Dependency Approaches To Laos

To the extent that political scholarship on Laos reflects a concern for the world system, then that distinction rests with the French political economist, Jean Pierre Barbier, whose thesis "Dix-sept ans d'aide économique au Laos, un pays malade de l'aide etrangère" (1973) betrays an intellectual debt to the French-trained Marxist, Samir Amin. Barbier sets out to establish the relationship between aid and development in the Kingdom of Laos between 1955 and 1971. Drawing upon the broad categories of Samir Amin's analysis of "unequal exchange" between the metropolitan center and the neo-colonial periphery, Barbier argues that during the colonial period, owing to the predominance of "traditional" forms in a little urbanized society, the disarticulation of the Lao economy had not proceeded to a great extent. Only under the impact of massive American aid, first begun in 1950, did "deep structural disequilibrium" of the economy occur, most notably in the spheres of consumption, production and external commerce (Barbier 1973:471). As a consequence, local traditional production responded less and less to the needs expressed by the urban population, who soon revealed a preference for imported deluxe consumer commodities. The decline in local artisinal production, he continued, was matched by the growth of tertiary sector activity, notably in import-export activities, but at the expense of long-term investments in the secondary sector (Barbier 1973:140). The Lao ruling class, which had by now become entirely dependent upon foreign aid, consisted of members of the government, certain deputies, high functionaries and military and police officers. This group was, in turn, divided among the traditional aristocracy, the national bourgeoisie and foreign-trained intellectuals (Barbier 1973:570). Tensions within this ruling class, however, were exploited by foreign powers to obtain their own political ends, while self-enrichment of the ruling class preempted any real notions of development (Barbier 1973:509). Unsurprisingly, the Lao economy was unable to absorb this aid which had transformed Laos into the highest per capita recipient of foreign aid in the world, while local importers became the major local beneficiaries of the aid arrangement. The real ability to turn this into profit, however, lay outside of the Lao economy, in the hands of Thai and Japanese traders. Barbier concludes that only via the path of state capitalism or socialism could Laos build a national sector. This would involve the transformation of the comprador bourgeoisie into a national bourgeoisie. In reality, this could only be accomplished by the path of primitive accumulation of capital derived from a surplus that would flow from a modernized agricultural sector. Capital investment in industrial development would have to respond to local conditions, forms of production and energy sources (Barbier 1973:524).

Guidicelli, also working in the same broad paradigm of imperialism studies, sees the disaggregation of social homogeneity and economic disarticulation alike as the twin consequences of the impact of American aid. Echoing Barbier's analysis, Guidicelli shows that aid only aggravated cleavages in the social space between town and countryside and between Vientiane and the provinces. Given the urban bias of this aid, the benefits for the 85 percent of the population which was rural was therefore marginal. Specifically, economic disarticulation since 1955 under the US Agency for International Development took place in the domains of consumption, production and external trade. Thus, the consumption patterns of the urban population revealed a preference for imported luxuries. Manpower, accordingly, was increasingly oriented towards servicing the tertiary sector. Foreign aid thus added to the prosperity of those engaged in the import-export business. Local productive activities increasingly became oriented away from local needs and redirected towards satisfying the new urban consumer needs. Thus while traditional productive activities withered, Laos became even more dependent upon the donor countries. As import taxes covered 50-70 percent of budget receipts, no diminution of economic dependence was countenanced by the political right. In short, Giudicelli saw American aid as a device to consolidate "local reactionary forces" while the conditional nature of aid ensured that an economically dependent class remained a politically dependent client (Guidicelli 1975:78-82).

Khieu Samphan, by contrast, addresses the question of the predominant mode of production in the colonial periphery with reference to Cambodia in his 1959 Sorbonne dissertation "Cambodia's Economy and Industrial Development." At a general level of analysis Samphan clearly reveals an intellectual debt to Samir Amin. Although concerned with Cambodia's autocentric development through state sponsorship under what he calls the leadership of forces "neither bureaucratic nor administrative" and allied with a "broad democracy" relying on the broad support of the "masses" (Samphan 1979:112), he argues from an ultra-nationalist position.

Samphan contends that colonial capitalist penetration of Cambodia actually reversed the trend towards the division of labor in the countryside as evidenced by the destruction of what he characterized as a relatively advanced handicrafts sector, and that which would otherwise have led to an autonomous national development of the country in the manner that class differentiation had developed in pre-colonial India and Vietnam. Colonial capitalist impact, he continues, in fact reinforced the pre-capitalist economy. He then proceeded to raise the question: To what extent did the colonial development program contribute to the generalization of capitalist circulation in the Cambodian economy? Contrary to conventional wisdom, he concluded; very little.

Samphan did not see any radical disruption of the feudal mode of production in the countryside (1979:41), rather, he saw to degrees that the feudal mode of production was strengthened. The peasantry was thus locked into "semi-servitude," land-rent and usury. Cambodia's colonial economy he viewed as a:

> ....backward agricultural one where two different sectors coexist; an atrophied capitalist sector and a predominating precapitalist sector, both, in addition, being integrated into foreign capitalism by means of foreign trade...."
>
> (*Samphan* 1979:48).

While in the years of prosperity — 1924-28 — a large "rich class" emerged from among administrative personnel and in the retail trade, there were logical and historical reasons, why foreign investments gravitated towards production for export, towards trade and investment related to import-export or in the sphere of servicing "tertiary" needs in the way of satisfying the consumption of luxuries.

Although Barbier, Guidicelli and Samphan differed on the political programme required to achieve a break-out from political and economic dependence, they shared a tendency to view a predominance of conservation effects in the countryside, particularly in the colonial era. Accordingly, each saw no option but to promote an autocentric industrialization — in Laos and Cambodia respectively — based upon a program of primitive accumulation outside of the State sector but under the auspices of a strong State. But while the Khmer Rouge, as legatees of State power in Cambodia, largely succeeded in crude economic terms in fulfilling the most radical reading of the breakout from the world system between 1975 and 1978, events were otherwise under the stewardship of the Pathet Lao in the post-revolutionary period.

Theory and Practice in Lao Communist Social Science

As mentioned, the debate on the development of socio-economic formations in Laos and Vietnam has been embedded in the communist histories of these two countries. How do Lao and Vietnamese today see the social evolution of their societies?

In Vietnam, at least, Marxist social science versions of the development of socio-economic formations are rich and variegated. As Phan Huy Le has written in a study of Vietnamese social science approaches to the question, no debate in Vietnam exists to challenge the notion that, in concert with the rest of the world during antiquity, the first socio-economic formation was "primitive-communalism." He outlines five shemata reflecting alternative views on the pre-capitalist socio-economic setting in Vietnam: viz.

1. primitive communalism — slave-owning system-feudalism
2. primitive communalism — feudalism
3. primitive communalism — Asiatic Mode of Production — feudalism
4. primitive communalism — Asiatic Mode of Production
5. primitive communalism — pre-capitalist

This shows that Vietnam social scientists, ethnologists in particular, have been prepared to entertain non-teleological and multilinear approaches to Marx's broad schemata of stages of historical evolution. Writing of the vestiges of pre-capitalist forms, Phan Huy Le has observed that it was the multilayer structure of social forms which "delayed the development of the social division of labor and social differentiation of the detachment of the town from the countryside, retarded the appearance and development of the embryos of capitalism" (Phan Huy Le 1986:87).

While the Lao have been less forthcoming in the elucidation of class society out of communal (tribal) society, than their Vietnamese counterparts, social scientists in both countries have been fundamentally concerned with political problems relating to the mobilization of the minorities and their incorporation into socialist systems. The unity of theory and practice in the social sciences is of course axiomatic (Gunn 1982:72). Evans has remarked that the ideological demands of Vietnamese communist nationalism has tended to deflect Vietnamese anthropologists from more strictly scientific concerns (Evans 1985:127).

In discussions with Lao historians at the Institut de Pedagogie in Vientiane in January 1981, the author was advised that Lao history was now seen as conforming to three periods. First, the *Sakdina* or "feudal" period (1353-1893), second, the semi-feudal/semi-colonial period (1893-1975) and, third, the period from 1975 or the period of building socialism (Gunn 1982:78).

To arrive at a more precise understanding of the period Stalinist conceptualization of social and class relations in Indochina, we will draw out the salient points on this question as contained in two ICP documents, one pertaining to Indochina in general and one pertaining to Laos in particular.

In the first document, actually submitted to the Macau Congress of the ICP held in 1935, a three-fold characterization of the Indochinese social formation emerged. The first comprised the "primitive and natural economy" said to be found among the Moi (Kha) of the Upper Donnai region and among the Man (Yao) and Meo of Tonkin. The second comprised the "feudal economy with survivals of a tribal system" and said to be found among the Muong, the Tai and the Kha. Their economy was based in part on a tribal regime and in part on a feudal regime. They have no clear class differentiation. The third category is that of the "incipient capitalist economy with numerous feudal survivals" and is found in Laos and Cambodia as well as in other locations such as at Caobang and Langson in Tonkin. Relative to the strength of the proletariat found in the Vietnamese-settled parts of Indochina, the proletariat in the third category was found to be qualitatively and quantitatively weak, consisting largely of agricultural coolies and workers engaged in transport activities. However, it was conceded that class differences had already emerged in the rural milieu and took the form of rich peasants, middle and poor peasants and agricultural workers:

> But in spite of the diversity of particular economic conditions particular to each population, the economic system of imperialist and feudal exploitation which reigns universally in Indochina is located in an agricultural economy.

Accordingly, the document continues, the local peasant population, including the montagnards, were liable to crushing taxes and corvees and the industrial proletariat as well as the petit-bourgeoisie and poor intellectual classes were exploited and led a miserable life. With respect to the feudalists, the French imperialists had delegated power to the mandarins, not the tribal chiefs and other communal agents, to oppress the population. This they achieved by creating a class of *collaborateur* (such as represented by Prince Phetsarath in Laos) and by resorting to divide and rule tactics, setting off ethnic groups against each other (AOM Paris Slotfom 111, 54, annex to NP 35, 2nd tri 1935, "Projet de Resolution soumis au Congress du PCI au sujet du travail parmi les minorites ethniques").

As presented in a second document drawn up in 1934, the ICP held that in Laos, as in Annam, there were two kinds of political power (1) that of the French imperialists and (2) that of the Lao feudalists. Accordingly, the French "imperialists" administered the population through the intermediary of the "feudalists". The strength of indigenous "professional" workers, it was noted, was very limited while the cultural level of workers and peasants alike was seen as "little evolved and lacking any spirit of solidarity. The political economy of the country was described as "strongly retarded". Commerce, apart from the activities of a small number of indigenous traders was in the hands of the French, Chinese, and in lesser numbers, the Vietnamese. Industry, however, was monopolized by the French. While a certain amount of agricultural holdings were in the hands of the *colons* and the missionaries, other lands were in the hands of the *chaomuong* and other functionaries. Property tax, however, had not been applied all over the country because of the incomplete land survey and was therefore only collected in the areas around the towns. Writing of the year 1934, which we have seen was a time of depression in Laos, the report noted that certain taxes, namely those on forestry products, customs, markets, vehicles, wood and charcoal had doubled. Market taxes realized 10-12,000 piasters in Vientiane alone. In 1930-31, the total tax revenue was 560,000 piasters for all Laos, while personal tax was fixed at $7.90 per registered tax payer. While the spirit of solidarity among the few workers in Laos was said to be "almost non-existent," the Party was encouraged by signs of struggle (AOM SLOTFOM, annex to NP no.35, "Rapports-Conference des Representants du Laos", 7-9 Septembre 1934).

As a general statement, the workerist bias of the Party vis-à-vis the role of the peasantry in the 1930s was not challenged until the banner of armed struggle was taken up even before the Japanese *coup de force* of March 1945.

As elaborated in the 1980s by the leading Lao official spokesperson, Kaysone Phomvihane — and in the absence of an autonomous social science tradition in Laos — in a pre-colonial time, Laos was a feudal state, decentralized and divided into several small kingdoms including montagnard tribes. The economy was purely "individual, dispersed and autarchic" of pre-feudal character. Under French domination, Kaysone continued, Lao society revealed features of "old style colonialism and feudalism" as the French relied on the feudal class to impose their domination. Under American domination, an attempt was made to transform "feudal and military bureaucrats" into compradors "to create a social base for their neo-colonialism." Laos thus revealed a "neo-colonial-semi-colonial" character. Clearly, the identification of "fundamental contradictions" or the enemy (foreign aggressors plus bourgeois comprador and feudal elements) was to serve the liberation struggle in the period after the defeat of the Japanese until 1975 (Kaysone 1980 and see Phoumi Vongvichit, 1968).

With liberation in 1975, the fundamental problem, aside from defending the gains of the revolution, was to usher in the transition to socialism. This was to take the form of by-passing capitalism.[3] Following Vietnamese Marxist precepts and in line with the prevailing Soviet orthodoxy, the Lao sought to usher in a triple revolution in the area of productive relations, science and ideology. The timetable for the transition was never made explicit but the pace for the first three or four years of the post-revolutionary period was fast, running into the resistance of those Lao peasants caught up in cooperativization and those minority peasant involved in sedentarization exercises.

While the first tentative reappraisals of the nature of the transition were broached in Laos in 1979, one official spokesperson told the author in an interview in 1981:

> We surmise that it will take 20-25 years to develop socialism but that would depend upon the world situation, less time if the world situation is favorable.
>
> (interview with Ouneheune Phounsavath, LPDR acting Minister for Information, Propaganda, Culture and Tourism, 13 February 1981).

In the present climate such a view would be seen as a grossly erroneous reading of Laos' development potential. One awaits the labors in this area of enquiry of the newly founded Commission for the Study of the History of the Lao People's Revolutionary Party under the chairmanship of Sisana Sisane.

Looking back in November 1986 on the occasion of the "historic" Fourth Party Congress of the Central Committee of the Lao People's Revolutionary Party, Kaysone outlined those features of the economy inherited from the past which had blocked the easy transition to socialism over the preceding ten years. Laos, he asserted, had emerged under socialism (in 1975) "from a colonial and feudal society in which the economy was in the main one of small-scale production with a natural and self-sufficient character." Under socialism, only little progress had been made in converting the "natural self-supplied economy to commodity production." Further delaying the transition was the low level of development of productive forces, weak division of labor and rudimentary tools of production. Barter was still common, meaning the commodity-money relationship had not been developed. Regional differentials between mountain and lowland areas, between areas with a commodity economy and a natural economy were marked. As such, a unified national market had not yet come into being. Signally, Kaysone declared, Laos still experienced "nearly all the modes of production from primitive to contemporary mankind has gone through." Laos is now seen as being at the first stage of the transition period to socialism (Kaysone 1986).

The upshot in Laos, then, of the reformist wind sweeping the socialist world is the acknowledgement of the necessity to make use of transitional forms, that is to allow and encourage the coexistence of socialist and non-socialist sectors. In Laos this means that even handicrafts have their role to play. Again the line between social science and politics is invisible. Kaysone's recall of the weight of pre-capitalist modes of production and his general concern with reevaluating the transition goes hand in hand with Lao programme of socio-economic renovation or reform.

NOTES

1. The tenor of these criticisms owe to Kelvin Rowley, although he may not yet be persuaded by my defense.

2. We would not fundamentally contradict Petras' thesis that socialist revolution grows out of "the more dynamic encounters with capitalism" rather than as products of backwardness (Petras 1978:298). In Laos the prime bearers of the Leninist doctrine were Vietnamese immigrants, peasants turned part-proletarians as well as members of the intelligentsia. To be sure, accumulation under French monopoly capitalism, forced requisitions in cash and in kind, the displacements occasioned by the Japanese intervention and the massive destruction and uprooting caused by US imperialism in Vietnam, had their counterparts in Laos (Petras 1978:298). But whether or not anti-capitalist forces as opposed to anti-colonial national forces were propelled in their confrontation with capital into the "maelstrom" of revolution remains to be proven. Such exaggerated claims for spontaneity or consciousness would not be offered up even by official Lao historians. Nevertheless our thesis has been to emphasize the "political" preparation of otherwise pre-political primitives by their wretched encounter with colonial capitalism in the early expansion stage.

3. The doctrine of by-passing capitalism to achieve socialism upheld by Laos and other countries of the "socialist periphery" has a mixed ancestry. Soviet writers purport to find the origins of the concept in Marx's *Communist Manifesto*. But surely the most explicit statement of this question was by Lenin at the Second Congress of the Comintern in 1920 in discussions on the national and colonial question. He wrote: "With the aid of the proletariat of the advanced countries, backward countries can go over to the Soviet system, and through certain stages of development to communism without having to pass through the capitalist stage".

Lenin, of course, had in mind not only such countries as Egypt and India but the Soviet Republics, backward by comparison with the old Czarist heartland.

But when the Soviet Union — in competition with China — sought leadership in the Third World, the doctrine was resurrected. Specifically, this was in 1960 at the Moscow Meeting of the Communist and Worker's Parties. Applied to such countries as South Yemen, Tanzania, Angola, Mozambique, etc. the doctrine offered not only a convenient rationalization for Soviet leadership in the Third World, particularly in competition with China, but a tantalizing prospect of a shortcut to socialism for the backward and underdeveloped countries.

Laos, and the Vietnamese-installed People's Republic of Kampuchea, are but the most recent of the communist bloc countries to fully embrace the doctrine. Aside from the Soviet Republics, the first was the Mongolian People's Republic, the Democratic Republic of Vietnam and the Democratic People's Republic of Korea. In Indochinese communism the origins of the doctrine can be traced back to the First Programme of the Indochinese Communist Party in 1930. In Laos, the concept was first written into Party documents at the Second Party Congress in 1972.

Thus in 1986, and with reference to the doctrine, Party Chairman Kaysone Phomvihane could note that "....assistance from the fraternal socialist countries is indispensable." Not having chosen the route of breakout from the international division of labor, Laos indubitably remains a leading exemplar of "dependent socialism" (Gunn 1988).

Appendix

French Colonial Commandants, Résidents Supérieurs and Commissioners in Laos

1 June 1895	Tournier, M.A.A. is named Commandant Supérieur of Lower Laos. Vacle, J. is named Commandant Supérieur of Upper Laos.
10 March 1897	Luce, P.L. is named interim replacement for Vacle who returns on 11 October 1898.
11 February 1899	Tournier, M.A.A. assumes the office of Résident Supérieur of Laos.
25 August 1903	Mahe, G.M.J. is named interim Résident Supérieur of Laos.
21 April 1906	Laffont, L.S. assumes interim replacement for Mahe who returns on 1 April 1907.
24 August 1910	Outrey, E. assumes interim replacement for Mahe who returns on 27 July 1911.
9 January 1912	Aubry de la Noe, L. is named interim Résident Supérieur.
4 July 1913	Garnier, C.L. is invested with responsibility for managing daily affairs.
9 October 1913	Bourcier-Saint-Chaffray, J.E. is named interim Résident Supérieur of Laos.
31 May 1914	Garnier, L.C.L. assumes an interim position of authority.
9 October 1917	Bosc, J. is named Résident Supérieur of Laos.
26 April 1921	Daroussin, J. named interim replacement for Bosc who returns in January 1923.
8 April 1925	Dauplay, J.J. named interim replacement for Bosc who returns in January 1926.
14 May 1928	Le Boulanger, P.R.O. is named interim replacement for Bosc who returns on 12 December 1928.
6 March 1931	Le Boulanger named interim office holder.

26 March 1931	Pages, P.A.M. named Résident Supérieur.
27 March 1931	Chatel, Y. replaces Pages declared *hors cadre.*
27 May 1931	Le Boulanger named interim office holder.
4 November 1931	Thiebault, J.N. replaces Boulanger on 18 October, the day of the latters' death.
21 November 1931	Le Fol, A.E. is named Résident Supérieur of Laos.
16 December 1933	Roques, A.A.M. assumes responsibility for the management of daily affairs.
19 December 1933	Eckert, L.F. is named Résident Supérieur.
7 April 1934	Eutrope, E.H.R. is named Résident Supérieur.
19 July 1934	Roques, A.A.M. assumes responsibility for the management of daily affairs until the arrival of Eutrope on 4 August 1934.
3 November 1934	Marty, L.F.C.G. is named interim replacement for Eutrope who returns on 13 October 1935.
5 April 1938	Touzet, A. is named Résident Supérieur.
16 November 1940	Roques is named interim replacement for Touzet who was relieved of his position on the same day.
29 December 1941	Brasey, L.A.M. is named Résident Supérieur.
29 August 1945	Imfeld (Colonel) is named Commissioner of the French Republic in Laos.
6 April 1946	Raymond, J.L.F.M. is named Commissioner of the Republic.
29 July 1947	Michaudel, M.M.A. is named interim Commissioner of the French Republic in Laos.
20 March 1948	Valmary, A.J.G. assumes interim responsibility.
8 August 1949	Regnier, R. is named Commissioner of the French Republic in Laos.
27 April 1953	Pereyra, M.J. is named High Commissioner of the French Republic in Laos.
6 January 1954	Breal, M.G.E. is named High Commissioner of the French Republic in Laos.

(Source: *Sources de l'histoire de l'Asie et de l'Oceanie dans les Archives et Bibliotheques Francaises,* I, Archives, Paris, K.G. Saur, 1981:552-3).

Bibliography

1. Archives
2. Unpublished materials
3. Published materials
A. Bibliographies and guides
B. Official publications
4. Newspapers
5. Periodicals
6. Books

1. ARCHIVES

a. Holdings of the Résidence Supérieure au Laos in Aix-en-Province (Aix) are classified as follows:

Series

A Official Acts
B General correspondence
C General administration
E Provincial administration
F Political affairs
G Justice
H Public works
I Mines
J Transport
K Posts and telegraph
L Commerce, industry and tourism
M Labor, settlement and land regulation
N Agriculture
O Navigation

Q Military affairs
R Education
S Health services
T Customs services
U Documents relating to the history of Indochina

b. (i) Archives Nationales de France, Section Outre-Mer, Indochine (Paris) or AOM Indochine Paris are classified as above.

(ii) Service de Liaison avec les Originaires des Territoires francaises d'Outre-Mer (Slotfom)

(iii) Le Service Historique des Troupes de Marine (SHTM), Versailles

(iv) Service Historique de la Marine (SHM), Vincennes

(v) Archives Nationales (AN) Paris

(vi) Public Record Office (PRO) London

2. UNPUBLISHED MATERIAL

Theses

Barber, M.J.P. "Migrants and Modernisation: A Study of Changes in Lao Society", Ph.D. submitted to University of Hull, 1979.

Cam Van Thu. "Les problemes de la main d'oeuvre dans les perspectives de developpment économique du Laos", Montpellier, 1973.

Dore, A. "La divination dans l'état du Lane Xang Hom Khao", Université de Paris, Doctorat de troisiéme cycle, 1972.

Gunn, G.C. "Testing Chalmers Johnson's Theory of Revolutionary Change: The Case of Laos", thesis submitted in partial fulfillment of the requirements of M.Soc.Sci. (Asian Government), University of Queensland, 1978.

Guidicelli, R. "Le Neutralisme au Laos: Ses Implications Politiques et Economiques depuis L'Accord de Vientiane", Memoire pour le Diplome d'Etude Supérieure de Sciences Economiques, Université de Paris I, September 1975.

Inche, F. "Le Statut Politique et International du Laos Francais: Sa Condition Juridique dans la Communaute du Droit des Gens", Thèse pour le doctorat en droit, Université de Toulouse, 1935.

Kahn, J.S. "Conceptualizing Agrarian Structure in Colonial Indonesia", paper presented at ASAA 6th Biennial Conference, University of Sydney, 11-16 May, 1986.

Moppert, F. "Mouvement de résistance au pouvoir colonial francais de la minorité proto-Indochinoise du plateau des Bolovens au Sud-Laos: 1901-1936", Thèse pour le doctorat de 3 éme cycle en histoire, Université Paris, 1978.

Sarin Chhakh, "Le Trace de la Frontiere Cambodgienne avec le Laos et le Sud-Vietnam", Université de Paris, Doctorat de science politique, 1964.

Vongsay Kithong. "La Formation de l'Etat Laotienne", Thèse en vue du doctorat en science politique, Toulouse, 1967.

Colonial Reports

(Angeli Report), "Rapport du Colonel Angeli sur sujet des operations entreprises dans le Haut Laos contre les Meo", nd., (SHTM, Versailles, Indochine 3PCX1).

(Barthelemy Report), "Rapport du Lieutenant Barthelemy concernant les problems que pose l'actuelle la frontiere separant les provinces Laotienne de Savannakhet et Vietnamienne de Quangtri", Tchepone, 31 December 1947, (AOM Aix Laos F14).

(Dorey Report), "Rapport de Dorey sur les operations du detachement du Laos pendant l'hiver 1920-1921 et sur la pacification de la region de la province de Luang Prabang", Hanoi, 5 June 1921, (SHTM, Versailles, Indochine 3 PCX1 353).

(Moretti Report: education), "Rapports de l'Inspecteur Moretti sur l'enseignement au Laos, le remplacement progressif des Annamites par des Lao", Rapport no.23, 13 March 1936, (AOM Paris Indochine H12 NF 287 2494 [2]).

(Moretti Report: fiscal), "Rapports de l'Inspecteur Moretti sur le regime fiscale au Laos et sur la situation financiere au Laos", 10 June 1936", (AOM Paris Indochine NF 286 2493).

(Saint-Chaffray Report), "AS du mouvement Meo de Lai Chau et Sonla, Saint-Chaffray to the Governor General, Hanoi, 10 February 1919", (SHTM, Versailles 3PCX1 353 F).

3. PUBLISHED MATERIALS

A. *Bibliographies and Guides*

Laos 1945-1975: chronologie, Association France-Laos amitié et solidarité, nd.

A Guide to Research Materials on Thailand and Laos, New York, Asia Library Services, 1977.

Lafont, P. *Bibliographie du Laos*, Tome I (1666-1961), 2nd edition, Paris, Ecole Francaise d'Extrême-Orient, 1978.

Mogenet, L. *Bibliographie Complementaire du Laos (1962-1973)*, Vientiane, Bibliothèque Nationale, 1973.

Sources de l'histoire de l'Asie et de l'Oceanie dans les Archives et Bibliotheques Francais, K.G.Saur, UNESCO, 1981.

B. *Official Publications*

Annuaire Statistique de l'Indochine, Hanoi: Imprimerie d'Extrême-Orient.

Annuaire Statistique de la France, Paris.

Department of State: *Foreign Relations of the United States: 1952- 54*, Vol.VI, Washington, US Government Printing Office.

Devoirs en matière fiscale des autorités provinciale francaises et laotiennes et des autorities cantonales et communales laotiennes. Résidence Supérieur au Laos, Vientiane, 1940.

Discours Prononcé par M. le Résident Supérieur Eutrope à l'overture de la session ordinaire (9e session) de l'Assemblée Consultative du Laos, 22 Octobre 1937.

Discours Prononcé par M. le Résident Supérieur Eutrope à l'overture de la 10e session de l'Assemblée Consultative Indigène du Laos, September 1938.

Geographical Handbook Series: Indochina, Naval Intelligence Divsion, USA, December 1943.

Indochine, 1931.

Laos: Rapport sur la Situation Administrative, Economique et Financière au Laos durant la periode 1929-1930, (1931-1932 and 1933), Imprimerie d'extrême-orient, Hanoi.

Mission Pavie, 1903. Geographie et Voyages, (7 volumes), Paris, Leroux, 1903.

Political Report of the Central Committee of the LPDR presented at its Fourth Party Congress, by Comrade Kaysone Phomvihan, General Secretary, Vientiane, 13 November 1986.

Teimoinages, np., 1941.

The Liberation Struggle of the Pathet Lao, The Pathet Lao Propaganda Committee for World Peace, October 1952.

Les Trentes Années de la Révolution Lao, Khaosan Pathet Lao, 12 October 1975.

4. NEWSPAPERS

L'Argus Indochinois

L'Alerte

Correspondance Internationale
La Depêche Coloniale
Far Eastern Economic Review (FEER)
L'Impartial
L'International Communiste
La Lutte
The Nation
L'Opinion
La Presse Indochinoise

5. PERIODICALS

Adas, M. "From Avoidance to Confrontation: Peasant Protest in Precolonial and Colonial Southeast Asia", *Comparative Studies in Society and History*, Vol. 23, No. 2, April 1981.

Anon. "La Province des Hua Phan: Laos", *Extrême Orient*, Nouvelle Serie, No. 14, August 1927.

Anon. "La Question de l'Opium", *Bulletin de la Société des Etudes Indochinois de Saigon*, Series I, pp. 5-28, 1916-17.

Anon. "Folklore", *Bulletin de l'Association Franco-Lao d'Amitié et de Solidarité, No. 5, 3 tri, 1978*.

de Barthelemy. "Note sur la decentralisation et une politique des races au Laos", in *Comptes Rendus et Rapports du Congress de l'Organisation Coloniale*, Vol.1, pp. 139-140, nd.

Berberuglu, B. "The Controversy over Imperialism and Capitalist Industrialization", *Journal of Contemporary Asia*, Vol.14, no.4, pp.399-407, 1984.

Berg, R. & Rowe, J.C. (eds), "American Representation of Vietnam", *Cultural Critique*, no.3, Spring, 1986.

Chandler, D. "The Assassination of Resident Bardez (1925): A Premonition of Revolt in Colonial Cambodia", *Journal of Siam Society*, Vol. 70, parts 1 and 2, pp. 35-49, January-July 1982.

Chovanes, A. B. "On Vietnamese and other Peasants", *Journal of Southeast Asian Studies*, Vol.XVII, No.2, September 1986.

Colburn, F.D. "Current Studies of Peasants and Rural Development", *World Politics*, Vol. XXXIV, No. 3, pp. 138-449, April 1982.

Colonna, M. "Monographie de la Province de Saravane", *Bulletin des Amis du Laos*, No. 2, pp. 81-121, 1938.

Coulet, G. "Les Chinois en Indochine", *Extrême Asie, Revue Indochinoise*, No. 35, 457-64, May 1929.

Dang Nghiem Van. "Notes on Ethnic Groups in Tay Nguyen", *Vietnam Courier*, No. 11, pp. 19-25, 1982.

__________ . "An Outline of the Thai of Vietnam", *Vietnam Studies*, pp. 143-196, 1972.

Deutsch, K.W. "Social Mobilisation and Political Development", *The American Political Science Review*, Vol. LV, No. 3, September 1961.

Devereux, G. "The Potential Contributions of the Moi to the Cultural Landscape of Indochina", *The Far Eastern Quarterly*, Vol. VI, No. 4, pp. 390-395, August 1947.

Dufosse. "Monographie des Peuplades Kouys du Cambodge", *Extrême Asie* tome VIII, No. 83, pp. 553-568, Feburary 1934.

Evans, G. "Vietnamese Communist Anthropology", *Canberra Anthropology*, 8 (182), pp. 116-147, 1985.

Fall, B. "Problemes politiques des Etats poly-ethniques en Indochine", *France-Asie*, No. 172, pp. 129-152, March-April, 1962.

Fineman, H. and Lord, M. "A Secret Search for MIA's", *Newsweek*, 1 June 1981.

Gunn, G.C. "Ideology and the Concept of Government in the Indonesian New Order", *Asian Survey*, Vol. XIX, No. 8, pp. 751-769, August 1979.

__________ . "Resistance Coalitions in Laos", *Asian Survey*, Vol. XX111, pp. 316-340 , No. 3, March 1983.

__________ . "Approaches to Tai-Lao Studies: From Orientalism to Marxism", *Review*, XII, 4, pp.503-533, Fall 1989.

__________ . "Laos in 1987: Socialist Dependence and Underdevelopment", *Southeast Asian Affairs*, pp.135-149, 1988.

Haudebert. "Monographe de la province de Bassac", Extrême-Asie, tome VII, No. 80-81, September-November 1933, pp. 407-426; 474-479, September-November 1933.

Herbert, P. "The Hsaya San Rebellion (1930-1932) Reappraised", Working Paper, Centre of Southeast Asian Studies, Monash University, 1982.

Lee, G.Y. "Ethnic Minorities and National Building in Laos: The Hmong in the Lao State", *Peninsule*, No.11/12, pp.215-232, 1985/6.

Martin, R. "Le Banque de l'Indochine au Laos", in *La Revue Francaise de l'élite Europeane*, no. 203, October 1967.

Moerman, M. "Who are the Lue?", *American Anthropologist*, 67, pp. 1215-1230, 1965.

Mogenet, L. "Les impôts coloniaux et les incidents au Sud-Laos en 1937", *Peninsule*, no. 1, pp. 73-93, Octobre, 1980.

Moppert, F. "Position de thèse", Mouvement de résistance au pouvoir colonial francais de la minorité proto-indochinoise du plateau des Bolovens au Sud-Laos: 1901-1936, *Asie du Sud-est et monde Insulindien*, Vol. IX, No. 1-2, pp. 255-7, 1977-8.

Morèchand, G. "Principaux traits du Chamanisme meo blanc en Indochine", in *Bulletin de L'Ecole Francaise d'Extrême Orient,* Vol. XLVII, 2, pp. 509-546, 1955.

Murdoch, J.B. "The 1901-1902 'Holy Man's' rebellion", *Journal of the Siam Society,* Vol. 62, part 1, pp. 47-65, January 1974.

Phan Huy Le. "The Development of Socio-Economic Formations in the History of Vietnam", *Vietnam Social Sciences,* 142, 1986, pp.77-90.

Phimasone Phouvong. "Ethnies et Nationalities au Laos" in *Revue Juridique politique Independence et Cooperation,* tome 25, no. 4, pp. 653-658, December 1971.

Pietrantoni, E. "Note sur les classes de revenues au Laos et au Tonkin avant 1945", *Bulletin de la Societé des Etudes Indochinoises,* NS, Tome XLIII, No.3, 3 Trimestre, pp. 1-14, 1968.

Roux, H.J. "Deux Tribus de la Région de Phongsaly (Laos Septentrional)", *Bulletin de L'Ecole Francaise d'Extrême Orient,* XXIV, 1924.

Roux, H. and Tran Van Chu. "Quelques minorites ethniques du nord de l'Indochine", *France Asie,* 92-93, Saigon, 1954.

Scott, J. "Hegemony and Peasantry", *Politics and Society,* 7:3, pp. 273-275, 1977.

____________. "Revolution in the Revolution, Peasants and Commissars", *Theory and State,* 7:1 and 2, January-March 1979.

So, A.Y. "The Process of Incorporation into the Capitalist World System: The Case of China in the Nineteenth Century", *Review,* Vol VIII, No. 1, 1984.

Solarz, S.J. "When to Intervene", *Foreign Affairs,* No. 63, pp.24-5, Summer 1986.

Taillard, C. "Le Village Lao de la Région de Vientiane: Un Pouvoir Local au Face au Pouvoir Etatique", *L'Homme,* Vol. XVII (2-3), pp. 71-100, August-September 1977.

Tapp, N. "Political Participation Among the Hmong of Thailand: Some Ideological Aspects", *Journal of Siam Society,* Vol.76, pp.145-161, 1988.

____________. "L'espace social: quelques reflexions à propos de deux exemples au Laos", *Asie du Sud-est et Monde Insulindien, 8 (2) 1977.*

Viet Chung. "National Minorities and Nationality Policy in the Democratic Republic of Vietnam", *Vietnamese Studies,* No. 15.

Vinh Nguyen. *Vietnam Courier,* No.3 1986.

Woodside, A. "Review" in *Pacific Affairs,* Vol. 55, No. 4, pp. 748-751, 1982-3.

Yaj Txooj Tsab. "La guerre de Pa Tyay", *Nouvelle de la Solidarité Hmong,* pp.25-51, 8 June, 1984.

Zawawi Ibrahim. "Perspectives towards integrating Malay peasant ideology and the bases of itș production in contemporary Malaysia", *Journal of Contemporary Asia,* Vol.13, no.2, 1983.

6. BOOKS

Adams, N.S. "Patrons, Clients, and Revolutionaries: The Lao Search for Independence, 1945-1954" in N.H. Adams and A.W. McCoy (eds), *Laos: War and Revolution*, New York, Harper and Row, 1970, pp.100-120.

Alleton, I. "Les Hmong aux confins de la Chine et du Vietnam: la revolte du 'Fou' (1918-1922)" in Pierre Brocheux (ed), *Histoire de l'Asie du Sudest: Révoltes, Réformes, Révolutions*, Lille, Presses Universitaires de Lille, 1981, pp. 31-46.

Amin, S. *Unequal Exchange: An Essay on the Social Formations of Peripheral Capitalism*, Sussex, The Harvester Press, 1976.

Andreyev, I. *The Non-capitalist Way: Soviet Experience and the Liberated Countries*, Moscow, Progress Publishers, 1977.

Anon. *Mission du Mandarinat Laotien*, Hanoi, Imprimérie d'Extrême Orient, 1942.

Anon. *Laos: An Outline of Ancient and Contemporary History*, Hanoi, Foreign Languages Publishing House, I982.

Archaimbault, C. *The New Year Ceremony at Basak (South Laos)*, Data Paper: Number 78, Southeast Asia Program, Ithaca, New York, Cornell University, 1971.

Ayme, G. *Monographie du Ve Territoire Militaire (Phongsaly, Laos)*, Hanoi, IDEO, 1930.

Ayrolles, L.H. *L'Indochine ne repond plus*, Saint-Brieuc, Prud'Homme, 1949.

Barney, G.L. "The Meo of Xieng Khouang Province, Laos", in Peter Kundstadter (ed), *Southeast Asian Tribes, Minorities, and Nations*, Princeton, New Jersey, Princeton University Press, 1967, pp. 271-194.

de Barthelmy, Marquis P. *Le Laos*, Plon, 1898.

Bell, H. *Foreign Colonial Administration in the Far East*, London, Edward Arnold, 1928.

Le Boulanger, P. *Histoire du Laos Francais*, Paris, Libraire Plon, 1931.

Bourotte, B. *History of the Mountain People of Southern Indochina up to 1945*, 1951 (mss. translated from French by USAID).

Branfman, F.R. *Voices from the Plain of Jars: Life Under an Air War*, New York, Harper Colophon, 1972.

Bunnag, T. *The Provincial Administration of Siam 1892-1915*, Kuala Lumpur, Oxford, 1977.

Burchett, W.G. *En Remontant le Mekong*, Hanoi, 1957.

Charbonneau-Bauchar, R. *Le Dernier Convoi d'Opium*, Paris, Editions SES, 1960.

Chattip Nartsupha, "The Ideology of Holy Men Revolts in North East Thailand", in A. Turton and S. Tanabe (eds), *History and Peasant Consciousness in South East Asia*, Osaka, Senri Ethnological Studies, No. 13, National Museum of Ethnology, March 1984.

Cheah Boon Kheng, *The Peasant Robbers of Kedah 1900-1929: Historical and Folk Perceptions*, Singapore, East Asia Historical Monographs, Oxford University Press, 1988.

Chit Phumisak. *Chomna sakdina thai* (The True Face of Thai Feudalism), Bangkok, chamrom nagsue saengtawan, 1974.

Clarence-Smith, W.G. *Slaves, Peasants and Capitalists in Southern Angola 1840-1926*, Cambridge, Cambridge University Press, 1979.

Condominas, G. *L'Espace Social à propos de l'Asie du Sud-est*, Paris, Flammarion, 1980.

____________. "The Lao" in N.S. Adams and A.W. McCoy (eds), *Laos: War and Revolution*, New York, Harper Colophon, 1970, pp.9-27.

Dassé, M. *Montagnards, Révoltes et Guerres Revolutionnaires en Asie du Sud-est Continentale*, Bangkok, D.K. Book House, 1976.

Dauplay, J.J. *Les Terres Rouges du Plateau des Bolovens*, Saigon, 1929.

Deloncle, P. "La Mise en valeur du Laos" in *Le Laos*, Jean Renaud, Paris, Libraire de la Revue Francaise, Alexis Redier, 1930.

D'esme, J. *Les Dieux Rouges*, Paris, La Renaissance du Livre, 1923.

Despuech, J. *Le traffic de Piastres*, Paris, Deux Rives, 1953.

Devilliers, P. *Histoire du Viet-Nam de 1940 à 1952*, Paris, Editions du Seuil, 1952.

Deydier, H. *Lokapala, Génies, Totems et Sorciers du Nord Laos*, Paris, Plon, 1954.

Dufumier, M. *Premiers Transformations Socialiser de l'Agriculture en PDRL*, Associations d'Amitie et de Solidarite France-Laos, Paris 1981.

Dumarest A. *La Formation des Classes Sociales en pays Annamites*, Lyon, Imprimerie P. Ferreol, 1935.

Elliott, D. *Thailand: Origins of Military Rule*, London, Zed Press, 1978.

Ennis, T. *French Policy and Developments in Indochina*, Chicago, University of Chicago Press, 1936.

Evans, G. *The Yellow Rainmakers: Are Chemical Weapons being used in Southeast Asia*, London, Verso, 1983.

Fletcher, D. and Gunn, G. *Revolution in Laos: The 'Fourth Generation' of People's War?*, Southeast Asian Monograph Series, No. 8, Townsville, 1981.

Friedman, J. "Tribes, States and Transformations" in M. Bloch (ed), *Marxist Analysis and Social Anthropology*, London, Malaby Press, 1975.

Forest, A. *Le Cambodge et la Colonisation Francais*, L'harmattan, Paris, 1980.

Garnier, F. *Voyage d'exploration en Indochine.....* Paris, Hachette, 1873.

de Galembert, J. *Les Administrations et les Services Publics Indochinois*, Hanoi, Mac Dinh Tu, 1924.

Girling, J.L.S. *Thailand, Society and Politics*, Ithaca, Cornell University Press, 1981.

Gosselin, C. *Le Laos et le protectorate francais*, Paris, Perrin, 1900.

Grossin, P. *Notes sur l'histoire de la province de Cammon (Laos)*, Hanoi, IDEO, 1933.

Guillemet,. *Sur les Sentiers Laotiens*, Hanoi-Haiphong, Imprimérie d'Extrême Orient, 1924.

Gunn, G.C. "Theravadins and Commissars: The State and National Identity in Laos" in M. Stuart-Fox (ed), *Contemporary Laos*, St. Lucia, University of Queensland press, 1982, pp.76-100.

____________. *Political Struggles in Laos (1930-1954): Vietnamese Communist Power and the Lao Struggle for National Independence*, Editions Duang Kamol, Bangkok, 1988.

Hagopian, M.N. *The Phenomenon of Revolution*, New York, Dodd Mead and Co., 1975.

Hamel, B. *Résistance en Indochine, 1975-1980*, Paris, IREP, 1980.

Hémery, D. *Revolutionnaires Vietnamiens et pouvoir colonial en Indochine*, Paris, Maspero, 1975.

Heudebert, L. *L'Indochine Francaise*, Paris, Dujarric, 1939.

Hickey, G.C. *Sons of the Mountains: Ethnohistory of the Vietnamese Central Highlands to 1954*, New Haven and London, Yale University Press, 1982.

Hue-Tam Ho Tai, *Millenarianism and Peasant Politics in Vietnam*, Cambridge, Havard University Press, 1983.

Ileto, I. *Paysan and Revolution: Popular Movements in the Philippines, 1840-1910*, Ateneo de Manila Press, Manila, 1979.

Ishii, Y. "A note on Buddhistic Millenarian Revolts in Northeast Siam", in S. Ichimura (ed), *Southeast Asia: Nature, Society and Development*, Honolulu, The University Press of Hawaii, 1977, pp. 67-75.

____________. *Sangha, State and Society, Thai Buddhism in History*, Kyoto University, Monographs of the Center for Southeast Asian Studies, No. 15, Honolulu, University Press of Hawaii, 1986.

Jacoby, E. *Agrarian Unrest in Southeast Asia*, New York, Columbia University Press, 1949.

Kahn, J.S. *Minangkabau Social Formations: Indonesian Peasants and the World Economy*, Cambridge, Cambridge University Press, 1982.

Khan, A.R. and Lee, E. *Employment and Development in Laos, Bangkok, ILO, 1980.*

Kaysone Phomvihane. *La Révolution Lao*, Editions du Progres, 1980.

Keyes, C.F. *The Golden Peninsula: Culture and Adaptation in Mainland Southeast Asia*, Macmillan, New York, 1977.

Lartéguy, J. and Yang Dao. *La Fabuleuse Aventure du Peuple de l'Opium*, Paris, Presse de la Cité, 1979.

Lee, G.Y. "Minority Policies and the Hmong", in M. Stuart-Fox (ed), *Contemporary Laos*, St. Lucia, University of Queensland Press, 1982, pp.199-219.

Lemoine, J. *Un village Hmong Vert du haut laos: milieu technique et organisation sociale*, Paris, CNRS, 1972.

Levy, P. *Histoire du Laos*, Paris, Presse Universitaires de France, 1974.

Lingat, R. *L'esclavage privé dans le vieux droit Siamois (avec un traduction des anciennes lois siamois sur l'esclavage)*, Paris, Domat Montchrestien, 1931.

Littauer, R. and Uphoff, N. (eds), *The Air War in Indochina*, Boston, Beacon Press, 1972.

Luce, E.P. *Le Droit Administratif Laotien*, Vientiane, Lao Offset Printing, 1974.

Luther, H. *Peasants and State in Contemporary Thailand; From Regional Revolt to National Revolution?*, Hamburg Mitteilungen des insitits fur Asienkundes, 1978.

Manivanna, Keo. "Aspects socio-economique du Laos medieval" in *Sur le "mode de production asiatique*, Centre d'Etudes et de Recherches Marxistes, Paris, Editions Sociales, 1974.

Marr, D. *Vietnamese Anti-colonialism, 1885-1925*, Berkeley, University of California Press, 1971.

Marx, K. *The Eighteenth Brumaire of Louis Bonaparte*, Peking, Foreign Languages Press, 1978.

Maybon. *L'Indochine*, Paris, Collection France d'Outre-mer, Larosse, 1931.

Mazzeo, D. and Antonini, C.S. *Monuments of Civilisation: Ancient Cambodia*, New York, Grosset and Dunop, 1978.

Melotti, U. *Marx and the Third World*, London, Macmillan, 1977.

Meyer, R. *Indochine Fracaise: Le Laos*, Hanoi, IDEO, 1930.

McAleavy, H. *Black Flags in Vietnam*, New York, Macmillan, 1968.

McCoy, A.W. *The Politics of Heroin in Southeast Asia*, New York, Harper and Row, 1972.

____________. "French Colonialism in Laos, 1893-1945", in N.H. Adams and A.W. McCoy (eds), *Laos: War and Revolution*, New York, Harper and Row, 1970, pp.67-98.

Menger, M.J. *Valley of the Mekong*, Vientiane, Catholic Mission, Vicar Apostolic, 1969.

Mole, R.J. *The Montagnards of South Vietnam*, Tokyo, Tuttle, 1970.

Moppert, F. "Le révolte des Bolovens (1901-1936)" in P. Brocheux (ed), *Histoire de l'Asie du Sud-est: Révoltes, Réformes, Révolutions*, Lille, Presses Universitaires de Lille, 1981.

Mottin, J. *History of the Hmong*, Bangkok, Odeon, 1980.

Mouhot, H. *Travels in the Central Parts of Indo China (Siam), Cambodia and Laos*, London, J. Murray, 1864.

Murray, M. *The Development of Capitalism in Colonial Indochina (1870-1940)*, Berkeley, University of California Press, 1981.

d'Orleans, Prince Henri. *Around Tonkin and Siam*, London, Chapman, 1894.

Osborne, M. *River Road to China*, New York, Liveright, 1975.

Persell, S.M. *The French Colonial Lobby, 1889-1938*, Hoover Institute Press, Stanford University, 1983.

Petras, J. *Critical Perspectives on Imperialism and Social Class in the Third World*, New York, Monthly Review Press, 1978.

Phoumi Vongvichit. *Le Laos et la Lutte Victorieuse du Peuple Lao contre le Neocolonialisme Americain*, np. Editions du Neo Lao Haksat, 1968.

Picanon, A.E. *Le Laos Francais*, Paris, Callamel, 1901.

Polanyi, K. *The Great Transformation*, New York, Reinholt, 1957.

Poole, P.A. *The Vietnamese in Thailand*, Ithaca, Cornell University Press, 1970.

Popkin, S.L. *The Rational Peasant*, Berkeley, University of California Press, 1979.

Pratt, J.C. *Vietnam Voices: Perspectives on the War Years, 1941- 1982*, New York, Penguin/Viking, 1984.

Raquez, A. *Pages laotiennes: le Haut Laos, le Moyen Laos, the Bas Laos*, Hanoi, Schneider, 1902.

de Reinach, L. *Le Laos*, Paris, Charles, 1901 (1911).

____________ . *Le Laos*, Paris, Libraire Orientale and Americaine, 1911.

Robequain, C. *The Economic Development of French Indochina*, London, Oxford University Press, 1944.

Robbins, C. *The Ravens: The Men who Flew in America's Secret War in Laos*, Pocket Books, New York, 1989.

Rochet, C. *Pays Laos, Le Laos dans le Tourmente, 1939-45*, Paris, Jean Vigneau, 1946.

Samphan, Khieu (trns.intro. L. Summers). *Cambodia's Economy and Industrial Development*, Ithaca, New York, Data Paper No. 111, Southeast Asia Program, March 1979.

Sartono Kartodirdjo, *Protest Movements in Rural Java*, Singapore, Institute of Southeast Asian Studies/Oxford University Press, 1973.

Savina, F.M. *Histoire des Miao*, Hong Kong, Imprimerie de la Société des Missions Etrangères, 1924.

Sawer, M. *Marxism and the Question of the Asiatic Mode of Production*, The Hague, Martinus Nijhoff, 1977.

Scott, J.C. *The Moral Economy of the Peasant: Rebellion and Subsistence in Southeast Asia*, New Haven and London, Yale University Press, 1976.

____________ .*Weapons of the Weak: Everyday Forms of Peasant Resistance*, New Haven, Yale University Press, 1985.

Shawcross, W. *Sideshow: Kissinger, Nixon and the Destruction of Cambodia*, London, Fontana, 1979.

Suret-Canale, J. *French Colonialism in Tropical Africa, 1900-1940*, London, Hurst, 1971.

Taillard, C. "Pouvoirs et espaces en Laos: La Partie de Vientiane", in *Etat Pouvoir et Espace dans le Tiere Monde*, Paris, Presses Universitaires de France, 1977.

Tambiah, S.J. *The Buddhist Saints of the Forest and the Cult of Amulets: A Study in Charisma, Hagiography, Sectarianism and Millenial Buddhism*, Cambridge, Cambridge University Press, 1984.

Taylor, J.G. *From Modernization to Modes of Production*, London, Macmillan, 1983.

Thompson, V. *French Indochina*, London, Allen and Unwin, 1937.

___________ . *Labour Problems in Southeast Asia*, New York, Yale University Press, 1947.

Toye, H.,Laos: *Buffer State or Battleground*, London, Oxford University Press, 1968.

Truong Chinh and Vo Nguyen Giap, *The Peasant Condition (1937- 1938)*, Data Paper: No. 94, Southeast Asia Program, Department of Asian Studies, Cornell University, Ithaca, New York, 1974.

Turton, A., Fast, J. and Caldwell, M. (eds.), *Thailand: Roots of Conflict*, Nottingham, Spokeman, 1978.

___________ . "Thai Institutions of Slavery", in J.L. Watson (ed), *Asian and African Systems of Slavery*, Berkeley, University of California Press, 1980.

___________ . and Tanabe, S. (eds), *History and Peasant Consciousness in South East Asia*, Senri Ethnological Studies, No.13, National Museum of Ethnology, Osaka, March 1984.

Wall, B. *Les Nya Hon*, Vientiane, Vithagna, 1975.

Warren, B. *Jim Thompson: The Legendary American of Thailand*, Bangkok, Asia Books, 1970.

Werner, J. S. *Peasant Politics and Religious Sectarianism: Peasant and Priest in the Cao Dai in Viet Nam*, Monograph Series, no.23/Yale University Southeast Asia Studies, 1981.

Westermeyer, J. *Poppies, Pipes, and People: Opium and its Use in Laos*, Berkeley, University of California, Press, 1982.

White, C.P. "The Vietnamese Revolutionary Alliance: Intellectuals, Workers and Peasants", in J.W. Wilson (ed), *Peasant Rebellions and Communist Revolution in Asia*, Stanford, Stanford University Press, 1974, pp.77-95.

Whitmore, J. "The Thai-Vietnamese Struggle for Laos in the Nineteenth Century", in N.H. Adams and A.W. McCoy (eds), *Laos: War and Revolution*, New York, Harper and Row, 1970.

Winnington, A. *The Slaves of the Cool Mountains*, Berlin, 1959.

Woodside, A.B. *Vietnam and the Chinese Model*, Cambridge, Mass., Harvard University Press, 1971.

___________ . *Community and Revolution in Modern Vietnam*, Boston, Houghton Mifflin Co., 1976.

Wolf, E. *Peasant Wars of the Twentieth Century*, New York, Harper and Row, 1969.

Yacano, X. *Les Etapes de la Decolonisation Francaises*, Paris, Presses Universitaires de France, 1971.

Yang Dao. *Les Hmong du Laos face au development*, Vientiane, Edition Siaosavath, 1975.

Zheng Lan, *Travels Through Xishuangbanna*, Beijing, Foreign Languages Press, 1981.

Map I: The *debloquement* or opening up of Laos

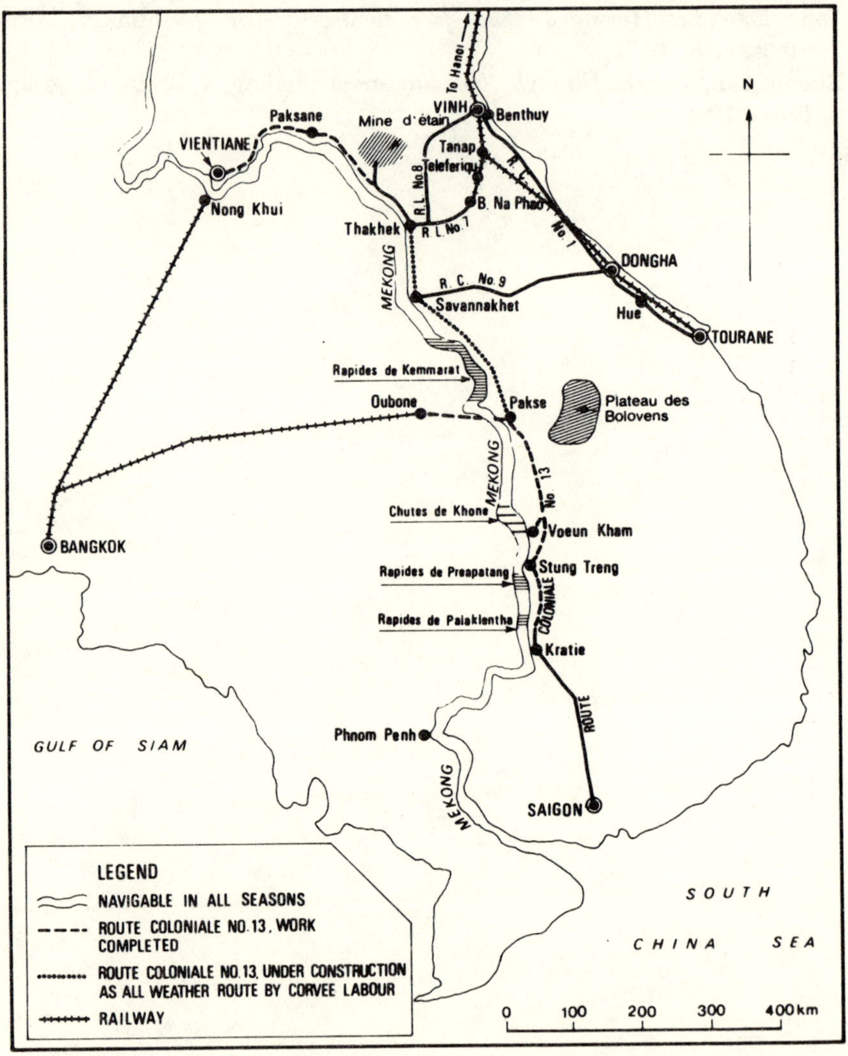

Map II: Indochina by Ethnicity

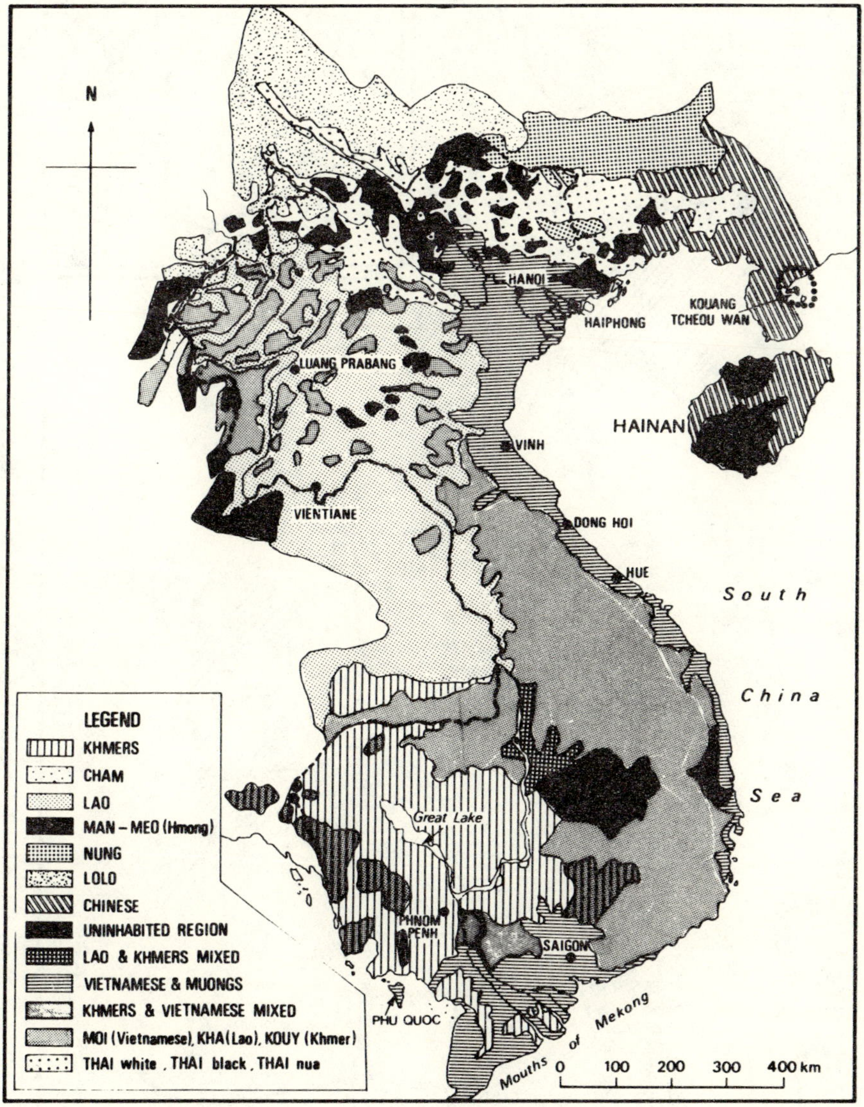

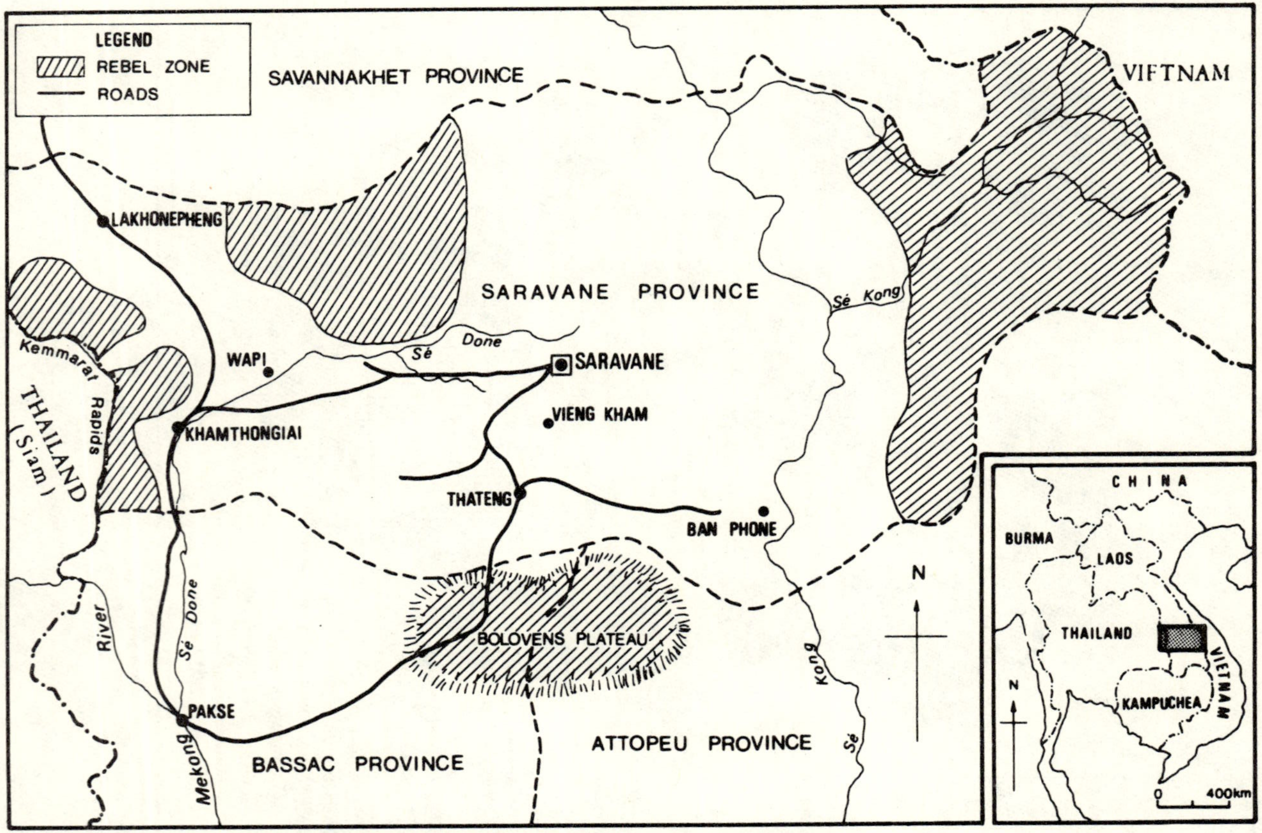

Map III: Montagnard Rebel Zones in Southern Laos, 1910s

Map IV: Military Deployments during the Batchai Rebellion, 1920

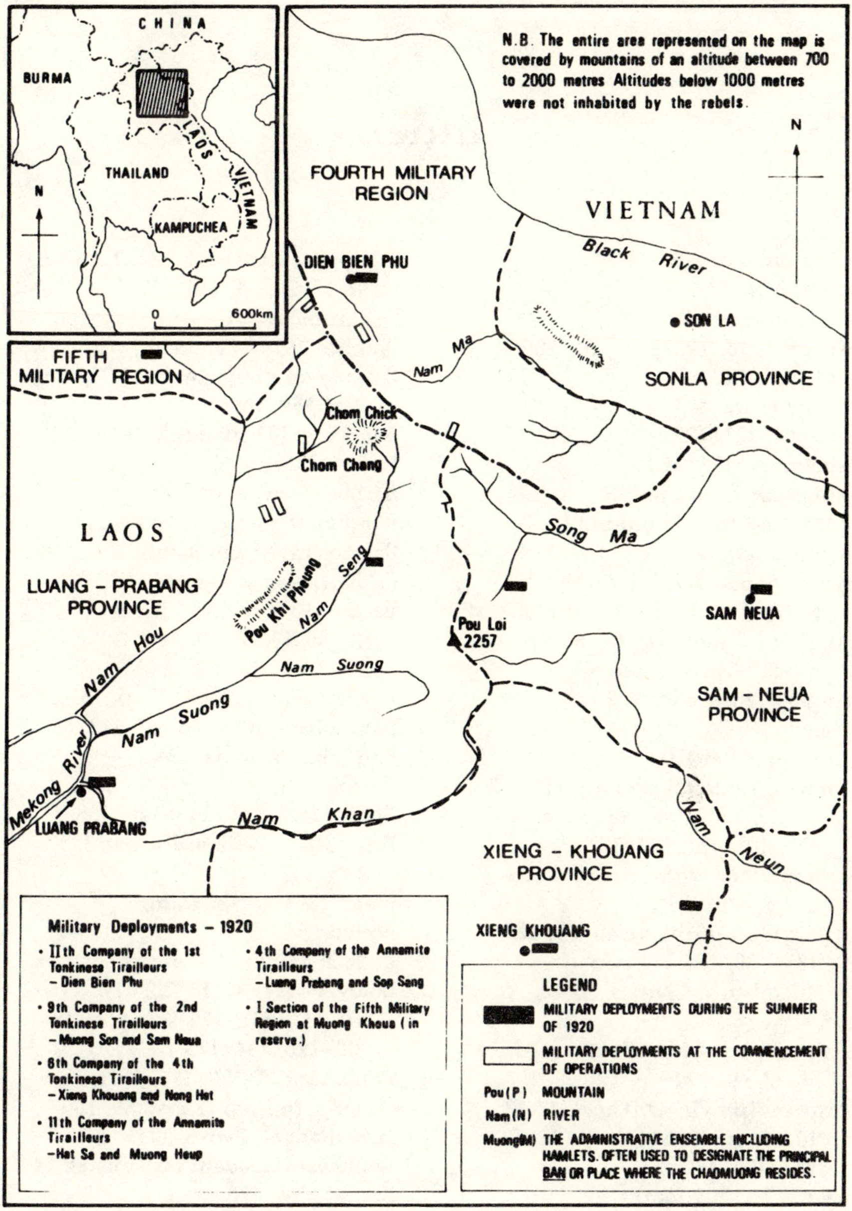

Index

Accumulation, 29, 42
Adas, M., 142-143
Afghanistan, 174
Africa, 1, 14, 19, 23, 39, 56, 185
Aid, 187-189
Air America, 171
Aircraft, 121, 127
Alleton, I., 156, 158
Althusser, Louis, 69, 93
AMP. See Asiatic mode of production
Amin, Samir, 1-2, 20, 23-24, 65, 68-69, 71, 74, 81, 82n, 184, 187, 189
Angkor [Cambodia], 66, 68
 mode of prodution, 67
Anglo-French rivalry, 13
Angola, 55-56, 181
Animism, 108-109
Annam [central Vietnam], 11-13, 15, 18, 25, 37, 41, 48, 61, 74, 83-85, 105, 108, 111, 122, 127, 136
 boundary with Laos, 134-135
 Court of, 135
Annamite Cordillera, 40, 62, 127, 135, 138, 172-173, 185
Archaimbault, Charles, 73
Archives, 6
Asiatic mode of production (AMP), 66-67, 69, 190
Attopeu (province) [Laos], 12-13, 15-16, 41, 49, 114, 117, 122, 124, 127, 128, 140n
Ayuthya (Kingdom), 11

Bac My (Ong Keo), 109-112, 114
Banditry, 103-104, 136, 142-143
Bangkok [Thailand], 12, 22, 28, 40, 46-47, 70, 74, 110, 112
Bankruptcies, 91
Ban Me Thuot [Vietnam], 134
Banque de l'Indochine, 23-24, 31n, 97n, 159, 163
Ban Vinai [Thailand], 7, 176
Barber, Martin, 67
Barbier, Jean P., 187-188
Barquez (Inspector), 136-137
Barthelemy (Lieutenant), 136, 138
de Barthelemy, Marquis P., 158
Bassac (k) (province) [Laos], 15-16, 18, 49-50, 70, 108, 111, 139
 King of, 118, 139, 140n
Batchai (Patchai) rebellion, 151-160
Battambang [Cambodia], 113
Baudoin, Francois, 134
Benjoin, 28
Black Flags, 145, 148, 149, 158
Black River [China, Vietnam], 12, 145, 147
Black Tai (See Tai Dam)
Bolivia, 55
Bollaert (High Commissioner), 46
Bolovens [Laos], 13, 28, 31n, 41, 92, 102, 110-112, 116-117, 122-123, 125-126, 134, 173
Bombing, 172-173, 176, 181n
Boneng, (mines) [Laos], 85, 185
le Boulanger, Pierre, 142
Bouloche (Resident Superieur), 14
Boundaries, 173
Bourgeoisie, 192
Bourotte, B., 49
Bourse, 25-26

Braudel, Fernand, 2
Brevie, J. (Governor General), 132
Brocheux, Pierre, 106
Brown, Macalister, 176
Brown, Radcliffe, 81
Buddharaja, 66
Buddhism (Theravada), 62, 64, 66
  education role, 38
  and religious hegemony of, 93-97
Budget, 42-47, 88-89, 94
  subvention, 86-89
Buell, Edgar, 170
Burma, 83, 92-93
Burmese, 12, 114
  and dynastic role, 68

Calu [Vietnam], 72
Cam Van Thu, 33-35
Cambodia, 11-13, 15, 18, 22, 25, 27, 37-38, 43, 46, 48-49, 56, 57n, 63, 70, 72, 74, 77, 82n, 85, 94-95, 103-104, 107, 118, 122, 172, 174-175, 178, 180-181
  Cambodians, 114, 121, 127, 140n
  and economy, 189-190
Cammon (province) [Laos], 12, 15-16, 103, 150
Cao Dai, 3, 94-95
Capitalism, 6
  and colonialism, 10-31
  as mode of production, 20, 25, 65
Chakkri [dynasty], 12
Cham (minority) [Cambodia], 108-123, 136, 189
Chamber of Deputies, 130-131
Champassak, 90, 180
Chaofa of Muong Sing, 143-144
Chao Lao, 179
Chaomuong (explained), 17
Chandler, David, 140n
Chatthip Nartsupha, 113
Chayanov, A.V., 75
Cheah Boon Kheng, 8n
Chemical agents, 176
Chiang Mai [Thailand], 40, 94
China, 7, 11, 13, 15, 21, 56n, 62, 72, 74, 96, 107, 109, 142, 147-148, 151, 155, 175, 178
  commodities, 19
  mandarins, 152
  merchants, 22, 28, 30, 84, 192
  rebels, 144-149
  revolution, 148
  republic, 148
  role in resistance 178-179
Chovanes, A.B., 81, 106
Christian Science Monitor, 174
Circulation, 24
Clarence-Smith, W.G., 55-56
Class formation/class-divided society, 65, 78-79
  relations, 2-3
Cochinchina [south Vietnam], 1, 11, 19, 22, 28, 37, 43, 48, 74, 84-85, 92, 95, 106, 111, 126-127, 130, 134, 136, 138
Coffee, 28, 31n
Colonial process, 32-54
Commoditization of labor, 14, 32, 54
Commodity mode of production, 65, 71-75
Communism, 7, 54, 107, 186, 193
Comptoir Nationale d'Escompte, 23
Condominas, Georges, 107
Conservation effects, 30, 65
Convention of 7 May 1886, 13
Cooperativization, 193
Cornell Air Way Study Group, 172
Corvee, 41-42, 48, 50-3, 87, 89, 126, 136, 143
  Kha role in, 116-117, 119, 131, 137
  peasant responses to, 89-92
Counterfeiters, 92
Customs laws, 19, 84

Dalat [Vietnam], 134, 136
Dang Nghiem Van, 141n
Darlac, 134, 141n
Dauplay, J.J., 76, 110, 114, 116
David, G.E., 170-171
Decoux, (Admiral), Jean, 137
Deloncle, P., 39-40

Delpit, 44
Demography, 34 (table), 62, 135
Deo Van Khang, 154
Deo Van Long, 160
Deo Van Tri, 12, 151, 154, 167n
La Depeche Colonial, 36
Dependency theory/approaches, 2, 187-190
Depression in Laos, 19, 62, 186, 192
  depression rebellions, 106
Devaluation, 24
Dien Bien Phu [Vietnam], 3, 68, 145, 153-155, 157
Dissolution effects, 1, 6, 30, 65
Dong Son (Dongson), 66, 107
Doumer administration, 42
Dubost, 26-27
Durkheim, E., 63, 81

Eastwood, C., 175
Education, 37, 38 (table), 39
Embezzlement, 89
Ennis, T., 28, 3in
Eutrope, E.H.R., 41, 52, 88
Evans, Grant, 170, 176, 191
Exploration, 12-13

Faydang Lobliyao, 160-161, 168
Feudalism, 66
  as mode of production, 68-69, 189, 192
Forest, Alain, 41, 57n
Forestry, 23, 27, 74
France, 12-14, 19, 21, 49
  administration of Laos, 18-19, 70-71, 119, 135, 151, 153, 159, 162, 171
  business role, 28, 192
  military, 31n, 54, 137, 144
  peasantry in, 96
Franco-Lao Agreement of 6 February 1950, 54
Franco-Siamese Treaty of 5 October 1893, 30n
Frank, Andre G., 2
Friedman, Johnathan, 5-6
Functionalism, 4

Garde Indigene (See also military), 14-5, 95, 122, 124, 126-7, 129, 149, 161, 167n, 163
Garnier, Francis, 74
Geneva Accords of 1962, 170
Gia Long (Emperor), 12
Godelier, Maurice, 3
Gold, 71
Gourou, Pierre, 75
Gramsci, Antonio, 93
Gritz, J., 175
Guidicelli, R., 188-189

Hagopian, M.N., 141n
Hamel, B., 176
Handicraft production, 71-73
Hanoi [Vietnam], 41, 113
Harmand (explorer), 13
Health, 35, 131
Hemery, Daniel, 24
Henri, Y., 75
Hickey., G.C., 107, 126-127, 129, 134-135
Historiography, 102, 126, 149
Hmong (Meo) (ethnic group), 7, 44, 52, 55, 62, 66, 73, 80, 92, 94, 146, 179
  in anti-communist resistance, 168-169, 175
  clan rivalry, 160-161
  and opium, 162-165
  messianism, 170
  rebellion, 102-103
  social sytem, 149-151
Ho Chi Minh Trail, 171-172
Hoa Binh [Vietnam], 145-147
Hobsbawm, E.J., 101
Holy Man's Uprising (See Phou Mi Boun)
Hong Kong, 47
Hua Phan (See Sam Neua)
Hue, 13
  Court of, 133, 139

ICP (See Indochinese Communist Party)
Ileto, R., 8n

Inche, F., 18
Incomes, 76-77
India, 189
Indigenous Consultative Assembly, 17, 88, 158
Indigenous Consultative Council, 17, 161
Indonesia, 73, 75, 97n
Industrialization theory, 2
Isan [northern Thailand], 114
Ishii, Yoneo, 103, 123
Indochinese Communist Party (ICP), 77, 106, 185-6, 191
Ivory, 28

Japan,
  agents, 113
  commodities, 19, 40, 74, 188
  occupation, 19, 45, 91, 126, 137, 186

Kahn, A.R., 177
Kahn, Joel, 3-5, 75
Kaysone Phomvihane, 192-194
Kengkok [Laos], 90, 104, 130
Keyes, C., 125
Kha (ethnic designation), 38, 48, 52, 62, 66, 87-88, 90, 107, 179
  craft, 72
Kha Alack, 110-112, 114
Kha Loven, 114, 120-121, 126, 140n
Kha Leu, 72, 120, 135-136, 172
Kha peasant rebellion,
  social structure, 108-109
  women, 156
Khamu (ethnic group), 103, 123
Khantabouli [Laos], 90
Khe Sanh [Vietnam], 72, 172-173, 182
Khmer Rouge, 178, 180, 190
Khone (Khong) [Laos], 14-15, 23, 37, 51, 103
Khon Khene [Thailand], 40
King's Council, 17
Kommadan (Ong), (Chief), 102, 109, 112, 129, 139, 173, 184, 187
  as millenarian rebel, 123-125
  political program, 116
  revolt, 114-126
Kommasang, 114-115
Kontum (province) [Annam], 127, 134
Korat [Thailand], 74, 113
Kouang Tcheou-Wan, 11

L'Alerte, 130-1
La Depeche Colonial, 36-37
L'Impartiale, 116, 122, 131
La Lutte, 130-131
La Pensee, 67
La Presse Indochinoise, 77
Labor dues (See prestations)
Labor process, 32-37
  bosses (cai),
  strikes, 90
de Lagree, Doudart, 12-13
Lai Chau [Vietnam], 12, 153-154
Lambert (administrator), 145-8
Land, 51
Lansdale, Edward, G., 169-170
Lan Xang (See Luang Prabang)
Lao Bao [Vietnam], 131
Lao Issara, 45-46, 102, 104, 138, 168, 186
Laokay [Vietnam], 153
Lao Loum (ethnic designation), 62-65, 71
Lao Nhay, 39
Lao People's Democratic Republic (LPDR), 7, 168, 174, 177-178
Lao People's Liberation Army (LPLA), 169, 179
Lao Soung (ethnic designation) (See Hmong)
Lao Theung (ethnic designation), (See Kha)
Laos,
  budget and monopoly system in, 42-47
  colonial development project in, 39-42
  development of colonial capitalism in, 10-57
  Kingdom of, 54
  labor process in, 32-37
  legal status of, 18

modes of state intervention in, 83-97
peasant rebellion in, 101-141
political development of, 11-18
political economy of, 18-30
pre-capitalist modes of production in, 61-82
tax and corveé system, 47-54
Lapomarade, 11
Larteguy, J., 175-176
Leang San, 145-147
Lee, Eddy, 177
Lee, Gary, 150-151, 161, 167
Lefevre (journalist), 131
Lenin, V.I., 3, 65, 187
Levy, P., 65-68
Li (clan), 160
Lingat, R., 70
Livestock, 28, 51, 72-73, 84-85
Lo (clan), 160-161
Long Chen, 175-176
Lu (ethnic group), 38, 52, 102
revolt of, 192-194
Luang Nam Tha (province) [Laos], 179
Luang Prabang, 7, 13-14, 18, 44, 71, 74, 87, 91, 108, 105, 160-162, 164
and Kingdom of (Lan Xang), 11-12, 16-17, 40-41, 48, 66-68, 120, 123, 157
Luther, Hans, 113-114, 177
Luxemburg R., 65

Macau Congress of 1935, 191
McCoy, Alfred, 30n, 46, 160, 169
MACG (See Mixed Airborne Command Group)
Macnamara, Robert, S., 169
Malaysia, 93
Manivanna, Keo, 67-68, 70
Market penetration, 16-21
Marx(ism), 2-4, 33, 54, 69, 80, 96, 185-186, 193
as social science, 190
Mekong, 2, 11-13, 21-22, 50, 62-63, 112, 116
Meo (ethnic group), (See Hmong)
Meray, M., 15, 21
Merchant capital, 21-22
Messianism (See also millenialism and shamans), 1, 106, 139, 153, 166, 168, 170, 179
Miao (ethnic group), (See Hmong)
Military regions, 16, 113, 125
military (See also Garde Indigene), 154-155
Millenialism (See also messianism and shamans), 96, 110
Kommandan's revolt as, 123-125
millenial Buddhism, 101
Migration, 123, 135, 150, 164, 178
Minority rights, 129
Mise en valeur (explained), 20-21
discussed, 40, 54
Missing-in-action, 174-5
Missionaries, 97, 98n, 140n, 159
Mixed Airborne Command Group (MACG), 169-170
Modernization theory, 2, 106
Modes of production, 4, 65
Moi (ethnic designation), 122, 134
Monetary system, 23-24
currency, 73
monetization, 165
Monopoly (Regie) (See Opium Regie), 42-47, 161-164, 166
Monopoly capital, 21-2
Montagnard policy, 134-138
Moore, Barrington, 1, 81, 93, 96
Moppert, F., 107, 109
Moretti, 36, 50, 88
Mouhot, Henri, 12-13
Mu Gia Pass [Laos-Vietnam], 40, 172, 185
Muong (system), 63-64
Muong Hoa (province) [Laos], 15
Muong La [China], 144, 152
Muong Sing, 142-144
Murdoch, J.B., 109
Murray, Martin, 19, 23, 25, 30, 42, 47-48

Naiban, explained, 17
role of, 53

Nakhon Phanom [Thailand], 172
Nam Patane (mining region) [Laos], 10, 23, 25-27, 3in, 33, 73, 185
National Institute of Social Sciences (of Laos), 7
Nationalism, 7
ethno-nationalism, 184
proto-nationalism, 183, 187
Natural economy, 29, 64-65, 72-73
Net, P.M., 13
New Economic Anthropology, 3
Nghe-Tinh (provinces) [Vietnam], 83-85, 105, 122, 14in, 163, 185
Nong Het (Nonghet) [Laos], 111, 12, 160, 167n
Nong Khai [Thailand], 74
Nya Hon (Nhaheun) (ethnic group), 24, 72, 114, 120, 128, 140n, 173

Ong Keo (See Bac My)
Ong Man, 112-114
Operation Lam Son, 173
Opium, 23, 42-45, 48, 55, 57n, 75, 80-81, 146, 151, 158
Opium Regie, 149
Oubon (Ubon) [Thailand],

Pacification, (and SEE military), 14, 28, 92, 96, 111, 121, 125- 128, 134-135
Pa(c)klay [Laos], 13
Pakse [Laos], 15, 41, 92, 114-115, 117, 128
Pareto, V., 78
Parson, Talcott, 81
Pathet Lao, 1-2, 7, 54, 102, 138, 140n, 168, 176-177, 187, 190
Pau Conference, 46
Pavie, Auguste, 12, 14, 20, 143
Peasants (defined), 4
condition of, 75-77
discovery of, 4
Marx' analysis, 96
studies, 6, 96, 184
Pentagon Papers, 169
Percell, S.M., 21
Petras, James, 194n
Phan Huy Le, 190
Phetisarath (King), 108
Phetsarath (Prince), 17, 80, 92, 119, 161, 167, 186, 186, 192
Phi cult, 64, 94, 121
Phi Noi, 128
Phocaduot, 102, 104-105
Phong Saly (province) [Laos], 16, 73, 150
Phontiou [Laos], 85, 185
Ph(o)u Bia [Laos], 168, 178
Phou Louang, 125-126
Phoumi Nosavan, 180
Phoumi Vongvichit, 49, 65, 73
Phnom Penh [Cambodia], 70, 74, 76-77, 94, 108
Phu Mi Boun (See messianism, millenialism), 109, 121, 139, 141n, 156, 166
Phuthai (ethnic group), 108, 136, 145
Piaster, 23-4
redemption of, 91
Pietrantoni, E., 78-81
Plain of Jars, 170, 172, 175-176
Pleiku [Vietnam], 134
Popkin, Samuel, 5-6, 61, 105-106, 183
Popular Front, 130
Poverty, 80-81
Pre-capitalist modes of production, 24-29, 61-82
Press, 45, 97, 104, 130, 141n, 181
Prestations (labor dues), 1, 47-49, 55, 77, 84, 87, 90, 124, 128, 130, 133, 167
Prices, 85
Primitive capital (accumulation), 6, 65, 101, 107, 116, 137, 190
Primitive communal mode of production, 107, 133
Prisoners, 138, 186
Proletariat, 81, 191
Protectionism, 21
Provost, 129
Public works, 87

Quang Tri (province) [Vietnam], 135
Quynh Nhai [Vietnam], 153

Race, Jeffrey, 6
Radcliffe-Brown, A.R., 81
Rambo, 175
Reagan Doctrine, 168, 174-181
defined, 174
Rebellion in Laos, discussed, 101-107
de Reinach, Lucien, 16, 43, 51
Refugees, 170, 172, 176
Relations of production, 4-5
Reproduction, 23-24
Resistance, right wing, 174-181
Review, 8n
Rey, P.P., 4
Reynaud, P., 18
Rhade (ethnic group), 118, 125
Rice, 98, 122, 165
export, 24, 27-28, 51
RLG (See Royal Lao Government)
Roads, 42, 50, 55-56, 62, 64, 92, 173
Robbins, C., 181
Robequain, Charles, 19, 25, 27, 3in, 41, 63, 75, 97
Rochet, Charles, 45
Roux, H.J., 158
Rowley, Kelvin, 56n
Royal Lao Government (RLG), 170, 173, 176-177
Rubber, 28
Rusk, Allan, W., 169
Rusk, Dean, 169

Saigon [Vietnam], 11, 27, 41, 44, 56, 85, 136
Sakdina, 69, 191
Salt, 42-44, 133, 136
Sambran, 103, 126-130, 141n
Sam Neua (province) [Laos], 12, 15-16, 41, 73, 103, 144-146, 148, 150, 160
Samphan, Khieu, 72, 189-190
Sangha, 64, 94-95
Saravane (province) [Laos], 13, 15-16, 50, 71, 111, 120, 127-128
scandal of, 130-133
Sartono, Kartodirdjo, 8n
Savannakhet [Laos], 15-16, 40-41, 50, 91, 104, 113, 134-136
Savina, F.M., 157-159
Sawer, M., 69
Scott, James, 3-6, 61, 83, 93, 101, 105-107, 129, 139n, 166, 168, 183-184
Scott (British administrator), 143
Sebanghien (river) [Laos], 13
Sedentarization, 137, 176
Sekong (river) [Laos], 13, 41, 127-128
Shamans/sorcerers (See also messianism, millenialism), 152-157, 168
Shawcross, William, 173
Siam (See Thailand)
Si Chiang Mai [Thailand], 84
Silver, 24, 57n, 162
Sip Song Chau Thai [Vietnam], 14, 68, 150, 167n
Sip Song Panna [China], 7, 68, 143-145
Sisana Sisane, 193
Sisavang Vong (King), 18
Sithon Kommadan, 126, 140n, 187
Slaves, 48-49, 117
Slave mode of production, 69-71, 73, 107
Smuggling, 164
So, Alvin, 5
Social differentiation/stratification, 63
Social formation, 4
Lao-Tai example, 73-74
Social science in Laos, 190-195
Social space, defined, 63
Song Tou, 160
Sonla (Son La) [Vietnam], 76, 145, 153-154
Souligna Vongsa (King), 68
Souphanouvong (prince), 187
Stalinism, 191
State Agricultural Service, 27
State Forestry Service, 27
Strung Treng, 15, 49, 70, 118
Subsistence ethic, 105, 114
economy, 164
crisis, 97

Sudan, 39
Sun Yat Sen, 148
Suret-Canale, J., 14, 19

Tai Dam (ethnic group), 7
Tai-Lao mode of production, 69
  political structures, 66-69
  social formation, 74
Taillard, Christian, 63, 150-151
Tai Neua (ethnic group), 94, 144
Tambiah, S.J., 124-125, 141n
Tasseng (explained), 17
  roles, 53
Tax, 1, 19, 42, 47-54, 177, 192
Taylor, John. G., 68
Tchepone [Laos], 136, 173
Thailand (Siam), 11-13, 16, 21-22, 38-9, 49, 62, 70, 73, 84, 89, 92, 103-194, 109, 112-114, 123, 179, 181, 188
  dynasty, 68
  military, 113
  traders, 85
Thakek [Laos], 31n, 40-41, 85
Theravada Buddhism (See Buddhism)
Thompson, Virginia, 18, 33
Timber, 27
Tin, 73 (See Boneng, Nam Patene)
Tobacco, 42-43, 52, 85
Tonkin [northern Vietnam], 1, 11-12, 14-15, 25-26, 37, 41, 48, 82n, 85, 111, 130, 138
  social differentiation in, 78-81
Touby Lyfoung, 160-162, 167n, 168-169
Tourane (Danang) [Vietnam], 41
Trade, 67, 73-74
Tran Ninh (Xieng Khouang) [Laos], 7, 15-16, 28, 31n, 73, 103, 150-152, 155, 160, 164, 169
Treaty of 3 October 1893, 13, 30n
Treaty of 24 October 1904, 13
Tributary mode of production, 65-69, 71
  tribute, 135, 137, 152
Truong Chinh, 85
Turton, A., 70

Ubon (Oubon, 40, 49, 172
Udorn [Thailand], 113
Uneconomic imperialism, 55-56
United Lao National Liberation Front, 180
United States Agency for International Development (USAID), 188
United States, 54, 151, 179-180
  agencies/forces, 168, 170-174, 178-179
USAID (See United States Agency for International Development), 188

Vang Pao (General), 168-171, 175-180
Van Na Poum, 142
Vientiane [Laos], 15-17, 40, 68, 73, 84-85, 104, 108, 118, 120, 150, 181
  Kingdom of, 12, 13, 118, 135
Viet Minh, 47, 78, 129, 135, 138, 187
Vietnam (See also Annam, Cochinchina & Tonkin)
Vietnam area, 46, 51, 62-63, 72, 93, 96, 105, 122, 134, 136, 138, 148, 150, 170, 172, 181, 183, 189
Vietnamese, 14, 22
  in Laos, 34, 35 (table), 36, 103, 127, 192, 194n
  communists, 178
  dynasty, 68
  labor, 54
Vinh [Vietnam], 41
Vo Nguyen Giap, 76

Wall, Barbara, 24, 128, 140n, 173
Wallerstein, Immanuel, 2-3
Westermeyer, J., 162
Weinberger, C., 162
Werner, J.S., 6, 95
White, C.P., 187
Winnington, Allan, 82n
Wolf, E., 6, 75, 184
Woodside, Alexander, 107, 138
World system, 2, 4-5, 81

Xieng Khouang (See Tran Ninh)

Yacano, X., 29
Yang Dao, 150-151, 167n, 175-176
Yao [ethnic group], 7, 52, 62, 80, 147, 153, 155, 178-179
Yunnan [China], 44
 border, 103
 lords, 151, 166
 merchants, 37, 74-75, 158
 railhead, 40-41

Zazloff, J.J., 176
Zawawi, Ibrahim, 3